The Tale of Sarcastic Halli

Original Text, Translations, and Word Lists

Translated by
Matthew Leigh Embleton

Copyright ©2025 Matthew Leigh Embleton. All rights reserved.

The Tale of Sarcastic Halli

The Tale of Sarcastic Halli (*Old Norse*)..4
Word List (*Old Norse to English*)..48
Word List (*English to Old Norse*) 68
The Tale of Sarcastic Halli (*Old Icelandic*) 84
Word List (*Old Icelandic to English*)...128
Word List (*English to Old Icelandic*)...148
A Word Comparison of Old Norse and Old Icelandic Words 165

Cover: Old Norse text over an outline of Iceland. Author's design.

The original Old Norse and Old Icelandic texts are in the public domain.
These translations ©2022 Matthew Leigh Embleton
©2025 Matthew Leigh Embleton (This Edition)

Acknowledgments

I have long been fascinated by languages and history, and I am very grateful to the special people in my life who have supported and encouraged me in my work. Thank you for believing in me. You know who you are.

Introduction

Old Norse is a North Germanic language spoken by inhabitants of Scandinavia from about the 7th to the 15th centuries. Old Icelandic is a variety of Old West Norse that emerged during the Norse settlement of Iceland in the second half of the 9th century. The rich tradition of Icelandic literature survived by oral tradition over several centuries before being written down in the 13th Century. The Tale of Sarcastic Halli (*Sneglu-Halla þáttr*) is one of the many Tales of Icelanders or *Íslendingaþættir*. The word '*þáttr*' (plural: '*þættir*') translates as a strand of rope or a yarn, comparable to the word 'yarn' in English sometimes used to refer to a story.

This book contains:
- The Tale of Sarcastic Halli (*Sneglu-Halla þáttr*) (Old Norse Version)
- An Old Norse to English Word List
- An English to Old Norse Word List
- The Tale of Sarcastic Halli (*Sneglu-Halla þáttr*) (Old Icelandic Version)
- An Old Icelandic to English Word List
- An English to Old Icelandic Word List
- A Word Comparison of Old Norse and Old Icelandic words

The texts are presented in their original form, with a literal word-for-word line-by-line translation, and a Modern English translation, all side-by-side. In this way, it is possible to see and feel how the worked and how it has evolved. This book is designed to be of use and interest to anyone with a passion for the Old Norse or Old Icelandic language, Norse history, or languages and history in general.

The Tale of Sarcastic Halli (*Old Norse*)

Old Norse	Literal	English
1	**1**	**1**
Þat er upphaf þessarrar frásagnar, at Haraldr konungr Sigurðarson réð fyrir Noregi.	It is beginning this from-saying, of Harald the-king Sigurdson ruled over Norway.	The beginning is to say that King Harald Sigurdson ruled Norway.
Þat var í þann tíma, er Magnús konungr frændi hans var andaðr.	It was in that time, that Magnus the-king's kinsman his was dead.	It was in that time that Magnus the king's kinsman was dead.
Svá er sagt, at Haraldr konungr var allra manna vitrastr ok ráðigastr;	So is said, that Harald the-king was of-all men the-wisest and well-advising;	So it is said that King Harald was the wisest of all men and of advice.
varð þat ok flest at ráði, er hann lagði til.	was it also the-most that advised, that he became to.	Also most of what he had counselled had become good.
Hann var skáld gott.	He was a-poet good.	He was a good poet
Jafnan kastaði hann háðyrðum at þeim mönnum, er honum sýndist;	Equally cast he mocking to they the-people, as he thought;	and also mocked whoever he thought to.
þoldi hann ok allra manna bezt, þótt at honum yrði kagtat klámyrðum, þá er honum var gott í skapi.	endured he also all men best, though that he was cast obscene-words, then that he was good of mood.	And when he was in a good mood, he endured most men even though obscenities were cast at him.
Hann átti þá Þóru, dóttur Þórbergs Árnasonar.	He married then Thora, daughter Thorberg's Son-of-Arni.	He was then married to Thora, daughter of Thorberg, Arni's son.
Honum þótti mikit gaman at skáldskap, ok hafði jafnan þá með sér er kveða kunnu.	He thought much delight in poetry, and had always then with him that compose could.	He took much delight in poetry and always had people about him who could compose poetry.
Þjóðólfr hét maðr;	Thjodolf was-named a-man;	There was a man named Thjodolf.
hann var íslenzkr, ok ættaðr ór Svarfaðardal, kurteiss maðr ok skáld mikit.	he was an-Icelander, and descended from Svarfadardal, polite man and poet great.	He was an Icelander whose family came from Svarfadardal, a polite man and a great poet.
Hann var með Haraldi konungi í hinum mestu kærleikum.	He was with Harald the-king in the most dear-friendship.	He had great friendship with King Harald.

The Tale of Sarcastic Halli (Old Norse)

Old Norse	Literal	English
Hann kallaði konungr höfuðskáld sitt, ok virði hann mest allra skálda.	Called the-king him chief-poet his, and worthied him most of-all poets.	The king called him his chief poet, and valued him most of all the poets.
Hann var ættsmár, ok menntr vel, öfundsjúkr við þá, er til komu.	He was family-small, and educated well, un-infatuated with then, who to came.	He was from a humble family and well educated, he was envious of newcomers.
Haraldr konungr elskaði mjök íslendinga;	Harald the-king loved much Icelanders;	King Harald loved Icelanders very much.
gaf hann til Íslands marga góða gripi, klukku góða til Þingvalla;	gave he to Iceland many good things, a-bell good for Thingvellir;	He gave many good things to Iceland, including a good bell for Thingvellir.
ok þá er hallæri þat hit mikla kom á Ísland, er ekki hefir slíkt komit annat, þá sendi hann út til Íslands fjóra knörru, hlaðna af mjöli, sinn í hveru fjórðung, ok lét flytja burt fátœka menn sem flesta af landinu.	and then when famine that the greatest came to Iceland, that not had such come another, then sent he out to Iceland four knorrs, ladened with meal, then to each fourth, and had carried brought poor men which most off the-land.	And when the greatest famine came to Iceland, which was like no other, he then sent four knorrs loaded with flour, one to each quarter, and had brought over many of the poorest men from the land.

2

Bárðr hét maðr, ok var hirðmaðr Haralds konungs.	Bard was-named a-man, and was court-man Harald's the-king's.	There was a man named Bard who was a court man of King Harald's.
Hann sigldi til Íslands, ok kom út at Gásum, ok vistaðist þar um vetrinn.	He sailed to Iceland, and came out to Gasir, and found-a-place there about winter.	He sailed to Iceland and came out to Gasir and found a place there for the winter.
Sá maðr tók sér far með honum, er Halli hét, ok var kallaðr Sneglu-Halli;	So a-man took himself passage with him, was Halli named, and was called Sarcastic-Halli;	So a man took passage with him who was named Halli, and he was called Sarcastic Halli.
hann var kallaðr skáld gott ok orðgreppr mikill.	he was called a-poet good and word-bold much.	He was a good poet and very bold with words.
Halli var hár maðr ok hálslangr, herðalítill ok handsíðr ok ljótlimaðr;	Halli was high man and long-neck, narrow-shouldered and long-armed and ugly-limbed;	Halli was a tall man with a long neck, narrow shoulders, long arms, and ill-proportioned limbs.

The Tale of Sarcastic Halli (Old Norse)

Old Norse	Literal	English
hann var ættaðr ór Fljótum.	he was descended out-of Fljot.	His descendants were from Fljot.
Þeir sigldu þegar (er þeir) váru búnir, ok höfðu langa útivist, tóku Noreg um haustit norðr við Þrándheim, við eyjar þær, er Hítrar heita, ok sigldu síðan inn til Agðaness ok lágu þar um nótt.	They sailed as-soon-as (was they) were prepared, and had long out-journey, took Norway about autumn north with Trondheim, with islands there, which Hitra named, and sailed since then to Agdanes and lay there about the-night.	They sailed as soon as they were ready and had a long passage, they reached Norway in the autumn north of Trondheim at the islands there which are called Hitra, and then sailed to Agdanes and laid up there for the night.
Enn um morgininn eftir sigldu þeir inn eftir firðinum lítinn byr;	Then about morning after sailed they then back-from the-fjord little fair-wind;	Then in the morning they sailed afterwards into the fjord with a light fair wind.
enn er þeir komu inn um Rein, sá þeir, at langskip þrjú röru innan eftir firðinum.	and when they came of about Reine, saw they, of longships three rowing in after the-fjord.	And when they came to Reine they saw three longships rowing back from the fjord.
Dreki var hit þriðja skipit.	Dragon was the third ship.	The third ship was a dragon ship.
Ok er skipin röru hjá kaupskipinu, þá gekk maðr fram ór lyftingunni á drekanum, í rauðum skarlatsklæðum, ok hafði gullhlað um enni, bæði mikill ok tiguligr.	And when the-ships rowing beside trading-ship, then got a-man from out lifting from the-dragon-ship, in red scarlet, and had gold-band about forehead, both great and dignified.	And when the ships were rowing beside the trading ship, a man came up out of the dragon ship in red scarlet with a gold band about his forehead, both great and dignified.
Þessi maðr tók til orða:	This man took to words:	This man spoke:
"Hverr stýrir skipinu eðr hvar váru þér í vetr, hvaðan ýttu þér, eðr hvar tóku þér fyrst land, eðr hvar lágu þér í nótt?"	"Who steers the-ship and where were you in winter, from-where pushed you, and where took you first land, and where laid you in the-night?"	"Who steers the ship, and where were you in winter, and where did you first take land, and where did you lay up last night?"
Þeim varð næsta orðfátt kaupmönnum, er svá var margs spurt senn.	They were next word-fallen the-trading-men, as so were many questions but.	The trading men were lost for words because there were so many questions, but
Halli svarar þá:	Halli answered then:	Halli answered them.

The Tale of Sarcastic Halli (Old Norse)

Old Norse	Literal	English
"Vér várum í vetr á Íslandi, enn ýttum af Gásum, enn Bárðr heitir stýrimaðr, enn tókum land við Hítrar, enn lágum í nótt við Agðanes?"	"We were in winter in Iceland, and pushed from Gasir, and Bard is-named steersman, and took land at Hitra, and laid about the-night at Agdanes?"	"We were in Iceland for the winter, and we pushed on from Gasir, and Bard is the name of the steersman, we took land at Hitra, and we laid up for the night at Agdanes".
Þessi maðr spurði, er reyndar var Haraldr konungr Sigurðarson:	This man asking, which actually was Harald the-king Sigurdson:	This man who was asking, was actually King Harald Sigurdson.
"Sarð hann yðr þá eigi hann Agði?"	"Wounded he you then not he Agdi?"	"Did Agdi not wound you?"
"Eigi enn þá?" sagði Halli.	"Not yet then?" said Halli.	"Not yet", said Halli.
Konungrinn brosti at, ok mælti:	The-king laughed and, also spoke:	The king laughed and also spoke:
"Er nökkurr til ráðs um, at hann muni enn síðar meir veita yðr þessa þjónustu?"	"Is something to agreement about, that he shall but afterwards more grant you this service?"	"Is there some agreement that he shall do you this service sometime later?"
"Ekki?" sagði hann Halli, "ok bar þó einn hlutr mest til þess, er vér fengum enga skömm af honum?"	"Not?" told he Halli, "and bears though one part there to this, that we travel not disgrace of him?"	Halli told him not, "and so it bears most in one part that we travel without suffering disgrace by him".
"Hvat var þat?"	"What was that?"	"What was that?"
sagði konungr.	said the-king.	said the king.
Halli vissi gerla, við hveru hann talaði.	Halli knew completely, with whom he talked.	Halli knew completely who he was talking to.
"Þat, herra?"	"That, lord?"	"That, lord",
sagði hann, "ef yðr forvitnar at vita, at hann Agði beið at þessu oss tignari manna, ok vænti yðar þangat í kveld, ok mun hann þá gjalda af höndum þessa skuld ótæpt?"	said he, "if you fore-knowing to know, that he Agdi waited for this us nobler men, and expected you from-there in the-evening, and shall he then pay of hand this debt unsettled?"	he said, "if you are curious to know, that Agdi was waiting for nobler men than us, and expected your arrival there this evening, and he shall pay you this debt fully".
"Þú munt vera orðhákr mikill?"	"You must be word-tall much?"	"You must be very brave of words",
segir konungr.	said the-king.	said the king.

The Tale of Sarcastic Halli (Old Norse)

Old Norse	Literal	English
Eigi er getit orða þeira fleiri at sinni.	Not is told words theirs more than these.	It is not told what more their words were than this.
Sigldu þeir kaupmennirnir inn til Kaupangs, ok skipuðu þar vöru upp, ok leigðu sér hús í bœnum.	Sailed they merchant-men then to Kapuang, and ships there were upped, and rented themselves a-house in town.	The merchants then sailed to Kaupang, upped their ships and rented themselves a house in town.
Fám nóttum síðar kom konungr inn aftr til bœjar, ok hafði hann farit til eyja út at skemta sér.	A-few nights afterwards came the-king then returning to the-town, and had he travelled to islands out to entertain himself.	After a few nights the king came returning to the town, as he had gone out to the islands to entertain himself.
Halli bað Bárð at fylgja sér til konungsins, ok kveðst vilja biðja hann vetrvistar;	Halli asked Bard to follow him to the-king, and said wished to-ask him winter-provisions;	Halli asked Bard to lead him to the king and said that he wished to ask him for winter lodgings.
enn Bárðr bauð honum með sér at vera.	but Bard invited him with himself to be.	But Bard invited him to stay with him.
Halli bað hann hafa þökk fyrir, enn kveðst með konunginum vilja vera, ef þess væri kostr.	Halli bid him having thanks for, but said with the-king wished to-be, if this was a-choice.	Halli thanked him but said that he wished to stay with the king if that was a choice.

3

Einn dag gekk Bárðr til konungs ok Halli með honum.	One day went Bard to the-king and Halli with him.	One day Bard went to meet the king and Halli went with him.
Bárðr kvaddi konung.	Bard greeted the-king.	Bard greeted the king.
Konungr tók vel kveðju hans, ok spurði margs af Íslandi, eðr hvárt hann hefði flutt útan nökkura íslenzka menn.	The-king received well greeting his, and asked many-things of Iceland, and whether he had brought out any Icelander men.	The king received his greeting well and asked many things of Iceland and whether he had brought any men from Iceland.
Bárðr sagðist flutt hafa einn íslenzkan mann;	Bard said brought had one Icelander man;	Bard said that he had brought one Icelander man
"ok heitir hann Halli, ok er nú hér, herra, ok vill biðja yðr vetrvistar?"	"and named he Halli, and is now here, lord, and wishes to-ask you winter-lodgings?"	"and he is named Halli, and he is now here lord, and wishes to ask you for winter lodgings".
Halli gekk þá fyrir konunginn ok kvaddi hann.	Halli went then before the-king and greeted him.	Halli then went before the king and greeted him.

The Tale of Sarcastic Halli (Old Norse)

Old Norse	Literal	English
Konungrinn tók honum vel, ok spurði, hvárt hann hefði svarat honum á firðinum, "er vér fundumst?"	The-king received him well, and asked, whether he had answered him in the-fjord, "when we met?"	The king received him well and asked whether he had answered him in the fjord "when we met".
"Sá er hinn sami?"	"So is the same?"	"I am the same",
segir Halli.	said Halli.	said Halli.
Konungrinn sagðist eigi spara mundu mat við hann, ok bað vera at búi sínu nökkuru.	The-king said not withhold would food from him, and invited to-be to estate his one-of.	The king said he would not withhold food from him and invited him to be on one of his estates.
Halli kveðst með hirðinni vilja vera, eðr leita sér annars ella.	Halli said with the-court to-be wished, or find himself another or-else.	Halli said that he wished to be at court or to find somewhere else.
Konungrinn kvað svá fara jafnan, at "mér er um kennt, ef várr vinskapr ferr eigi vel af hendi, þó at mér þykki varla svá vera.	The-king said so goes always, that "to-me is about blame, if our friendship goes not well of to-hand, though that to-me seems hardly so being.	The king said that it always goes "that I am to blame if our friendship does not go well, though that seems to me hardly to be.
Eru þér einráðir íslendingar ok ósiðblendnir.	They-are you one-decision Icelanders and un-custom-mixing.	You are single-minded, you Icelanders, and unsociable.
Nú ver, ef þú vill, ok ábyrgst þik sjálfr, hvat sem í kann gerast?"	Now be, if you wish, and responsible you yourself, what which about can be?"	Now be here if you wish, and you are responsible for yourself whatever will be".
Halli kvað svá vera skyldu, ok þakkaði konunginum.	Halli said so being would, and thanked the-king.	Halli said that it would be so, and thanked the king.
Var hann nú með hirðinni, ok líkaði hverjum manni vel til hans.	Was he now with the-court-men, and liked each man well to him.	He was now with the court men and he was liked by each of them.
Sigurðr hét sessunautr Halla, gamall hirðmaðr ok gæfr.	Sigurd was-named bench-companion Halli, old court-man and agreeable.	Halli's bench companion was named Sigurd, an old court man and agreeable.
Sá var siðr Haralds konungs, at eta einmælt;	So was the-custom Harald's the-king's, to eat one-meal;	It was Harald's custom to eat one meal a day.

The Tale of Sarcastic Halli (Old Norse)

Old Norse	Literal	English
var fyrst borin vist fyrir konung, sem vánligt var, ok var hann þá jafnan mjök mettr, er vistin kom fyrir aðra.	were first brought provisions for the-king, as expected was, and was he then usually much satisfied, when the-supply came before others.	First the food was brought before the king, as was expected, and he was usually very much satisfied when the food was brought to the others.
Enn þá er hann var mettr, klappaði hann með hnífskefti sínu á borðit, ok skyldi þá þegar ryðja borðin, ok váru margir þá hvergi nærri mettir.	But then when he was satisfied, rapped he with knife-handle his on the-table, and would then straight-away cleared tables, and were many then nowhere near satisfied.	But then when he was satisfied, he rapped his knife handle on the table, and then straight away the tables were cleared, and many people were then nowhere near satisfied.
Þat bar til eitt sinn, er konungr gekk úti um stræti ok fylgdin með honum,	It bore to once then, that the-king went out about the-street and followers with him,	It happened once that the king went out in the street with his followers, and many of them were nowhere near satisfied.
at þeir heyrðu í eitt herbergi deild mikla.	that they heard in one hostel room great.	They heard something great in an inn.
Þar váru at sútari ok járnsmiðr, ok þar næst flugust þeir á.	They were a tanner and ironsmith, and there near flew they to.	It was a tanner and an ironsmith, and they nearly flew towards eachother.
Konungrinn nam staðar ok sá á um stund.	The-king took place and saw for about awhile.	The king took his place and watched for a while.
Síðan mælti hann:	Afterwards spoke he:	Afterwards he spoke:
"Göngum burt,	"We-are-going away,	"Let us go away.
hér vil ek engan hlut at eiga;	here wish I none part to own;	I do not wish to be a part of this here,
enn þú, Þjóðólfr, yrk um þá vísu?"	but you, Thjodolf, write about then a-verse?"	but you Thjodolf write a verse about it".
"Herra?" segir hann, "eigi sómir þat, þar sem ek em kallaðr höfuðskáld yðart?"	"Lord?" said Thjodolf, "not common that, there as I am called chief-poet yours?"	"Lord", said Thjodolf, "I don't agree there, since I am called your chief poet".
Konungr svarar:	The-king answered:	The king answered:
"Þetta er meiri vandi enn þú munt ætla;	"This is more difficult than you should suppose;	"This is more difficult than you think.

The Tale of Sarcastic Halli (Old Norse)

Old Norse	Literal	English
þú skalt gera af þeim alla menn aðra en þeir eru:	you shall make of them completely men other than they are:	You shall make the men completely other than they are.
lát annan vera Sigurð Fáfnisbana, ok annan Fáfni, ok kenn þó hvárn til sinnar iðnar?"	have one be Sigurd Slayer-of-Fafnir, and another Fafnir, also know though each to his trade?"	Have one be Sigurd the Slayer of Fafnir, and another Fafnir, and also identify each one's trade".
Þjóðólfr kvað þá vísu:	Thjodolf recited then a-verse:	Thjodolf then recited a verse:
Sigurðr eggjaði sleggju snák váligrar brákar, enn skapdreki skinna skreið of leista heiði,	Sigurd urged the-hammer snake wretched breaker, but mood-dragon of-skins crawled off of-footwear the-heath,	Sigurd urged the-hammer snake wretched breaker, but mood-dragon of-skins crawled off of-footwear the-heath.
menn sásk orm, áðr ynni	people with-footwear the-serpent, before won	People with-footwear the-serpent before won
ilvegs búinn kilju nautaleðrs á naðri neflangr konungr tangar.	evil-ways prepared the-binding ox-skin of serpent long-nosed king's tongs.	evil-ways prepared the-binding, ox-skin of serpent long-nosed king's tongs.
"Þetta er vel kveðit?"	"That is well worded?"	"That is well composed",
segir konungr, "ok kveð nú aðra, ok lát þá annan vera Þór, enn annan Geirrauð jötun, ok kenn þó hvárn til sinnar iðnar.	said the-king, "and recite now another, and have now being one Thor, and another Geirrod the-giant, and know though each to their trade.	said the king, "and now recite another and have one being Thor and another Geirrod the Giant, and identify each with their trade".
Þá kvað Þjóðólfr vísu:	Then recited Thjodolf a-verse:	Then Thjodolf recited a verse:
Varp ór þrætu þorpi Þórr smiðbelgja stórra hvatt eldingum höldnum hafra kjöts at jötni;	Threw from threatening village Thor smith-bellows great encouraged lightning held goat flesh the giant;	Threw from threatening village Thor smith-bellows great lightning held goat flesh the giant.
hljóðgreipum tók húðar hrökkvi-skafls ór afli glaðr við galdra smiðju Geirrauðr síu þeiri.	sound-grippers (ears) took hide shaken of power glad with magic of-the-smith Geirrod sift of-them.	Sound-grippers (ears) took hide shaken of power glad with magic of-the-smith Geirrod sift of-them.
"Ekki ertú ámælisverðr um þat?"	"Not are-you talked about that?"	"You are not over talked about",
sagði konungr, "at þú ert órleysingr til skáldskapar?"	said the-king, "that you are over-praised as a-poet?"	said the king, "when you are praised as a poet".

The Tale of Sarcastic Halli (Old Norse)

Old Norse	Literal	English
Ok lofuðu allir, at vel væri ort.	And praised all, to well being worded.	And all praised him on how well it had been composed.
Ekki var Halli við þetta.	Not was Halli with this.	Halli was not present with them.
Ok um kveldit, er menn sátu við drykk, kváðu þeir fyrir Halla, ok sögðu hann eigi mundu svá yrkja, þótt hann þœttist skáld mikit.	And about evening, when men sat with drink, recited they for Halli, and told him not would so compose, though he thought a-poet great.	And that evening when men sat drinking they recited the poem for Halli and told him that he could not compose such a poem even though he thought of himself as a great poet.
Halli kveðst vita, at hann orti verr enn Þjóðólfr.	Halli said knew, that he worded worse than Thjodolf.	Halli said that he knew he composed worse poetry than Thjodolf
"Enn þó mun mér firrst um fara, ef ek em eigi við staddr yrkis-efnin?"	"In-the-end shall then to-me lost about going, if I seek not with to compose?"	"in the end I shall lose if I do not try to compose a verse, and if I am not present",
segir Halli.	said Halli.	said Halli.
Þetta var þegar sagt konungi, ok snúit svá, at hann þœttist eigi minna skáld enn Þjóðólfr.	This was then told-to the-king, and turned so, that he thought not less a-poet than Thjodolf.	This was then told to the king and turned around to say that he thought himself no less of a poet than Thjodolf.
Konungr kvað honum eigi at því verða mundu, "enn vera kann, at vér fáim þetta reynt af stundu?"	The-king said him not that therefore be would, "but be can-it, that we get that tested in awhile?"	The king said that he would not be that, "but it can be that we can test him in a while".

4

Þat var einn dag, er menn sátu yfir borðum, at þar gekk inn í höllina dvergr einn, er Túta hét;	It was one day, when people were sitting at-table, that there went then into the-hall dwarf one, who Tuta named;	It was one day when people were sitting at the table that a dwarf named Tuta went into the hall.
hann var frískr at ætt.	he was Frisian by descent.	He was Frisian by descent.
Hann hafði lengi verit með Haraldi konungi.	He had long been with Harald the-king.	He had been with King Harald a long time.

The Tale of Sarcastic Halli (Old Norse)

Old Norse	Literal	English
Hann var eigi hærri enn þrevett barn, enn allra manna digrastr ok herðamestr, höfuðit mikit ok elliligt, hryggrinn eigi allskammr, enn sýlt í neðan, þar sem fœtrnir váru.	He was not higher than three-winters-old child, but of-all men thick-set and most-hardy, head great and elderly, spine not very-short, but sleek of below, there where the-legs were.	He was no taller than a child of three years old, but he was the most thick set and hardy of all men, he had a large and elderly looking head, and his back was not very short, but sleek below where his legs were.
Haraldr konungr átti brynju, þá er hann kallaði Emmu;	Harald the-king hat coat-of-mail, then which he called Emma;	King Harald had a coat of mail which he called Emma.
hann hafði látit gera hana í Miklagarði.	he had had made her in Byzantium.	He had had it made in Byzantium.
Hon var svá síð, at hon tók niðr á skó Haraldi konungi, þá er hann stóð réttr;	She was so long, that she took down to shoes Harald's the-king, then when he stood upright;	It was so long that it reached down to King Harald's shoes when he stood upright.
var hon öll tvöföld, ok svá styrk, at aldrigi festi járn á.	was she all two-fold, and so strong, that never pierced iron-weapon an.	It was all double-thickness and so strong that it was never pierced by an iron weapon.
Konungrinn hafði látit fœra dverginn í brynjuna ok setja hjálm á höfuð honum, ok gyrði hann sverði.	The-king had had sent-for the-dwarf in coat-of-mail and set helmet on head his, and equipped him a-sword.	The king had ordered the dwarf to be in the coat of mail with a helmet set on his head and equipped with a sword.
Síðan gekk hann inn í höllina, sem fyrr var ritat, ok þótti maðrinn vera undrskapaðr.	After went he in to the-hall, as before was written, and thought the-man was wonder-created.	After he went into the hall as was written before, and the man was thought to be a wonder.
Konungrinn kvaddi sér hljóðs, ok mælti:	The-king called to be-heard, and spoke:	The king called to be heard and spoke:
"Sá maðr, er kveðr um dverginn vísu, svá at mér þykki vel kveðin, þiggi af mér kníf þenna ok belti?"	"So the-man, who words about the-dwarf a-verse, so that to-me seems well worded, receives of me knife this and belt?"	"So the man who composes a verse about the dwarf, so that I think it is a good verse, will accept of me this knife and a belt",
ok lagði fram á borðit fyrir sik gripina:	and laid from to table before him the-trinkets:	and he put the trinkets on the table for him,

The Tale of Sarcastic Halli (Old Norse)

Old Norse	Literal	English
"Enn vitit þat fyrir víst, ef mér þykkir eigi vel kveðin, at hann skal hafa óþökk mína, ok missa gripanna beggja?"	"But know that for certainly, if to-me seems not well worded, that he shall have un-thanks mine, and miss the-trinkets both?"	"but know for certain that if I don't think it is a good poem, he will have my displeasure and lose the trinkets both".
Ok þegar er konungr hafði flutt erindi sitt, kveðr maðr vísu útar á bekkinn, ok var þat Sneglu-Halli:	And as-soon-as when the-king had delivered message his, recited a-man a-verse out from the-bench, and was that Sarcastic-Halli:	And as soon as the king had delivered his speech, a man recited a verse outside of the bench, and it was Sarcastic-Halli:
Færðr sýndisk mér frændi Frísa kyns í brynju, gengr fyr hirð í hringum hjálmfaldinn kúrvaldi; flœr-at eld í ári úthlaupi vanr Túta, sé'k á síðu leika sverð rúghleifa skerði.	Brought seems to-me kinsman Frisian kin in chain-mail, going before the-court in circles the-helmet folded; fleeing the-fire in all-year out-running custom Tuta, see of side games sword rye-loaf cuts.	Brought seems to-me kinsman Frisian kin in chain-mail. Going before the-court in circles the-helmet folded. Fleeing the-fire in all-year out-running custom Tuta. See I of side games sword rye-loaf cuts.
Konungr bað fœra honum gripina:	The-king ordered brought to-him the-trinkets:	The king ordered the trinkets to be brought to him
"Ok skaltú ná hér á sannmæli, því at vísan er vel kveðin?"	"And shall-you obtain here in true-words, because it the-verse is well worded?"	"and you will find the truth here, because the verse is well recited".
Þjóðólfi fannst fátt um.	Thjodolf thought little about.	
Þat var einn dag, er konungrinn var mettr, at konungr klappaði knífi á borðit, ok bað ryðja.	It was one day, when the-king was finished-eating, that the-king struck knife on the-table, and ordered cleared.	One day when the king had finished eating he struck his knife on the table and ordered the tables to be cleared.
Þjónustumenn gerðu svá,	The-servants did so,	The servants did so.
Þá var Halli hvergi nærri mettr.	Then was Halli nowhere near satisfied.	Then Halli was nowhere near satisfied.
Tók hann þá stykki eitt af diskinum, ok helt eftir, ok kvað þetta:	Took he then piece one off the-plate, and held back, and recited this:	He then took a piece of food from the place and held it back and recited this:
Hirði ek eigi hvat Haraldr klappar, læt ek gnauða grön,	Care I not that Harald's hammering, have I gnawing moustache,	Care I not that Harald's hammering. Have I gnawing moustache.

The Tale of Sarcastic Halli (Old Norse)

Old Norse	Literal	English
geng ek fullr at sofa.	going I full to sleep.	Going I full to sleep.
Um morgininn eftir, er konungr var kominn í sæti sitt ok hirðin, gekk Halli í höllina fyrir konunginn.	About morning after, when the-king was coming to sit himself and courtiers, went Halli into the-hall before the-king.	About morning when the king had come to sit with his courtiers, Halli went into the hall and went before the king.
Hann hafði skjöld sinn ok sverð á baki sér.	He had shield his and sword about back his.	He had his shield and sword on his back.
Hann kvað vísu:	He spoke a-verse:	He spoke a verse:
Selja mun'k við sufli sverð mitt, konungr, verða, ok, rymskyndir randa, rauðan skjöld við brauði; hungrar hilmis drengi, heldr gangu vér svangir; mér dregr hrygg at hverju (Haraldr sveltir mik) belti.	Barter will of with-bread sword mine, the-king, becomes, and, quickly-cleared round, the-red shield with bread; hungry helmsman's boys, rather going are-we hungry; to-me draws the-spine that which (Harald starving me) belt.	Barter will I of with-bread sword mine, the-king, becomes, and quickly-cleared round the-red shield with bread. Hungry helmsman's boys. Rather going are-we hungry. To-me draws the-spine, that which, Harald starving me, belt.
Engu svarar konungr, ok lét sem hann heyrði eigi;	None answered the-king, and had as he heard not;	The king gave no answer and acted as though he had not heard,
enn þat vissu allir menn, at honum mislíkaði.	but though knew all people, that he mis-liked.	but all the people knew that he disliked this.
Litlu síðar var þat, at konungrinn gekk úti ok fylgdin með honum;	A-little afterwards was it, that the-king went out and followers with him;	A little while afterwards one day the king went out into the street and had his followers with him.
þar var ok Halli í för.	there was also Halli with going.	And there was also Halli going with them.
Hann snaraði fram hjá konunginum.	He rushed ahead nearby the-king.	He rushed ahead to be near the king.
Konungrinn kvað þetta:	The-king spoke this:	The king spoke this:
"Hvert stillir þú Halli?"	"Where heading you Halli?"	"Where are you heading Halli?"
Halli svarar:	Halli answered:	Halli answered:
"Hleyp'k fram at skyrkaupum?"	"running forwards to cow-buying?"	"I am running to buy a cow".

The Tale of Sarcastic Halli (Old Norse)

Old Norse	Literal	English
"Graut muntú gera láta?"	"Porridge would-you look-to have?"	"Will you look to have porridge?"
segir konungr.	said the-king.	said the king.
"Görr matr es þat, smjörvan?"	"Ready-made food is that, buttered?"	"It is a ready made meal, when buttered",
segir Halli.	said Halli.	said Halli.
Hleypr hann Halli þá upp í garðinn, ok þangat sem var eldahús;	Ran he Halli then up to garden, and from-there as was fire-house (kitchen);	Then Halli ran up to a house where there was a kitchen.
þar hafði hann látit gera graut í stórum katli, settist til ok át grautinn.	there had he had made porridge in stone-kettle and, sat to and eat the-porridge.	There he had made porridge in a stone kettle, and sat there to eat the porridge.
Konungr sér, at Halli hverfr upp í garðinn.	The-king saw, that Halli turned up-to the garden.	The king saw that Halli had gone into the house.
Hann kvaddi til Þjóðólf ok tvá menn aðra, at leita Halla.	He called to Thjodolf and two men other, to look-for Halli.	He called to Thjodolf and two other men to look for Halli.
Konungr veik ok upp í garðinn.	The-king turned also up to the-house.	The king also arrived at the house.
Þeir finna hann, þar sem hann át grautinn.	They found him, there as he ate porridge.	They found him there as he ate the porridge.
Konungr kom þá at, ok sá, hvat hann hafðist at.	The-king came then to, and saw, what Halli had to.	The king came to him and saw what Halli was doing.
Konungr var hinn reiðasti, ok spurði Halla hví hann fór af Íslandi til höfðingja, til þess at gera af sér skömm ok gabb.	The-king was the most-angry, and asked Halli if he travelled from Iceland to chieftains, to this that make of himself scandal and mockery.	The king was very angry and asked Halli if he had travelled from Iceland to visit chieftains and make scandal and mockery.
"Látit eigi svá, herra?"	"Let not so, lord?"	"Let it not be so",
segir Halli;	said Halli;	said Halli,
"jafnan sé ek yðr eigi drepa kendi við góðum sendingum?"	"always see I you not kill hands with good delivery?"	"always I see that you do not kill hands that deliver good food".

The Tale of Sarcastic Halli (Old Norse)

Old Norse	Literal	English
Halli stóð þá upp, ok kastaði niðr katlinum, ok skall við haddan.	Halli stood then up, and cast down the-kettle, and hit against the-lid.	Halli then stood up and threw down the kettle, and hit against the lid.
Þjóðólfr kvað þá þetta:	Thjodolf recited then this:	Thjodolf then recited this:
Haddan skall, enn Halli hlaut offylli grautar, hornspánu kveð'k honum hlýða betr enn prýði.	The-handle rattled, and Halli a-lot-of gluttony of-porridge, horn-spoon say to-him suits better than finery.	The-handle rattled and Halli a-lot-of gluttony of-porridge. Horn-spoon say I to-him suits better than finery.
Konungrinn gekk þá burtu ok var allreiðr,	The-king went then away and was all-angry,	The king then went away and was very angry.
ok um kveldit kom engi matr fyrir Halla, sem fyrir aðra menn.	and about evening came no food before Halli, as before other people.	And about evening there came no food for Halli as there had been for the other people.
Ok er menn höfðu snætt um stund, komu inn tveir menn, ok báru milli sín trog mikit, fullt grautar, ok með spán, ok settu fyrir Halla.	And when people had dined about awhile, came then two men, and carried between themselves trough great, full of-porridge, and with a-spoon, and set before Halli.	And when people had dined for a while, then came two men carrying between themselves a great through, full of porridge, and with a spoon set it before Halli.
Hann tók við ok át sem hann lysti, ok hætti síðan.	He took to and ate as he appetite, and stopped afterwards.	He took it and ate as much as his appetite would allow, and then stopped.
Konungr bað Halla eta meira.	The-king ordered Halli eat more.	The king ordered Halli to eat more.
Hann kveðst eigi mundu eta meira at sinni.	He said not would eat more for himself.	He said he himself would not eat any more.
Haraldr konungr brá þá sverði, ok bað Halla eta grautinn, þar til er hann spryngi af.	Harald the-king drew then a-sword, and ordered Halli eat porridge, there until that he burst of.	King Harald then drew a sword and ordered Halli to eat the porridge until he burst.
Halli kveðst eigi mundu sprengja sik á grauti, enn sagði konung ná mundu lífi sínu, ef hann væri á þat einhugi.	Halli said not would burst himself with porridge, but told the-king take could life his, if he would-be of that one-minded.	Halli said that he would not burst himself with porridge, but told the king that he could take his life if he was of a mind to do so.
Konungr sezt þá niðr ok slíðrar sverðit.	The-king sat then down and sheathed sword.	The king then sat down and sheathed his sword.

The Tale of Sarcastic Halli (Old Norse)

Old Norse	Literal	English
5	**5**	**5**
Nökkuru síðar var þat einn dag, at konungr tók disk einn af borði sínu, ok var á steiktr gríss, ok bað Tútu dverg at fœra Halla,	Somewhat later was it one day, that the-king took plate one off table his, and was it roasted pig, and ordered Tuta the-dwarf to bring Halli,	One day somewhat later, the king took a plate off his table, and on it was a roasted pig, he ordered Tuta the dwarf to bring it to Halli
"ok bið hann yrkja vísu, ef hann vill halda lífinu, ok hafa kveðit, áðr þú kemr fyrir hann, ok seg honum eigi fyrr enn þú kemr á mitt gólf?"	"and order him to-compose a-verse, if he wishes to-hold his-life, and have spoken, after you come before him, and tell him not before that you come to the-middle the-floor?"	"and order him to compose a verse if he wishes to hold his life, and recite it after you come before him, and tell him not before you are in the middle of the floor".
"Eigi em ek þess fúss?"	"Not am I this willing?"	"I am not willing to do this",
segir Túta, "því at mér líkar vel við Halla?"	said Tuta, "because that I like well with Halli?"	said Tuta, "because I like Halli".
"Sé ek",	"See I",	"I see",
segir konungr,	said the-king,	said the king,
"at þér líkar vel vísan ok þykkir góð, sú er hann orti um þik, ok muntú gerla heyra kunna.	"that you consider good verse yours that good, the-one is he worded about you, and shall-you completely hear know.	that you consider his verse good that he composed about you, and you know how to listen carefully.
Nú far burt í stað, ok ger sem ek býð?"	Now go away to the-place, and do as I command?"	Now to away and do as I command".
Túta tók við diskinum, ok gekk á mitt gólfið ok mælti:	Tuta took with the-plate, and went to the-middle of-the-floor and spoke:	Tuta now took the place and went to the middle of the floor and spoke:
"Þú, Halli, yrk vísu at boði konungs, ok haf ort, áðr ek kem fyrir þik, ef þú vill halda lífinu?"	"You, Halli, compose a-verse to order the-king's, and have worded, before I come before you, if you wish to-hold your-life?"	"You Halli are ordered by the king to compose a verse and have it composed before I come before you if you wish to hold your life".
Halli stóð þá upp, ok rétti hendr í móti diskinum, ok kvað vísu:	Halli stood then up, and extended hand to meet the-plate, and recited a-verse:	Halli then stood up and extended a hand to meet the plate and recited a verse:
Grís þá greppr at ræsi gruntrauðustum dauðan,	Pig then grasped of-the-ruler deep-red death,	Pig then grasped of-the-ruler deep-red death.

The Tale of Sarcastic Halli (Old Norse)

Old Norse	Literal	English
Njörðr sér börg á borði baglands fyr (sér) standa;	Njord sees the-city on the-table ring-land before (himself) standing;	Njord sees the-city on the-table ring-land before standing.
runa síður lít'k rauðar, ræð'k skjótt gera kvæði, rana hefir seggr af svíni (send heill, konungr) brenndan.	row since coloured red, speak rapidly made poem, the-trunk has said man swine (send health, king) burnt.	Row since coloured I red. Speak I rapidly made poem. The-trunk has said man swine, send health king, burnt.
Konungr mælti þá:	The-king spoke then:	The king then spoke:
"Nú skal gefa þér upp reiði mína, Halli, því at vísan er vel kveðin, svá skjótt sem til var tekit?"	"Now shall give you up anger mine, Halli, because that verse is well recited, so quickly as to was taken?"	"Now I will give up my anger for you, Halli, because the sentence is well recited as soon as it was taken".

6

Frá því er sagt einn dag, at Halli gekk fyrir konunginn, þá er hann var glaðr ok kátr.	From then is said one day, that Halli went before the-king, then as he was glad and cheerful.	From then it is said that one day Halli went before the king as he was glad and cheerful.
Þar var þá Þjóðólfr ok margt annarra manna.	There was then Thjodolf and many other people.	Then Thjodolf and many other people were there.
Halli sagðist hafa ort drápu um konunginn, ok bað sér hljóðs.	Halli said had worded drapa (poem) about the-king, and asked for-him be-heard.	Halli said that he had composed a drapa about the king and ask him for it to be heard.
Konungrinn spurði, hvárt Halli hefði nökkut kvæði fyrri ort.	The-king asked, whether Halli had anything composed before worded.	The king asked whether Halli had composed anything before.
Halli kveðst eigi hafa fyrri ort.	Halli said not had before worded.	He said he had not composed anything.
"Þat munu menn mæla?"	"It would people say?"	"Some people would say",
segir konungr, "at þú takist mikit á hendr, slík skáld sem ort hafa um mik áðr, eftir nökkurum málefnum;	said the-king, "that you take much in hand, such poets as worded have about me before, after some matters;	said the king, "that you take much in hand, as such poets have composed poems about me for various reasons.
eðr hvat sýnist þér Þjóðólfr?"	but what seems to-you Thjodolf?"	But what seems advisable to you Thjodolf?"
"Eigi kann ek, herra, at gefa yðr ráð?"	"Not can I, lord, to give you advice?"	"I can not give you advice, lord",

The Tale of Sarcastic Halli (Old Norse)

Old Norse	Literal	English
segir Þjóðólfr, "enn hitt mun hóti nær, at ek muna kunna at gefa Halla heilræði?"	said Thjodolf, "but then could not near, that I would know to teach Halli sound-advice?"	said Thjodolf, "but then I could give Halli some sound advice".
"Hvert er þat?"	"What is that?"	"What is that?"
sagði konungr.	said the-king.	said the king.
"Þat fyrst, herra, at hann ljúgi ekki at yðr?"	"That first, lord, that he lie not to you?"	"First of all that he not lie to you".
"Hvat lýgr hann nú?"	"What lies he now?"	"What does he lie about now?"
segir konungr.	said the-king.	said the king.
"Þat lýgr hann, at hann sagðist ekki kvæði ort hafa?"	"That lying he, that he said not composed words had?"	"He is lying when he says that he has not composed such words",
sagði Þjóðólfr, "enn ek segi hann ort hafa?"	said Thjodolf, "but I say he words has?"	said Thjodolf, "but I say that he has composed".
"Hvert er kvæði þat?"	"What is composed that?"	"What has he composed?",
segir konungr, "eðr um hvat er ort?"	said the-king, "and about what is worded?"	said the king, "and what is it composed about?"
Þjóðólfr svarar:	Thjodolf answered:	Thjodolf answered:
"Þat köllu vér Kollu-vísur, er hann orti um kýr, er hann gætti ut á Íslandi?"	"That call we cow-verses, which he worded about cows, that he guarded out in Iceland?"	"That which we call Cow-verses, which he composed about cows that he guarded out in Iceland".
"Er þat satt, Halli?"	"Is that true, Halli?"	"Is that true Halli?"
segir konungr.	said the-king.	said the king.
"Satt er þat?"	"True is that?"	"That is true",
segir Halli.	said Halli.	said Halli.
"Hví sagðir þú, at þú hefðir ekki kvæði ort?"	"Why said you, that you had not composed words?"	"Why did you say that you had not composed such words?"
sagði konungr.	said the-king.	said the king.

The Tale of Sarcastic Halli (Old Norse)

Old Norse	Literal	English
"Því" sagði Halli, *"at lítil kvæðismynd mundi á því þykkja, ef þetta skal heyra, ok lítt mun því verða á loft haldit?"*	"Because" said Halli, "that little poem-image would be therefore seemed, if it should heard, and little would therefore worth of praised held?"	"Because", said Halli, "that such a little poem would seem if heard worth little praise".
"Þat viljum vér fyrst heyra?"	"That wish we first to-hear?"	"We wish to hear that first",
segir konungr.	said the-king.	said the king.
"Skemt mun þá fleira?"	"Entertainment should then more?"	"Then there should be more than one amusement",
segir Halli.	said Halli.	said Halli.
"Hverju þá?"	"What then?"	"What then?"
segir konungr.	said the-king.	said the king.
"Kveða mun Þjóðólfr þá skulu Sorptrogs-vísur, er hann orti úti á Íslandi?"	"Recite should Thjodolf then should food-trough-verses, which he worded out in Iceland?"	"Thjodolf should then recite Food-trough-verses which he composed out in Iceland",
segir Halli, "ok er þat vel, at, Þjóðólfr leitaði á mik eða af virði fyrir mér, því at upp eru svá í mér bitar ok jaxlar, at ek kann vel at svara honum jöfnum orðum?"	said Halli, "and is that well, that, Thjodolf sought to me but disrespected before me because, that up we-are so coming that my bite and molars, that I can well to answer him even words?"	said Halli, "and it is well that Thjodolf sought to disrespect me, but because my bite and molars are up I can answer him well with words".
Konungr brosti at, ok þótti gaman at etja þeim saman.	The-king smiled at, and thought enjoyment to provoke them together.	The king smiled and thought it was enjoyable to provoke them against eachother.
"Hveru veg er kvæði þat, eðr um hvat er ort?"	"What way is composed that, and about what are words?"	"What is it composed about and what are the words?"
segir konungr.	said the-king.	said the king.
Halli svarar:	Halli answered:	Halli answered:

The Tale of Sarcastic Halli (Old Norse)

Old Norse	Literal	English
"Þat er ort um þat, er hann bar út ösku með öðrum systkinum sínum, ok þótti þá til einkis annars fœrr fyrir vitsmuna sakir, ok varð þó um at sjá, at eigi væri eldr í, svá at mein yrði at, því at hann þurfti allt vit sitt í þann tíma?"	"That is worded about that, which he bore out ashes with other siblings his, and thought then to nothing other accomplished before intellect sake, and became though about to see, that not would fire about, so that mean should that, because that he needed all wit his at that time?"	"It is composed about carrying out ashes with his other siblings, and he was thought capable of accomplishing nothing more for the sake of his intellect, and it was necessary to see that there was no fire about because he needed all his wit at that time".
Konungr spyrr ef þetta væri satt?	The-king asked if that was true	The king asked if that was true.
"Satt er þat, herra?"	"True is that, lord?"	"That is true, lord",
segir Þjóðólfr.	said Thjodolf.	said Thjodolf.
"Hví hafðir þú svá óvirðuligt verk?"	"Why had you so unworthy work?"	"Why did you have such unworthy work?"
segir konungr.	said the-king.	said the king.
"Því, herra?"	"Because, lord?"	"Because lord",
segir Þjóðólfr,	said Thjodolf,	said Thjodolf,
"at ek vilda flýta oss til leika, enn eigi váru verk á mik lagin?"	"that I wished quickly us to play, and not was work to me assigned?"	"that I wished to get us quickly out to play, and no work was assigned to me".
"Þat olli því?"	"That cause therefore?"	"It caused",
segir Halli,	said Halli,	said Halli,
"at þú þóttir eigi hafa verkmanns vit?"	"that you thought not had workman's wit?"	that you were thought not to have the sense of a worker".
"Ekki skulu þit við talast?"	"Not should you-two against speak?"	"You must not argue",
segir konungr, "enn heyra vilju vér kvæðin bæði?"	said the-king, "but hear wish we poems both?"	said the king, "but we want to hear both the poems".
Ok svá varð at vera.	And so became to be.	And so it was.
Kvað þá hvárr sitt kvæði;	Recited then each their poems;	Then each recited their poems.

The Tale of Sarcastic Halli (Old Norse)

Old Norse	Literal	English
ok er lokit var kvæðunum, mælti konungrinn:	and when concluded was the-poetry, spoke the-king:	And when the poems were finished, the king said:
"Lítit er kvæðit hvárttveggja, enda munu lítil hafa verit yrkisefnin, ok þat þó enn minna, er þú hefir ort, Þjóðólfr?"	"Little is poem each-way, ended would little have been the-themes, and is though the lesser, is you have worded, Thjodolf?"	"The poems are little on both sides, because the themes were small, and the lesser one is the one that you have composed Thjodolf".
"Svá er ok, herra?"	"So is also, lord?"	"And so it is, lord",
segir Þjóðólfr, "ok er Halli orðhvass mjök.	said Thjodolf, "and is Halli sharp-tongued much.	said Thjodolf, "and Halli is very sharp tongued.
Enn skyldara þætti mér honum, at hefna föður síns, enn at eiga sennur við mik hér í Noregi?"	But should seems to-me of-him, to avenge father his, but that not chatter with me here in Norway?"	But I think it's more important for him to avenge his father than to have a fight with me here in Norway".
"Er þat satt, Halli?"	"Is that true, Halli?"	"Is that true Halli?"
segir konungr.	said the-king.	said the king.
"Satt er þat, herra?"	"True is that, lord?"	"That is true, lord",
segir Halli.	said He.	he said.
"Hví fórtu af Íslandi til höfðingja við þat, at þú hafðir eigi hefnt föður þíns?"	"Why went-you from Iceland to chieftains with than, that you have not avenged father yours?"	"Why did you go from Iceland to meet the chieftains when you had not avenged your father?"
segir konungr.	said the-king.	said the king.
"Því, herra?"	"Because, lord?"	"Because, lord",
"at ek var barn at aldri, þá er faðir minn var veginn, ok tóku frændr (mínir) málit, ok sættust á fyrir mína hönd.	"said Halli that I was a-child, in age when father mine was, killed and took (kinsman) the-matter, and settled it before my hand.	said Halli, "I was a child in age when my father was killed, and my cousins took the case and settled on my behalf.
Enn þat þykkir illt nafn á váru landi, at heita griðníðingr?"	But it considered ill named in our land, to call truce-breaker?"	But it is considered ill called in our land to be a truce-breaker".
Konungrinn svarar:	The-king answered:	The king answered:

The Tale of Sarcastic Halli (Old Norse)

Old Norse	Literal	English
"Þat er nauðsyn at ganga eigi á grið eðr sættir, ok er ór þessu allvel leyst?"	"It is necessary to go not to peace or settlements, and that from this all-well answered?"	"It is necessary to go to peace or reconciliation and this is well resolved".
"Svá hugða ek, herra?"	"So thought I, lord?"	"So I thought, lord",
segir Halli, "enn vel má Þjóðólfr tala stórmannliga um slíka hluti, því at öngvan veit ek jafngreypiliga hefnt hafa föður síns sem hann?"	said Halli, "and well may Thjodolf speak big-man-like about such a-thing, since that none know I equally-badly revenge had his father as he?"	said Halli, "and well may Thjodolf speak arrogantly about such a thing since no one I know has equally badly avenged his father as him".
"Víst er Þjóðólfr líklegr til, at hafa þat hraustliga gert?"	"Certainly is Thjodolf likely to, that have that boldly done?"	"Certainly Thjodolf is like to have done that boldly",
segir konungr;	said the-king;	said the king,
"eðr hvat er verkum gert um þat, at hann hafi þat framar gert enn aðrir menn?"	"but what are actions done about it, that he has that from done than other people?"	but what actions did he take unlike other people?
Þat helzt, herra?	That rather, lord?	"Rather, lord",
segir Halli, "at hann át föðurbana sinn".	said Halli, "that he ate his father's-killer".	said Halli, "that he ate his father's killer".
Nú œptu menn upp, ok þóttust aldrei slík undr heyrt hafa.	Now called-out people up, and thought never such wonder heard had.	Now people rose up and called out and thought they had never heard of such a wonder.
Konungrinn brosti at, ok bað menn vera hljóða.	The-king grinned at, and ordered men to-be calm.	The king grinned and ordered people to be calm.
"Ger þetta satt, er þú sagðir, Halli?"	"Does this true, that you said, Halli?"	"Do so that what you say is true Halli",
segir konungr.	said the-king.	said the king.
Halli mælti:	Halli spoke:	Halli spoke:
"Þat hygg ek, at Þórljótr héti faðir Þjóðólfs.	"That think I, that Thorljot named father Thjodolf's.	"I think that Thjodolf's father was named Thorljot.
Hann bjó í Svarfaðardal á Íslandi, ok var hann fátœkr mjök, enn átti fjölda barna.	He lived in Svarfadardal in Iceland, and was he fee-taken much, and had many children.	He lived in Svarfadardal in Iceland and he was very poor and had many children.

The Tale of Sarcastic Halli (Old Norse)

Old Norse	Literal	English
Enn þat er siðr á Íslandi á haustum, at bœndr þinga til fátœkra manna, ok var þá engi fyrri til nefndr, enn Þorljótr, faðir Þjóðólfs;	But it is a-custom in Iceland in autumn, that farmers assemble to the-poor people, and was then none before to named, than Thorljot, father Thjodolf's;	But it is a custom in Iceland in the autumn for farmers to hold meetings for poor people, and there was no one better than Thorljot, Thjodolf's father,
ok einn bóndi var svá, stórlyndr, at hann gaf honum sumargamlan kálf.	and one farmer was so, large-repaying (generous), that he gave him one-summer-old a-calf.	and one farmer was so generous that he gave him a summer-old calf.
Síðan sœkir hann kálfinn ok hafði í taumi, ok var lykkja á enda taumsins;	Then sought he the-calf and had a leash, and was noose at the-end the-leash;	Then he fetched the calf and had it on a leash and there was a loop at the end of the leash.
ok er hanu kom heim at túngarði sínum, hefr hann kálfinn upp á garðinn, ok var furðanliga hár garðrinn;	and when he came home to hayfield-wall his, had he the-calf up on the-wall, and was extremely high the-wall;	And when he came home to his yard wall he had the calf up on the wall, and it was extremely high,
þó var hærra fyrir innan, því at þar hafði verit grafit torf til garðsins.	though was higher before inside, because that there had been dug turf up-to the-wall.	but it was higher on the inside because the turf had been dug up to the wall.
Síðan ferr hann inn yfir garðinn;	Afterwards went he then over the-wall;	Then he went into the yard,
enn kálfrinn veltr út af garðinum.	but the-calf hung outside of the-wall.	but the calf tumbled out of the yard.
Enn lykkjan, er á var taums-endanum, brást um háls honum Þorljóti, ok kenndi hann eigi niðr fótum;	Then the-noose, that about was the-leash, transformed about neck his Thorljot, and felt he not down feet;	But the loop that was on the end of the leash snapped around Thorljot's neck and he didn't fall to his feet.
hekk nú sínum megin hvárr, ok váru dauðir báðir, þegar er til var komit.	hung now his side each, and were dead both, already then until who came.	Now each hung separately and both were dead by the time it was over.
Drógu börnin heim kálfinn, ok gerðu til matar, ok hygg ek, at Þjóðólfr hefði óskerðan sinn hlut af honum?"	Drew the-children home the-calf, and made into food, and think I, that Thjodolf had the-whole his share of him?"	The children brought the calf home and made it for dinner, and I think Thjodolf had his share of it intact".
"Nærri hófi mundi þat"	"Close-to reasonable should-be that"	"That would be more reasonable",
segir konungr.	said the-king.	said the king.

The Tale of Sarcastic Halli (Old Norse)

Old Norse	Literal	English
Þjóðólfr brá sverði, ok vildi höggva til Halla.	Thjodolf drew sword, and wished to-strike to Halli.	Thjodolf drew his sword and wanted to attack Halli.
Hljópu menn þá í milli þeira.	Ran men then in between them.	Men ran in between them.
Konungr kvað hvárigum hlýða skyldu, at gera öðrum mein:	The-king said neither obeying should, to do eachother harm:	The king said that neither should do eachother harm if they obeyed him.
"Leitaðir þú, Þjóðólfr, fyrr á Halla?"	"Seek you, Thjodolf, went-before to Halli?"	"Thjodolf, you went for Halli first".
Varð nú svá at vera sem konungr vildi.	Was now so as being as the-king willed.	Then it was now as the king wished.
Færði Halli drápuna, ok mæltist hon vel fyrir, ok launaði konungr honum góðum penningum.	Performed Halli the-drapa (poem), and recited it well for, and rewarded the-king him good payment.	Halli performed the drapa and it was well received, and the king paid him good money.
Leið nú á vetrinn ok var allt kyrrt.	Passed now to winter and was all peaceful.	It now passed to winter and everything was quiet.

7

Einarr er maðr nefndr, ok var kallaðr fluga.	Einar was a-man named, and was called Fly.	There was a man named Einar who was called Fly.
Hann var son Háreks ór Þjóttu.	He was son Harek's from Thjotta.	He was the son of Harek from Thjotta.
Hann var lendr maðr, ok hafði sýslu á Hálogalandi ok Finnferð af konungi, ok var nú í kærleikum miklum við konung, enn þó eldi þar jafnan ýmsu á.	He was land man, and had business in Halogaland and Finland-voyages of the-king's, and was now in friendship much with the-king, but though fire there equally about was.	He was a land owning man and had business in Halogaland and voyages to Finland, and was now in great friendship with the king, but there was always something going on there.
Einarr var óeyrðarmaðr mikill.	Einar was unreliable much.	Einar was very unreliable.
Drap hann menn, ef eigi gerðu allt, sem hann vildi, ok bœtti öngan mann.	Killed he men, if not did all, as he wished, and compensated no man.	He killed people if they didn't do everything he wanted and gave compensation to no man.
Einars var ván til hirðarinnar at jólunum.	Einar was expected to court at Yule.	Einar was expected at court during Yule.

The Tale of Sarcastic Halli (Old Norse)

Old Norse	Literal	English
Þeim Halla og Sigurði sessunaut hans varð talat til Einars.	They Halli and Sigurd bench-companion his were talking about Einar.	Halli and his bench companion Sigurd were talking about Einar.
Sagði Sigurðr Halla frá, at engi maðr þyrði at mæla í móti Einari eðr í aðra skál at leggja enn hann vildi sjálfr, ok hann bœtti eigi fé fyrir víg eðr rán.	Told Sigurd Halli from, that no man dared to speak to against Einar or that other shall to allow but he wished himself, and he compensated not payment for slaying or robbery.	Sigurd told Halli that no man dared to speak against Einar or to allow anything other than what he wished, and that he paid no compensation for slaying or robbery.
Halli svarar:	Halli answered:	Halli answered:
"Vændis höfðingjar mundu slíkir kallaðir á váru landi?"	"Wicked chieftains would such be-called in our land?"	"Such a chieftain would be called wicked in our land".
"Mæl þú varliga, félagi?"	"Speak you warily, companion?"	"Speak carefully, friend",
segir Sigurðr, "því at hann er lítilþægr at orðum, ef honum eru í móti skapi?"	said Sigurd, "because that he is little-behaving that words, if he is to against mind?"	said Sigurd, "because he doesn't mix his words if he's in a bad mood".
"Þó at þér séit allir svá hræddir?"	"Though that you look all so afraid?"	"Although you are all so afraid",
segir Halli, "at engi yðarr þori, at mæla eitt orð í móti honum, þá segi ek þér þat satt, at ek skylda kæra, ef hann gerði mér rangt, ok þess get ek, at hann bœti mér?"	said Halli, "that none of-you dare, to say one word to against him, then say I to-you this true, that I would accuse, if he did me wrong, and this get I, of him compensate me?"	said Halli, "that none of you dare to say a word against him, I tell you that I would complain if he did me wrong and I expect him to make it up to me".
"Hví þér enn öðrum?"	"Why to-you than others?"	"Why are you different from others?"
segir Sigurðr.	said Sigurd.	said Sigurd.
"Þat mundi honum sýnna?"	"That would to-him appear?"	"That shall become apparent to him",
segir Halli.	said Halli.	said Halli.
Þar til þræta þeir hér um, at Halli býðr Sigurði at veðja.	They to argued them here about, that Halli offered Sigurd to wager.	They argued amongst themselves until Halli offered to make a wager with Sigurd about it.

The Tale of Sarcastic Halli (Old Norse)

Old Norse	Literal	English
Leggr Sigurðr hér við gullhring, er stóð hálfa mörk, enn Halli leggr við höfuð sitt.	Laid Sigurd here with a-gold-ring, in place half a-mark, and Halli laid with head his.	Here, Sigurd placed a gold ring that stood at half a mark, but Halli placed his head.
Einarr kemr at jólum, ok sitr hann á hœgri hönd konungi, ok menn hans út frá honum.	Einar came at Yule, and sat he by other hand the-king's, and people his about from him.	Einar came at Yule and he sat by the king's hand with his people around him.
Var honum öll þjónusta veitt sem konungi sjálfum.	Was he all service given as the-king himself.	He was given every service as much as the king himself.
Ok jóladag, er menn váru mettir, mælti konungrinn:	And Yule-day, when people were finished-eating, spoke the-king:	And on Yule day when people had finished eating the king spoke:
"Nú viljum vér hafa fleira til gamans, enn drekka.	"Now wish we to-have more to amusement, than drinking.	"Now we wish to have more amusement than drinking.
Skaltú nú, segja oss Einarr, hvat til tíðinda hefir orðit í förum yðrum?"	Shall-you now, Einar tell Us, what to news have worded on journey yours?"	Einar, you shall now tell us what word you have of news on your journey.
Einarr svarar:	Einar answered:	Einar answered:
"Ekki kann ek þat í frásagnir at fœra, herra, þó at vér knúskim bú-Finna eðr fiskimenn?"	"Not can I that as stories to bring, lord, though that we knocked-down farmers and fishermen?"	"I don't know how to tell stories, lord, even though we knocked down some farmers and fishermen".
Konungr svarar:	The-king answered:	The king answered:
"Segit settliga, því at vér erum lítilþægir at, ok þykkir oss gaman at því öllu, þó at yðr þykki lítilsvert, er jafnan standit í stríði?"	"Tell sedately, because that we are easily-satisfied by, and seems to-us a-delight that therefore all, though that you think little, is always standing in battles?"	"Tell us calmly because we are easily satisfied by it and it all seems to us a delight even though you think it is of little worth, and as you are constantly in battles".
"Þat er þá, herra, helzt at segja?"	"It is though, lord, rather to say?"	"However, lord, I prefer to say",
segir Einarr, "at í fyrra sumar, er vér komum norðr á Mörkina, mœttum vér Íslands-fari einu, ok höfðu þeir orðit þangat sæhafa, og setit þar um vetrinn.	said Einar, "that of last summer, when we came north of The-border, met we Iceland-voyage one, and had they become from-there sea-scattered, and sat there about winter.	said Einar, "that last summer when we came north of the border we met a ship journeying from Iceland, and they had been sea-scattered and were there since winter.

The Tale of Sarcastic Halli (Old Norse)

Old Norse	Literal	English
Bar ek á hendr þeim, at þeir mundu kaup átt hafa við Finna, fyrir útan yðart lof eðr mitt;	Bore I to hand them, that they would had having traded with The-Sami, for without your permission or mine;	I put it to them that they had traded with the Sami people without your permission or mine,
enn þeir duldu ok gengu eigi við;	that the denied and went not with;	which they denied and would not agree with,
enn oss þóttu þeir ótrúligir, ok beidda ek þá rannsóknar;	but we thought them un-truthful, and asked I then a-search;	but we thought they were untruthful, and I asked to search them,
enn þeir synjuðu þverliga.	but they refused crossly.	but they flatly refused.
Ek sagða þá, at þeir skyldi hafa þat, er þeim væri verra ok makligra, ok bað ek mína menn vápnast ok leggja at þeim.	I said then, that they should have it, what for-them being worse and well-deserved, and ordered I my men armed and lay at them.	I then said that they should have what was worse and more deserved for them, and I asked my men to arm themselves and attack them.
Ek hafða fimm langskip, ok lögðu vér at á bæði borð, ok léttum eigi fyrr enn hroðit var skipit.	I had five longships, and laid we to at both boards, and let-up not before that cleared was the-ship.	I had five longships and we anchored on both sides and did not let up until the ship was cleared.
Ok einn íslenzkr maðr, er þeir kölluðu Einar, varðist svá vel, at hans maka fann ek aldrigi, ok víst var skaði at um þann mann, ok eigi hefðim vér unnit skipit, ef slíkir hefði allir verit innanborðs?"	And one Icelander man, that they called Einar, guarded so well, that he equal found I never, and certainly was harm to about that man, and not have we won the-ship, if such had all been onboard?"	And one Icelander man, that they called Einar, guarded so well that I have never found his equal, and it was certainly a loss for that man, and we would not have won the ship if such men as him had all been aboard".
"Illa gerir þú þat, Einarr"	"Badly done you it, Einar"	"You did badly, Einar",
segir konungr, "er þú drepr saklausa menn, þó at eigi geri allt sem þér líkar bezt?"	said the-king, "when you killed sake-less people, though that not did all as you liked best?"	said the king, "you kill innocent people who don't do everything you like best".
"Mun ek eigi?"	"Would I not?"	"I will not",
sagði Einarr, "sitja fyrir hættu þeiri;	said Einar, "settle for danger theirs;	said Einar, "sit before that danger.
enn mæla þat sumir menn, herra, at þér gerit eigi allt sem guðréttligast;	and say it some people, lord, that you do not all as good-rightly;	But some people say, sir, that you don't do everything in the most godly way.

The Tale of Sarcastic Halli (Old Norse)

Old Norse	Literal	English
enn þeir reyndust illa, ok fundu vér mikinn finnskrepp í skipinu?"	but they proved bad, also found we much Sami-goods in the-ship?"	But they turned out to be bad and we found a great amount of Sami goods in the ship".
Halli heyrði, hvat þeir tölluðu, ok kastaði knífinum fram á borðit ok hætti at eta.	Halli heard, what they spoke, and cast knife away from the-table and stopped of eating.	Halli heard what they were talking about and threw the knife on the table and stopped eating.
Sigurðr spurði, ef hann væri sjúkr.	Sigurd asked, if he was sick.	Sigurd asked if he was sick.
Hann kvað þetta sótt verra:	He said that not was:	He said it wasn't,
"Einarr fluga sagði lát Einars bróður míns, er hann kveðst fellt hafa á kaupskipinu í fyrra sumar, ok má vera at nú gefi til, at leita eftir bótunum við hann Einar?"	"Einar Fly told-of had Einar brother mine, that he said fell had on merchant-ship in before summer, and may be that now give to, of seeking after compensation with him Einar?"	"Einar Fly told about the death of my brother Einar, who he claims to have killed on the merchant ship last summer, and it may be that he now seeks to give compensation for Einar".
"Tala ekki um, félagi?"	"Speak not about, companion?"	"Do not speak about it, companion",
segir Sigurðr;	said Sigurd;	said Sigurd,
"sá mun vænstr?"	"so would-be promising?"	that would be the most promising.
"Nei?" segir Halli, "ekki mundi hann svá við mik gera, ef hann ætti eftir mik at mæla?"	"No?" said Halli, "not would he so with me doing, if he had after me the matter?"	Halli said no, "he would not do that with me if it was my case he was dealing with".
Hljóp hann þá fram yfir borðit, gekk innar fyrir hásætit ok mælti:	Jumped he then from over table, went in before high-seat and spoke:	He then jumped over the table, and went before the high seat and spoke:
"Tíðindi sögðu þér, Einarr bóndi, það er mik akta œrit mjök í drápi Einars bróður míns, er þér sögðuzt feldan hafa á kaupskipinu í fyrra sumar.	"News announced you, Einar master, that is me taxes greatly much by the-killing Einar's brother mine, who you said killed had in merchant-ship about last summer.	"You announced news which concerns me greatly, the killing of Einar, my brother, who you said you killed in the merchant ship last summer.
Nú vil ek vita, hvárt þú vill nökkuru bœta mér Einar bróður minn?"	Now wish I to-know, whether you will some compensation to-me Einar brother mine?"	Now I wish to know if you will pay me some compensation for my brother".

The Tale of Sarcastic Halli (Old Norse)

Old Norse	Literal	English
"Hefir þú eigi spurt, at ek bœti engan mann?"	"Have you not heard, that I compensate no man?"	"Have you not heard that I compensate no one",
segir Einarr.	said Einar.	said Einar.
"Eigi er mér skylt at trúa því?"	"Not I me should to believe accordingly?"	"I was not obliged to believe",
segir Halli, "at þér væri allt illa gefit, þó at ek heyrða þat sagt?"	said Halli, "that you were all evil given, though that I heard that said?"	said Halli, "that you were all evil, though I heard it said".
"Gakk burt maðr?"	"Go away man?"	"Go away man",
segir Einarr, "annarr mun verri?"	said Einar, "otherwise should-be worse?"	said Einar, "otherwise it shall be worse".
Halli gekk at sitja.	Halli went to sit.	Halli went to sit.
Sigurðr spyrr, hvé farit hefði.	Sigurd asked, how gone had.	Sigurd asked how it had gone.
Halli svarar, ok kveðst hafa hótun fyrir fébœtr.	He answered, and said had a-threat for compensation.	He answered and said that he had been given a threat as compensation.
Sigurðr bað hann eigi oftar koma á þetta mál, ok sé laus veðjanin.	Sigurd asked him not more come that this matter, and so lost the-wager.	Sigurd ask him not to persist in this matter any more, and the wager would be lost.
Halli kvað honum vel fara:	Halli said he well went:	Halli said it had gone well,
"enn á skal koma oftar?"	"but about shall come more?"	but there is more to come.
Ok annan dag eftir gekk Halli fyrir Einar ok mælti:	And the-next day after went Halli before Einar and spoke:	And the next day Halli went before Einar and spoke:
"Þat mál vil ek vekja, Einarr, ef þú vilt nökkuru bœta mér bróður minn?"	"The matter wish I awaken, Einar, if you will some compensation to-me brother mine?"	"I wish to raise the matter with you, Einar, whether you will give me some compensation for my brother".
Einarr svarar:	Einar answered:	Einar answered:
"Þú ert seinþreyttr at, ok ef þú dregst eigi brott, þá muntú fara slíka fór sem bróðir þinn eðr verri?"	"You are persistent this, and if you draw not away, then should fare such before as brother yours or worse?"	"You are persistent in this, and if you do not back away, then it should go the same way as you brother did or worse".

The Tale of Sarcastic Halli (Old Norse)

Old Norse	Literal	English
Konungrinn bað hann eigi svá svara:	The-king ordered him not so to-answer:	The king ordered him not to answer like that,
"Ok er þat frændunum ofraun, ok veit eigi, hvers hugar hverjum lér.	"And was it kinsmen too-much, and known not, how-so minds each leaned.	and it is too-much for the kinsmen and not known how each mind goes.
Enn þú, Halli, kom eigi oftar á þetta mál, því at stœrri bokkar verða at þola honum slíkt enn þú ert?"	But you, Halli, come not again of this matter, because that greater bigger-men have-been that enduring him such than you are?"	But you, Halli, do not raise this matter again because greater and bigger men have endured such as you are".
Halli svarar:	Halli answered:	Halli answered:
"Svá mun vera verða?"	"So should be becomes?"	"So it will have to be".
Gekk hann þá til rúms síns.	Went he then to rooms his.	Then he went to his rooms.
Sigurðr fagnar honum vel, ok spurði, hvé farit hefði.	Sigurd welcomed him well, and asked, how gone had.	Sigurd welcomed him well and asked how it had gone.
Halli kveðst hafa heitan fyrir fébœtr af Einari.	Halli said had threat for compensation of Einar.	Halli said that he had received a threat for compensation from Einar.
"Þótti mér þat í hug?"	"Thought me that in mind?"	"I thought that in my mind",
segir Sigurðr, "ok sé laus veðjanin?"	said Sigurd, "and so lost the-wager?"	said Sigurd, "and so the wager is lost".
"Vel ferr þér?"	"Well go you?"	"You behave well",
segir Halli, "enn enn skal ek koma í þriðja sinn?"	said Halli, "but for shall I come to a-third occasion?"	said Halli, "but I shall raise the matter a third time".
"Gefa vil ek þér nú til hringinn?"	"Give will I you now to the-ring?"	"I will now give you the ring",
sagði Sigurðr, "at þú látir vera kyrrt, er þetta hefir þó nökkut af mér til hlotizt í fyrstu?"	said Sigurd, "that you leave be peace, as this has though somewhat of me to part the first?"	said Sigurd, "so that you will let there be peace, because I am responsible for part of this.
Halli svarar:	Halli answered:	Halli answered:

The Tale of Sarcastic Halli (Old Norse)

Old Norse	Literal	English
"Sýnir þú í þessu, hverr maðr þú ert, ok eigi má þér um kenna, hversu sem til vegar ferr;	"Show you in this, what man you are, and not may you about know, how-so as to way go;	"You show what kind of man you are and you can't be blamed no matter what happens.
enn prófa skal enn um sinn?"	but prove shall one about occasion?"	But it must be tried one more time".
Ok þegar um morgininn eftir, er konungr tók handlaugar ok Einarr fluga, gekk Halli at honum, ok kvaddi konunginn.	And early about morning after, when the-king took hand-washing and Einar Fly, went Halli to him, and greeted the-king.	And early the next morning, when the king took to washing his hands along with Einar Fly, Halli went to him and greeted the king.
Konungrinn spyrr, hvat er hann vildi.	The-king asked, what is he wanted.	The king asked what he wanted.
"Herra?"	"Lord?"	"Lord",
segir Halli, "ek vil segja yðr draum minn.	said Halli, "I wish to-tell you dream mine.	said Halli, "I wish to tell you about my dream.
Ek þóttumst vera allr maðr annarr enn ek em?"	I seemed to-be all man another than I am?"	I thought I was a completely different person than I am".
"Hvat manni þóttist þú vera?"	"What man thought you to-be?"	"Who did you think you were?"
segir konungr.	said the-king.	said the king.
"Ek þóttumst vera Þórleifr jarls skáld, enn hann Einarr fluga þótti mér vera Hákon jarl Sigurðarson, ok þóttumst ek hafa ort um hann níð, ok munda ek sumt níðit, er ek vaknaða?"	"I thought being Thorleif the-earl's the-poet, but he Einar Fly seemed to-me to-be Hakon earl Sigurdson, and thought I had worded about him slander, and remembered I some the-slander, when I awoke?"	I thought I was Thorleif the poet, but Einar Fly was Earl Hakon Sigurdson, and I thought I had written about him, and I remembered some things when I woke up".
Snöri Halli þá útar eftir höllinni, ok kvað nökkut fyrir munni sér, ok námu menn eigi orðaskil.	Turned Halli then out after the-hall, and spoke something before mouth his, and took people not words-separated.	Halli then turned around outside the palace and said something in front of his mouth and the people did not understand any of it.
Konungr mælti:	The-king spoke:	The king spoke:
"Þetta var eigi draumr annarr enn hann dregr þessi dœmi saman;	"This was not a-dream another that he drew these examples together;	"This was not a dream, and he has drawn these examples together.

The Tale of Sarcastic Halli (Old Norse)

Old Norse	Literal	English
ok svá mun fara með ykkr, sem fór með Hákoni Hlaðajarli ok Þórleifi skáldi, ok þat sama gerir Halli:	and so should go with you, as went with Hakon Earl-of-Lade and Thorleif the-poet, and that same does Halli:	And so it should go with you as it went with Earl Hakon of Lade and Thorleif the poet, and Halli is doing the same thing.
hann svífst einkis, ok megu vit sjá, at bitit hefir níðit ríkari menn enn svá sem þú ert, Einarr, sem var Hákon jarl, ok mun þat munat, meðan Norðrlönd eru byggð, ok er verri einn kviðlingr, um dýran mann kveðinn, ef munaðr verðr eftir, enn lítil fémúta;	he shrinks-from nothing, and may we see, that biting has-been the-slander richer men than so as you are, Einar, as was Hakon earl, and would-be that remembered, as-long-as Northern-lands are settled, and is worse one short-poem, if remembered becomes after, then little money-bribe about, fine men composed;	He shrinks from nothing, and we may see how slander has bitten richer men than you are, Einar, as Earl Hakon was, and it would be remembered as long as the Northern Lands are settled, one short verse about powerful men, if it becomes remembered afterwards, is worse than paying a small bribe,
ok ger svá vel ok leys hann af með nökkuru?"	and do so well and repay him of with somehow?"	and so it would do well to repay him somehow".
"Þér skulut ráðar herra?"	"You should decide lord?"	"You will decide, lord"
segir Einarr, "ok seg honum, at hann taki þrjár merkr silfrs af féhirði mínum, er ek fekk honum síðast í sjóði?"	said Einar, "and tell him, that he takes three marks of-silver of fee-servant mine, that I give him the-last in purse?"	said Einar, "and tell him that he may take three marks of silver from my fee-servant in the purse I just gave him".
Þetta var sagt Halla.	This was told Halli.	This was told to Halli.
Gekk hann at finna féhirðinn, ok sagði honum sitt erindi.	Went he to find fee-servant, and told him his errand.	He went to find the fee-servant and told him.
Hann kvað vera fjórar merkr silfrs í sjóðnum.	He said be four marks of-silver in the-purse.	He said there were four marks of silver in the purse.
Halli kveðst þrjár hafa skyldu.	Halli said three have should-be.	Halli said that he was to have three.
Halli gekk þá fyrir Einar, ok sagði honum.	Halli went then before Einar, and told him.	Halli went before Einar and said to him:
"Hafa mundir þú þat, er í var sjóðnum?"	"Have would you that, which in was the-purse?"	"Have you taken what was in the purse?",
segir Einarr.	said Einar.	said Einar.

The Tale of Sarcastic Halli (Old Norse)

Old Norse	Literal	English
"Nei?" sagði Halli, "öðruvísi muntú ná lífi mínu, enn ek verða þjófr at fé þínu, ok sá ek, at þú hafðir ætlat mér þat?"	"No?" said Halli, "other-knowing shall-you obtain life mine, than I being thief of money yours, and saw I, that you have that intended to-me?"	Halli said no, "you will have to find another way to take my life than me being a thief of your money, and I saw what you intended for me".
Ok svá, var, at Einarr hafði þat ætlat Halla, at hann mundi hafa, þat er í sjóðnum var, ok þótti honum þat nóg bana-sök.	And so, was, that Einar had it intended Halli, that he would have that, which in was the-purse, and thought him that enough death-sentence.	And so it was that Einar thought that Halli would have taken whatever was in the purse, which he thought would be enough of an offence for a death sentence.
Gekk Halli nú til sætis síns, ok sýndi Sigurði féit.	Went Halli no to seat his, and showed Sigurd the-money.	Halli went now to his seat and showed Sigurd the money.
Sigurðr tók hringinn, ok kvað Halla hafa vel til unnit.	Sigurd took the-ring, and said Halli well had to won.	Sigurd took the ring and said that Halli had won it.
Hann svarar:	He answered:	He answered:
"Eigi eru vit þá jafnir þegnar, ok tak hring þinn, ok njót manna bezt.	"Not are-we with then equal men, and take the-ring yours, and enjoy man the-best.	"We are not equally good men, keep the ring and enjoy it, best of men.
Enn þér satt at segja, þá átta ek aldrigi skylt við þenna mann, er Einarr hefir drepit, ok vilda ek vita, ef ek næða fénu af honum?"	But to-you truth to say, then related-to I never should with this man, which Einar had killed, and wished I to-know, if I neared money of him?"	But to tell you the truth, I was never related to this man which Einar killed, and I wished to know if I could obtain money from him".
"Engum manni ertú líkr at prettum?"	"No man are-you like in trickery?"	"There is no one like you in trickery",
segir Sigurðr.	said Sigurd.	said Sigurd.
Einarr fór brott eftir jólin norðr á Hálogaland.	Einar went away after Yule north to Halogaland.	Einar went away after Yule north to Halogaland.

8

Um várit eftir bað Halli konung órlofs at fara til Danmerkr í kaupferð.	About spring after asked Halli the-king vacation to travel to Denmark on trading-voyage.	In the spring, King Halli asked for leave to go to Denmark on a trading voyage.

The Tale of Sarcastic Halli (Old Norse)

Old Norse	Literal	English
Konungr bað hann fara, sem hanh vildi, "ok kom aftr skjótt, því at oss þykkir gaman at þér, ok far varliga fyrir Einari flugu;	The-king bid he travel, as he wished, "and come back quickly, because that we consider fun that to-you, and travel warily because-of Einar Fly;	The king asked him to go as he wished "and come back quickly because we like you and be careful of Einar Fly.
hann mun hafa illan hug á þér, ok sjaldan veit ek honum jafnsleppt tekizt hafa"	he should have evil mind to you, and seldom know I him equally-slip taken has"	He will have a bad opinion of you and I rarely know of him slipping up".
Halli tók sér far með kaupmönnum suðr til Danmerkr, ok svá til Jótlands.	Halli took himself passage with trading-men south to Denmark, and so to Jutland.	Halli took found passage with merchants south to Denmark and then to Jutland.
Rauðr hét maðr, er þar hafði sýslu, ok réðst Halli þar til vistar.	Raud was-named a-man, who there had stewardship, and appointed Halli there to lodgings.	There was a man named Raud who had a stewardship there and appointed Halli there some lodgings.
Þat bar til eitt sinn, er hann skyldi hafa þing fjölmennt, ok er menn skyldu þar mæla lögskilum sínum, þá var svá mikit háreysti ok gap, at engi maðr mátti þar málum sínum fram koma;	It bore to one occasion, that he should have assembly followers, and that men should there matters legal-settlement theirs, then was so much commotion and gaping, that no man may there matter his from come-forward;	It happened day when he was supposed to have a large assembly and when people were supposed to discuss their legal issues there, there was so much shouting and gaping that no one was allowed to present their case there
ok fóru menn við þat heim um kveldit.	and went people with that home about evening.	and the people went home that evening.
Þat var um kveldit, er menn komu til drykkjar, at Rauðr mælti:	It was about evening, that men came to drink, that Raud spoke:	It was in the evening when people came to drink that Raud said:
"Þat væri ráðleitinn maðr, er ráð fyndi til, at fólk þetta allt þagnaði?"	"It being cunning man, who plan find to, that people these all silenced?"	"It would be a wise man who could find a way to keep all these people quiet".
Halli svarar:	Halli answered:	Halli answered:
"Þat fæ ek gert, þegar er ek vil, at hér skal hvert mannsbarn þagna?"	"That can I do, as-soon-as that I wish, that here shall each man's-son silence?"	"I can do that when I want every human being to be silent".
"Þat fær þú eigi gert landi?"	"That undertaking you not do the-land?"	"You will not get that done in this land",

The Tale of Sarcastic Halli (Old Norse)

Old Norse	Literal	English
segir Rauðr.	said Raud.	said Raud.
Um morgininn komu menn til þings, ok var nú slíkt óp ok gap sem hinn fyrra dag, ok varð engum málum skilat.	About morning came people to the-assembly, and were now such shouting and gaping as the before day, and were no matters settled.	In the morning, people came to the assembly and now there was such an uproar as the previous day and no issues were resolved.
Fóru menn við þat heim.	Went men with that home.	The men then went home.
Þá mælti Rauðr:	Then spoke Raud:	Then Raud spoke:
"Viltú veðja um Halli, hvárt þú fær hljóðit á þinginn eðr eigi?"	"Will-you wager about Halli, each you carry-out silence to the-assembly or not?"	"Will you wager, Halli, that you will get silence at the assembly or not?".
Halli kveðst þess búinn.	Halli said this settled.	Halli said this would be done.
Rauðr svarar:	Raud answered:	Raud answered:
"Legg við höfuð þitt, enn ek gullhring er stendr mörk?"	"Lay with head yours, and I gold-ring which stands one-mark?"	"Lay down your head, and I will lay down a ring which is worth one mark".
"Þat skal vera?"	"That shall be?"	"So it shall be",
segir Halli.	said Halli.	said Halli.
Um morgininn spurði Halli Rauð, ef hann vildi veðjanina halda.	About morning asked Halli Raud, if he wished wager to-hold.	In the morning, Halli asked Raud if he wanted to keep the wager.
Hann kveðst halda vilja.	He said hold wished.	He said that he wished to keep it.
Komu menn nú til þingsins, ok var nú slíkt óp eðr meira, enn hina fyrri dagana.	Came men now to the-assembly, and were not such shouting and more, than the before day.	Now people came to the assembly and there was as much shouting or more as the previous days.
Ok er menn varði sízt, hleypr Halli upp, ok œpir sem mest mátti hann:	And when people were least, ran Halli up, and cried-out as high as-might he:	And when the people were at their least, Halli ran up and shouted as loud as he could:
"Hlýði allir menn;	"Listen all people;	"Listen everyone.
mér er mikils málspörf;	for-me is great matter;	For me this is a matter of need.

The Tale of Sarcastic Halli (Old Norse)

Old Norse	Literal	English
ek skal kæra um óðindælu mína sjálfs;	I shall discuss about puzzle mine self's;	
mér er horfin hein ok heinar-sufl, skreppa ok þar með allr skreppu-skrúði, sá er karlmanni er betra at hafa, enn at missa?"	mine is lost hone and honing-grease, bag and there with all bag-tackle, so is a-man that better to have, than to lose?"	I have lost my hone and honing grease, and my bag with all its tackle, which is better for a man to have than lose".
Allir menn þögnuðu.	All people silenced.	All the people were silent.
Sumir hugðu, at hann mundi œrr orðinn, enn sumir hugðu hann mundu tala konungs erindi nökkur.	Some thought, that he could-be awed of-words, and some thought he could-be speaking the-king's errand some.	Some people thought that he was lost for words, and some thought that he could be speaking some message from the king.
Ok er hljóð fekkst, settist Halli niðr ok tók við hringnum.	And when silence received, settled Halli down and took with the-ring.	And when there was a sound, Halli sat down and took the ring.
Enn þegar menn sáu, at þetta var ekki nema dáruskapr, þá var háreysti sem áðr, ok komst Halli á hlaupi undan, því at Rauðr vildi hafa líf hans, ok þótti þetta verit hafa hin mesta ginning.	Then as-soon-as people saw, that this was nothing but mockery, then was commotion as before, and came Halli to running out-from, because that Raud wished to-have life his, and thought this become had the most deception.	But when people saw that this was nothing but a prank, Halli was as stubborn as before and ran away from Raud who wanted his head and thought that this was the greatest deception.
Létti hann eigi fyrr enn hann kom til Englands.	Let-up he not before that he came to England.	He did not let up until he came to England.

9

Old Norse	Literal	English
Þá réð fyrir Englandi Haraldr Guðinason.	Then ruled for England Harald Godwinson.	Then Harald Godwinson ruled England.
Halli ferr þegar á konungs fund, ok kveðst ort hafa um hann drápu, ok bað sér hljóðs.	Halli went straight-away to the-king to-meet, and said had composed about him a-drapa (poem), and asked for-him be-heard.	Halli went straight away to the king and said that he had composed a drapa about him and asked that it be heard.
Konungr lét gefa honum hljóð.	The-king had granted him a-hearing.	The king granted him a hearing.

The Tale of Sarcastic Halli (Old Norse)

Old Norse	Literal	English
Sezt nú Halli fyrir kné konungi, ok flutti fram kvæðit;	Sat now Halli before knee the-king's, and brought from the-poem;	Halli sat down before the king and recited the poem.
ok er lokit var kvæðinu, spurði konungr skáld sitt, er var með honum, hveru veg at væri kvæðit.	and when ended was the-poem, asked the-king the-poet this, that was with him, each way that being the-poem.	And when the poem was finished, the king asked his poet who was with him and what the poem was about.
Hann kveðst ætla at gott væri.	He said supposed that good was.	He said that he supposed it was good.
Konungr bauð Halla með sér at vera, enn Halli kveðst búinn vera til Noregs áðr.	The-king invited Halli with him to be, but Halli said prepared being to Norway back.	The king invited Halli to stay with him, but Halli said he has already prepared to return to Norway.
Konungr kvað þá þann veg fara mundu af hendi um kvæðislaunin "við þik, sem vér njótum kvæðisins, því at engi hróðr verðr oss at því kvæði, er engi kann.	The-king said then that way going would of hand about poem-reward "with you, as we benefit the-poem, because that none fame worthy to-us that before recited, as none knows.	The king said then that it would go the same way "in rewarding you for the poem, as we benefit from the poem, because we get no fame's worth from a poem that no one knows.
Sit nú niðr á gólfit, enn ek mun láta hella silfri í höfuð þér, ok haf þat, er í hárinu loðir, ok þykkir mér þá hvárt horfa eftir öðru, er vér skulum eigi ná at nema kvæðit?"	Sit now down on the-floor, then I will have poured silver on head yours, and have it, which in the-hairs of-your-hair, and seems to-me then each turn after the-other, that we shall not obtain to but the-poem?"	Now sit down on the floor, and I will have silver poured over your head, and keep whatever sticks to your hair, and it seems to me that it looks the same on both sides because we will not get to learn the poem".
Halli svarar:	Halli answered:	Halli answered:
"Bæði mun vera, at lítilla launa mun vert vera, enda munu ok þessi launin lítil vera.	"Both should be, that little reward should worth become, and shall this repay also little being.	"Both are small rewards due and that the rewards will be small.
Lofa munu þér, herra, at ek ganga út nauðsynja minna?"	Promise shall you, lord, that I go out needs mine?"	Will you promise me that I may go outside to attend to my needs".
"Gakk sem þú vill?"	"Go as you wish?"	"Go as you wish",
segir konungr.	said the-king.	said the king.

The Tale of Sarcastic Halli (Old Norse)

Old Norse	Literal	English
Halli gekk þar til, er skipsmiðir váru, ok bar í höfuð sér tjöru, ok skrýfði sem mest hárinu, ok gerði sem diskr væri;	Halli went there to, where ship-smiths were, and bore on head his tar, and scrawled as most hair, and made as a-plate being;	Halli walked to where the shipbuilders were and carried tar on his head and fashioned into the shape of a plate
gekk síðan inn, ok bað hella silfrinu yfir sik.	went afterwards in, and asked pour the-silver over him.	and then went back inside and asked for the silver to be poured over him.
Konungr kvað hann vera brögðóttan;	The-king said he was cunning;	The king said that he was cunning,
ok var nú heilt yfir hann, ok var þat mikit silfr, er hann fekk.	and was now rather over him, and was it much silver, that he got.	and now the silver was poured over him, and it was a lot of silver that he got.
Fór hann síðan þangað, er skip þau váru, er til Noregs ætluðu, ok váru öll burtu nema eitt, ok var þar ráðinn fjöldi manna með miklum þunga;	Went he afterwards from-there, to ship there where, that to Norway intended, and were all away except one, and was that appointed many men with much heavy-cargo;	He then went to where the ships were that were going to Norway, and they were all gone, except one that had many men with much heavy cargo.
enn Halli hafði of fjár, ok vildi gjarna í burt, því at hann hafði ekki kvæði ort um konung annat enn endileysu, ok mátti hann því eigi kenna þat.	but Halli had of fee, and wished gladly to away, because that he had not composed words about the-king other than nonsense, and may he therefore not teach it.	Halli had plenty of money and wished very much to travel away, because he had not composed words about the king other than reciting nonsense, and therefore could not teach it.
Stýrimaðr bað hann fá til ráð, at Suðrmenn gengi ór skipinu, ok kveðst þá vilja gjarna taka við honum.	Steersman bid him get to advice, that Southern-men walking out-of the-ship, and said then wished gladly take with him.	The steersman told him to find a scheme so that the southern men would leave the ship, then he would gladly take him.
Enn þá var komit at vetri.	But then was coming the winter.	But then winter was coming.
Halli var hjá þeim í herbergjum um hríð.	Halli was beside them in sleeping-quarters about awhile.	Halli stayed with them in sleeping quarters for a while.
Eina nótt lét Halli illa í svefni, ok var lengi áðr enn þeir fengu vakit hann.	One night had Halli badly in sleep, and was long before that they caught awake him.	One night, Halli felt sick in his sleep and it was a long time before they could wake him up.
Þeir spurðu, hvat hann hefði dreymt.	They asked, what he had dreamed.	They asked what he had dreamed.

The Tale of Sarcastic Halli (Old Norse)

Old Norse	Literal	English
Halli kvað lokit því, at hann mundi biðja þá fars héðan frá.	Halli said finished therefore, that he would ask then travel from-there from.	Halli said that he was finished with asking for passage from there,
"Mér þótti maðr koma at mér ógrligr, ok kvað þetta:	"To-me seemed a-man come that to-me terrible, and recited this:	It seemed to me that a terrible looking man came to me and recited this:
Hröng es, þar's hávan þöngul	Roaring is, there the harbour there	Roaring is there the harbour there
held ek siz'k fjörs selda'k sýn es,	think me about since that I life,	think me about, since that I life sold.
at sit'k at Ránar,	am-I one to Ran,	Disappeared am-I one to Ran.
sumir eru í búð með humrum;	some are in lodgings with lobsters;	Some are in lodgings with lobsters.
ljóst es lýsu at gista;	light is the-whitings with guest;	Light is the-whitings with guest.
lönd á'k út við ströndu;	lands I out from-the-shore;	Lands I out from-the-shore.
því sit'k bleikr í brúki,	because sit pale in use,	Because sit I pale in use.
blakkir mér þari um hnakka,	pale mine intestines about neck,	Pale mine intestines about neck,
blakkir mér þari um hnakka.	pale mine intestines about neck.	pale mine intestines about neck.
Ok er Suðrmenn vissu draum þenna, réðust þeir ór skipinu, ok þótti víss bani sinn, ef þeir fœri þar á.	And when The-southerners knew this-dream then, decided they out-of the-ship, and thought certain death theirs, if they went there in.	And when the southerners knew this dream, they got out of the ship and thought it would be their death if they went there.
Halli réðst þegar á skip, ok sagði, at þetta var prettr hans enn engi draumr.	Halli took straight-away in the-ship, and said, that this was trick his and no dream.	Halli took passage in the ship straight away, and said that it was a trick, and not a dream.
Ok tóku þeir út þegar, er þeir váru búnir, ok tóku Noreg um haustit;	And took they out from-there, were they were ready, and took Norway about autumn;	And they went out when they were ready and took to Norway in the autumn,
ok fór Halli þegar til Haralds konungs.	and went Halli then to Harald the-king.	and Halli immediately went to King Harald.
Hann tók vel við Halla, ok spurði, hvárt hann hefði ort um aðra konunga.	He received well with Halli, and asked, whether he had words about other kings.	He welcomed Halli and asked if he had written about other kings.
Halli kvað þetta:	Halli said this:	Halli said this:
"Orta ek eina um jarl?"	"Worded I one about an-earl?"	Worded I one about an earl
Þula	a-Thula (poem)	a-'thula' (poem).

The Tale of Sarcastic Halli (Old Norse)

Old Norse	Literal	English
verðr at drápu *með Dönum verri;* *föll eru fjórtán* *ok föng tíu;* *opit es ok öndvert,* *öfigt stígandi.* *Svá skal yrkja* *sá's illa kann.*	worthy that drapa (poem) with The-Danes worse; mistakes are fourteen and rhymes ten; open is and upside-down, reversed ascending. Then shall compose so badly knows.	Poorer drapa with The-Danes worse. Mistakes are fourteen and rhymes ten. Open is and upside-down, reversed ascending. Then shall compose so who badly knows.
Konungr brosti at, ok þótti honum jafnan gaman at Halla.	The-king smiled that, and thought him always entertaining of Halli.	The king smiled an thought he always found Halli entertaining.

10

Old Norse	Literal	English
Haraldr konungr fór um várit til Gulaþings;	Harald the-king went about spring to Gula-assembly;	In the spring Harald went to the Gulathing Assembly.
ok um daginn spurði konungr Halla, hversu honum yrði til kvenna um þingit.	and about the-day asked the-king Halli, how-so he became to women at the-assembly.	And one day the king asked Halli how he was with women at the assembly.
Halli svarar:	Halli answered:	Halli answered:
Gott es Gulaþing þetta: *giljum vér hverjar es viljum.*	Good is Gula-assembly this: beguile we that as we-wish.	Good is Gulathing this, beguile we that as we-wish.
Konungr fór þaðan norðr til Þrándheims.	The-king went from-there north to Trondheim.	The king went north from there to Trondheim.
Ok er þeir sigldu fyrir Stað, áttu þeir Þjóðólfr ok Halli búðarvörð at halda, ok var Halli sæsjúkr mjök, ok lá undir báti, enn Þjóðólfr varð at þjóna einn.	And when they sailed for Stad, had they Thjodolf and Halli shop-keeping to hold, and was Halli seasick much, and lay under the-ship's-boat, and Thjodolf came to serve alone.	And when they sailed for Stad, Thjodolf and Halli were assigned the cooking and serving, and Halli was very seasick and lay under the ship's boat, and Thjodolf had to serve alone.
Ok er hann bar vistina, fell hann um fót Halla, er stóð út undan bátnum.	And when he carried the-provisions, fell he about leg Halli's, which stood out under the-boat.	And when he was carrying the provisions, he fell on Halli's leg, which was standing out from under the boat.
Þjóðólfr kvað þá þetta:	Thjodolf spoke then this:	Thjodolf spoke this:
Út stendr undan báti ilfat.	Out standing under the-boat sole-bucket.	"Out standing under the-boat sole-bucket.

The Tale of Sarcastic Halli (Old Norse)

Old Norse	Literal	English
Muntú nú gilja?	Shall-you now beguile	Shall-you now beguile?"
Halli svarar:	Halli answered:	Halli answered:
Þjón geri'k þann at sveini: Þjóðólf læt'k mat sjóða.	Servant made then to this-lad: Thjodolf let food boil.	Servant made I then to this-lad, Thjodolf let I food boil.
Fór konungrinn nú leiðar sinnar, unz hann kom í Kaupang.	For the-king now on-way his, until he came to Kaupang.	The king now went on his way until he came to Kaupang.
Þóra drottning var nú með honum, ok var hon lítt til Halla;	Thora the-queen was not with him, and was she little towards Halli;	Queen Thora was now with him and she did not like Halli,
enn konungr var vel til hans, ok þótti gaman at Halla jafnan.	but the-king was well towards him, and seemed to-delight in Halli always.	but the king liked him and always delighted in Halli.
Þess er getit einn dag, at konungrinn gekk úti um stræti ok fylgdin með honum.	This is told one day, that the-king went out about the-street and followers with him.	It is said that one day the king went out into the street and his follower with him.
Halli var þar í för.	Halli was there in procession.	Halli was there in the procession.
Konungrinn hafði öxi í hendi, ok öll gullrekin, enn silfrvafit skaftit ok silfrhólkr mikill á forskeftinn, ok þar í ofan steinn góðr.	The-king had an-axe in hand, and all gold-inlaid, and silver-wound the-shaft and silver-band great in upper-shaft, and there in over a-stone good.	The king had an axe in his hand and all the shafts were gold, but the shaft was wrapped in silver, and a large silver cylinder on the foreshaft, and above it a good stone.
Þat var ágætr gripr.	It was excellent possession.	It was excellent possession.
Halli sá jafnan til öxarinnar.	Halli looked always to the-axe.	Halli kept looking towards the axe.
Konungr fann þat ok brátt, ok spurði, hvárt Halla litist vel á öxina.	The-king found that and soon, and asked, whether Halli looked well of the-axe.	The king soon found out and asked if Halla had a good look at the axe.
Honum kveðst vel á lítast.	He said well it looked.	He said it looked good.
"Hefir þú sét betri öxi?"	"Have you seen a-better axe?"	"Have you seen a-better axe?"
(segir konungr).	(said the-king).	(said the-king).
"Eigi ætla ek þat?" segir Halli.	"Not suppose I that?" said Halli.	"I suppose not", said Halli.

The Tale of Sarcastic Halli (Old Norse)

Old Norse	Literal	English
"Viltú láta serðast til öxarinnar?"	"Will-you allow to-get-hurt for the-axe?"	"Do you want to be hurt by the axe?"
segir konungr.	said the-king.	said the king.
"Eigi?" segir Halli;	"Not?" said Halli;	Halli said not,
"enn várkunn þykki mér yðr, at þér vilit svá selja sem þér keyptut?"	"but understandable seems to-me you, that you wish so to-sell same-as you bought?"	"but it's understandable to me that you would wish to sell it for the same as you bought it".
"Svá skal vera, Halli?"	"So shall be, Halli?"	"So it shall be Halli",
segir konungr;	said the-king;	said the king,
"tak við, ok njót manna bezt:	"take with, and enjoy man the-best:	take it with you and enjoy it, best man,
gefin var mér, enda skal svá selja?"	given was to-me, and shall so to-sell?"	it was given to me, and now shall it be given to you.
Halli þakkaði konungi.	Halli thanked the-king.	Halli thanked the king.
Um kveldit, er menn komu til drykkjar talaði drottning við konung, at þat væri undarligt	About evening, when men came to drink talked the-queen with the-king, that it was scandalous	In the evening, when the men came to drink, the queen spoke to the king that it was strange
ok eigi vel til skift, at gefa Halla þá gripi, "er varla er ótíginna manna at eiga, fyrir klámyrði sín;	and not well to exchange, to give Halli then treasure, "that hardly was un-ranking man that not, before obscene his;	and it is not a good idea to give Halli the those things to a lowly man hardly has for his obscenities,
enn þó fá sumir lítit fyrir góða þjónustu"	that then give some little before good service"	but then some people get little for good service".
Konungr kveðst því ráða vilja, hverjum hann gefi gripi sína:	The-king said therefore decided wished, each he gave possessions his:	The king said that he would decide who he would give his possessions to,
"Vil ek eigi snúa orðum Halla til hins verra, þeim er tvíræð eru"	"Wish I not return words Halli to his worst, they are ambiguous are"	for I do not wish to turn Halli's words to the worse, which are ambiguous in a bad sense".
Konungr bað kalla Halla, ok svá var gert.	The-king asked to-call Halli, and so was done.	The king asked to call Halli, and it was done.

The Tale of Sarcastic Halli (Old Norse)

Old Norse	Literal	English
Halli laut honum.	Halli bowed to-him.	Halli bowed to him.
Konungr bað Halla mæla nökkur tvíræðis-orð við Þóru drottningu:	The-king ordered Halli speak something ambiguous about Thora the-queen:	The king asked Halli to say some ambiguous words to Queen Thora
"ok vit, hversu hon þolir?"	"and know, how-so she endures?"	and know how she endures it.
Halli laut þá at Þóru ok kvað:	Halli bowed then to Thora and said:	Halli bowed then to Thora and said:
Þú ert makligust miklu, (munar stórum þat) Þóra, flenna upp at enni allt leðr Haralds reðra.	You are the-best much, (delight great that) Thora, to-extend up to brow all skin Harald's genitals.	You are the-best much, delight great that, Thora, to-extend up to brow all the skin of Harald's genitals.
"Takit hann ok drepit?"	"Take him and kill?"	"Take him and kill him",
segir drottning;	said the-queen;	said the queen.
"vil ek eigi hafa hrópyrði hans?"	"will I not have obscenities his?"	"I will not have his obscenities".
Konungr bað öngvan svá djarfan vera, at á Halla tœki hér fyrir:	The-king ordered none so daring be, that to Halli take force for:	The king ordered that no one should dare take Halli by force:
"Enn at því má gera, ef þér þykkir önnur makligri til at liggja hjá mér ok vera drottning, ok kanntú varla at heyra lof þitt".	"But that then may done, if you think another more-suitable that to lie beside me and be queen, and know-you hardly to hear praise yours".	"But then it may be done if you think another is more suitable to lie beside me and be queen, and you hardly know how to hear your praise".
Þjóðólfr skáld hafði farit til Íslands, meðan Halli var í burtu frá konungi.	Thjodolf poet had travelled to Iceland, while Halli was to away from the-king.	The poet Thjodolf had gone to Iceland while Halli was away from the king.
Þjóðólfr bafði flutt útan frá Íslandi hest góðan, ok vildi gefa konungi, ok lét Þjóðólfr leiða hestinn í konungsgarð, ok sýna konungi.	Thjodolf had brought out from Iceland a-horse good, and wished to-give the-king, and had Thjodolf lead the-horse to the-king, and showed the-king.	Thjodolf had brought a good horse from Iceland and wanted to give it to the king, and he had Thjodolf lead the horse to the king's garden and show it to the king.
Konungrinn gekk at sjá hestinn, ok var (hann) mikill ok feitr.	The-king went to see the-horse, and was (he) great and stout.	The king went to see the horse and it was big and fat.

The Tale of Sarcastic Halli (Old Norse)

Old Norse	Literal	English
Halli var þar hjá, er hestrinn hafði úti sinina.	Halli was there beside, when horse had extended-out tendon.	Halli was there when the horse extended its tendon.
Halli kvað þá:	Halli spoke then:	Halli then spoke:
Sýr er ávallt, *hefir saurigt* *allt hestr Þjóðólfs reðr* *hann es dróttins serðr.*	Sow as always, has filthy all horse Thjodolf's beam he is master wounder.	Sow as always, has filthy all horse Thjodolf's beam, he is master-wounder.
"Tví, tví?"	"Tut, tut?"	"Tut tut",
segir konungr, "hann kemr aldrigi í mína eign at þessu?"	said the-king, "he comes never in mine ownership at this?"	said the king, "he will not come into my ownership at this rate".
Halli gerðist hirðmaðr konungs ok bað sér orlofs til Íslands.	Halli became court-man the-king's and asked him vacation to Iceland.	Halli became the king's court man and asked him for leave to vacate to Iceland.
Konungr bað hann fara varlega fyrir Einari flugu.	The-king bid him travel warily because-of Einar Fly.	The king asked that he travel carefully because of Einar Fly.
Halli fór til Íslands ok bjó þar.	Halli went to Iceland and settled there.	Halli went to Iceland and settled there.
Eyddust honum penningar, ok lagðist hann í útróðr;	Spent his money, and lay he to out-rowing (fishing);	He spent his money and he took to fishing,
ok eitt sinn fekk hann andróða svá mikinn, at þeir tóku nauðliga land.	and one occasion had he difficulty so much, that they took necessarily land.	and on one occasion he had so much difficulty rowing back that they just reached land.
Ok um kveldit var borinn fyrir Halla grautr;	And about evening was brought before Halli porridge;	That evening porridge was brought before Halli,
ok er hann hafði etit nökkut lítit, hnígr hann aftrábak, ok var þá dauðr.	and as he had to-eat few bites, fell he back, and was then dead.	and when he had eaten a few bites, he fell back and was then dead.
Haraldr spurði lát tveggja hirðmanna sinna af Íslandi:	Harald learned had both court-men his from Iceland:	Harald learned of the death of both his court men from Iceland,
Bolla hins prúða ok Sneglu-Halla.	Bolli the Elegant and Sarcastic-Halli.	Bolli the Elegant, and Sarcastic Halli.
Hann svaraði svá til Bolla:	He answered so to Bolli:	He said of Bolli:

The Tale of Sarcastic Halli (Old Norse)

Old Norse	Literal	English
"Fyrir dörrum mun drengrinn hnigit hafa?"	"Before spears would the-boy fallen had?"	"The boy must have fallen to spears".
Enn til Halla segir hann svá:	And to Halli said he so:	And he said of Halli:
"Á grauti mundi greyit sprungit hafa?"	"On porridge would the-poor-thing burst have?"	"The poor thing must have burst eating porridge".
Lýk ek þar sögu Sneglu-Halla.	End I there the-story Sarcastic-Halli.	And there I end the story of Sarcastic Halli.
Brot ór Haralds-drápu *Svá lét und sik* *seggja dróttinn* *lönd öll lagin,* *liðs oddviti.*	Offence about Harald's-poem So gave up he said the-lord lands of-all the-songs company leader.	Offence about Harald's poem So gave he up said the Lord Lands of all the songs The leader of company.

Word List *(Old Norse to English)*

Old Norse	English

A, a

Old Norse	English
aðra	another, other, others
aðrir	other
af	disrespected, from, from, in, man, of, of, off, with
afli	power
aftr	back, returning
aftrábak	back
Agðanes	Agdanes (place)
Agðaness	Agdanes (place)
Agði	Agdi (name), Agdi (name)
akta	taxes
aldrei	never
aldri	a-child
aldrigi	never
alla	completely
allir	all, all
allr	all, all
allra	all, of-all
allreiðr	all-angry
allskammr	very-short
allt	all, all
allvel	all-well
andaðr	dead
andróða	difficulty
annan	another, another, being, one, the-next
annarr	another, another, otherwise
annarra	other
annars	another, other
annat	another, other
at	a, am-I, and, as, at, by, by, for, for, in, in, it, of, of, said, than, that, that, the, the, this, to, to, up, was, with

Á, á

Old Norse	English
á	about, an, at, be, by, for, from, in, it, of, on, that, to, was, with
á'k	I
ábyrgst	responsible
áðr	after, back, before
ágætr	excellent
ámælisverðr	talked
ári	all-year
Árnasonar	Son-of-Arni (name)
át	ate, ate, eat
átt	having
átta	related-to
átti	had, hat, married
áttu	had
ávallt	always

Æ, æ

Old Norse	English
ætla	suppose, supposed
ætlat	intended, that
ætluðu	intended
ætt	descent
ættaðr	descended
ætti	had
ættsmár	family-small

B, b

Old Norse	English
bað	asked, bid, invited, ordered
báðir	both
bæði	both
bafði	had
baki	back
bana-sök	death-sentence
bani	death
bann	he
bar	bears, bore, carried

Word List (Old Norse to English)

Old Norse	English
Bárð	Bard (name)
Bárðr	Bard (name)
barn	child, I
barna	children
báru	carried
báti	the-boat, the-ship's-boat
bátnum	the-boat
bauð	invited
bauglands	ring-land
beggja	both
beið	waited
beidda	asked
bekkinn	the-bench
belti	belt
betr	better
betra	better
betri	a-better
bezt	best, the-best
bið	order
biðja	ask, to-ask
bitar	bite
bitit	biting
bjó	lived, settled
blakkir	pale
bleikr	pale
boði	order
bœjar	the-town
bœndr	farmers
bœnum	town
bœta	compensation
bœti	compensate
bœtti	compensated
bokkar	bigger-men
Bolla	Bolli (name)
bóndi	farmer, master
borð	boards
borði	table, the-table
borðin	tables
borðit	table, the-table
borðum	at-table
börg	the-city
borin	brought
borinn	brought
börnin	the-children
bótunum	compensation
brá	drew
brákar	breaker
brást	transformed
brátt	soon
brauði	bread
brenndan	burnt
bróðir	brother
bróður	brother
brögðóttan	cunning
brosti	grinned, laughed, smiled
brot	offence
brott	away
brúki	use
brynju	chain-mail, coat-of-mail
brynjuna	coat-of-mail
búð	lodgings
búðarvörð	shop-keeping
bú-Finna	farmers
búi	estate
búinn	prepared, settled
búnir	prepared, ready
burt	away, brought
burtu	away
býð	command
býðr	offered
byggð	settled
byr	fair-wind

D, d

Old Norse	English
dag	day
dagana	day
daginn	the-day
danmerkr	Denmark, Denmark (place)
dáruskapr	mockery
dauðan	death
dauðir	dead
dauðr	dead
deild	room
digrastr	thick-set
disk	plate
diskinum	the-plate

Word List (Old Norse to English)

Old Norse	English
diskr	a-plate
djarfan	daring
dœmi	examples
Dönum	the-Danes (name)
dörrum	spears
dóttur	daughter
drap	killed
drápi	the-killing
drápu	a-drapa (poem), drapa (poem)
drápuna	the-drapa (poem)
draum	dream, this-dream
draumr	a-dream, dream
dregr	draws, drew
dregst	draw
drekanum	the-dragon-ship
dreki	dragon
drekka	drinking
drengi	boys
drengrinn	the-boy
drepa	kill
drepit	kill, killed
drepr	killed
dreymt	dreamed
drógu	drew
dróttinn	the-lord
dróttins	master
drottning	queen, the-queen
drottningu	the-queen
drykk	drink
drykkjar	drink
duldu	denied
dverg	the-dwarf
dverginn	the-dwarf
dvergr	dwarf
dýran	remembered

E, e

Old Norse	English
eða	but
eðr	and, but, or
ef	if, then
eftir	about, after, back, back-from
eggjaði	urged
eiga	not, own
eigi	not
eign	ownership
eina	one
Einar	Einar (name)
Einari	Einar (name)
Einarr	Einar (name), us
Einars	Einar (name), Einar's (name)
einhugi	one-minded
einkis	nothing
einmælt	one-meal
einn	alone, one
einráðir	one-decision
einu	one
eitt	once, one
ek	Halli (name), I, me
ekki	not, nothing
eld	the-fire
eldahús	fire-house (kitchen)
eldi	fire
eldingum	lightning
eldr	fire
ella	or-else
elliligt	elderly
elskaði	loved
em	am, seek
Emmu	Emma (name)
en	than
enda	and, ended, the-end
endileysu	nonsense
enga	not
engan	no, none
engi	no, none
Englandi	England (place)
Englands	England (place)
engu	none
engum	no
enn	and, but, fine, for, in-the-end, one, than, that, the, then, yet
enni	brow, forehead
er	age, are, as, I, in, is, that, then, to, was, were, what, when, where, which, who

Word List (Old Norse to English)

Old Norse	English
erindi	errand, message
ert	are
ertú	are-you
eru	are, are-we, is, so, they-are
erum	are
es	as, is, life
eta	eat, eating
etit	to-eat
etja	provoke
eyddust	spent
eyja	islands
eyjar	islands

F, f

Old Norse	English
fá	get, give
faðir	father, when
fæ	can
fær	carry-out, undertaking
Fáfni	Fafnir (name)
Fáfnis-bana	Slayer-of-Fafnir (name)
fagnar	welcomed
fáim	get
fám	a-few
fann	found
fannst	thought
far	go, passage, travel
fara	fare, go, goes, going, travel, went
farit	gone, travelled
fars	travel
fátœka	poor
fátœkr	fee-taken
fátœkra	the-poor
fátt	little
fé	money, payment
fébœtr	compensation
féhirði	fee-servant
féhirðinn	fee-servant
féit	the-money
feitr	stout
fekk	give, got, had
fekkst	received
félagi	companion
feldan	killed
fell	fell
fellt	fell
fémúta	composed
fengu	caught
fengum	travel
fénu	money
ferr	go, goes, went
festi	pierced
fimm	five
finna	find, found, the-Sami (name)
Finnferð	Finland-voyages (place)
finnskrepp	Sami-goods
firðinum	the-fjord
firrst	lost
fiskimenn	fishermen
fjár	fee
fjölda	many
fjöldi	many
fjölmennt	followers
fjóra	four
fjórar	four
fjórðung	fourth
fjörs	since
fjórtán	fourteen
fleira	more
fleiri	more
flenna	to-extend
flest	the-most
flesta	most
Fljótum	Fljot (place)
flœr-at	fleeing
fluga	Fly (name)
flugu	Fly (name)
flugust	flew
flutt	brought, delivered
flutti	brought
flýta	quickly
flytja	carried
föður	father, his
föðurbana	his
fœra	bring, brought, sent-for

Word List (Old Norse to English)

Old Norse	English
fœrði	performed
fœrðr	brought
fœri	went
fœrr	accomplished
fœtrnir	the-legs
fólk	people
föll	mistakes
föng	rhymes
fór	before, for, travelled, went
för	going, procession
forskeftinn	upper-shaft
fórtu	went-you
fóru	went
förum	journey
forvitnar	fore-knowing
fót	leg
fótum	feet
frá	from
frændi	kinsman
frændr	took
frændunum	kinsmen
fram	ahead, away, forwards, from
framar	from
frásagnar	from-saying
frásagnir	stories
Frísa	Frisian (name)
frískr	Frisian
fullr	full
fullt	full
fund	to-meet
fundu	found
fundumst	met
furðanliga	extremely
fúss	willing
fylgdin	followers
fylgja	follow
fyndi	find
fyr	before
fyrir	because-of, before, for, me, over
fyrr	before, went-before
fyrra	before, last
fyrri	before
fyrst	first
fyrstu	first

G, g

Old Norse	English
gabb	mockery
gæfr	agreeable
gætti	guarded
gaf	gave
gakk	go
galdra	magic
gamall	old
gaman	a-delight, delight, enjoyment, entertaining, fun, to-delight
gamans	amusement
ganga	go
gangu	going
gap	gaping
garðinn	garden, the-house, the-wall
garðinum	the-wall
garðrinn	the-wall
garðsins	the-wall
Gásum	Gasir (place)
gefa	give, granted, teach, to-give
gefi	gave, give
gefin	given
gefit	given
Geirrauð	Geirrod (name)
Geirrauðr	Geirrod (name)
gekk	got, went
geng	going
gengi	walking
gengr	going
gengu	went
ger	do, does
gera	do, doing, done, look-to, made, make
gerast	be
gerði	did, made
gerðist	became
gerðu	did, made
geri	did
geri'k	made

Word List (Old Norse to English)

Old Norse	English
gerir	does, done
gerit	do
gerla	completely
gert	do, done
get	get
getit	told
gilja?	beguile
giljum	beguile
ginning	deception
gista	guest
gjalda	pay
gjarna	gladly
glaðr	glad
gnauða	gnawing
góð	good
góða	good
góðan	good
góðr	good
góðum	good
gólf	the-floor
gólfið	of-the-floor
gólfit	the-floor
göngum	we-are-going
görr	ready-made
gott	good
grafit	dug
graut	porridge
grautar	of-porridge
grauti	porridge
grautinn	porridge, the-porridge
grautr	porridge
greppr	grasped
greyit	the-poor-thing
grið	peace
griðníðingr	truce-breaker
gripanna	the-trinkets
gripi	possessions, things, treasure
gripina	the-trinkets
gripr	possession
grís	pig
gríss	pig
grön	moustache
gruntrauðustum	deep-red
Guðinason	Godwinson (name)
guðréttligast	good-rightly
Gulaþing	Gula-assembly (name)
Gulaþings	Gula-assembly (name)
gullhlað	gold-band
gullhring	a-gold-ring, gold-ring
gullrekin	gold-inlaid
gyrði	equipped

H, h

Old Norse	English
haddan	the-handle, the-lid
háðyrðum	mocking
hærra	higher
hærri	higher
hætti	stopped
hættu	danger
haf	have
hafa	composed, had, has, have, having, that, to-have, traded, well
hafða	had
hafði	had
hafðir	had, have
hafðist	had
hafi	has
hafra	goat
Hákon	Hakon (name)
Hákoni	Hakon (name)
halda	hold, to-hold
haldit	held
hálfa	half
Halla	Halli (name), Halli's (name)
hallæri	famine
Halli	Halli (name), he
Hálogaland	Halogaland (place)
Hálogalandi	Halogaland (place)
háls	neck
hálslangr	long-neck
hana	her
handlaugar	hand-washing
handsíðr	long-armed
hanh	he

Word List (Old Norse to English)

Old Norse	English
hann	called, Halli (name), he, him, Thjodolf (name)
hans	he, him, his
hanu	he
hár	high
Haraldi	Harald (name), Harald's (name)
Haraldr	Harald (name), Harald's (name)
Haralds	Harald (name), Harald's (name)
Haralds-drápu	Harald's-poem
Háreks	Harek's (name)
háreysti	commotion
hárinu	hair, the-hairs
hásætit	high-seat
haustit	autumn
haustum	autumn
hávan	the harbour
héðan	from-there
hefði	had
hefðim	have
hefðir	had
hefir	had, has, has-been, have
hefna	avenge
hefnt	avenged, revenge
hefr	had
heiði	the-heath
heill	health
heilræði	sound-advice
heilt	rather
heim	home
hein	hone
heinar-sufl	honing-grease
heita	call, named
heitan	threat
heitir	is-named, named
hekk	hung
held	think
heldr	rather
hella	pour, poured
helt	held
helzt	rather
hendi	hand, to-hand
hendr	hand
hér	force, here
herbergi	hostel
herbergjum	sleeping-quarters
herðalítill	narrow-shouldered
herðamestr	most-hardy
herra	lord
hest	a-horse
hestinn	the-horse
hestr	horse
hestrinn	horse
hét	named, was-named
héti	named
heyra	hear, heard, to-hear
heyrða	heard
heyrði	heard
heyrðu	heard
heyrt	heard
hilmis	helmsman's
hin	the
hina	the
hinn	the
hins	his, the
hinum	the
hirð	the-court
hirðarinnar	court
hirði	care
hirðin	courtiers
hirðinni	the-court, the-court-men
hirðmaðr	court-man
hirðmanna	court-men
hit	the
Hítrar	Hitra (place)
hitt	then
hjá	beside, nearby
hjálm	helmet
hjálmfaldinn	the-helmet
Hlaðajarli	Earl-of-Lade (name)
hlaðna	ladened
hlaupi	running
hlaut	a-lot-of
Hleyp'k	running
hleypr	ran
hljóð	a-hearing, silence
hljóða	calm

Word List (Old Norse to English)

Old Norse	English
hljóðgreipum	sound-grippers (ears)
hljóðit	silence
hljóðs	be-heard
hljóp	jumped
hljópu	ran
hlotizt	part
hlut	part, share
hluti	a-thing
hlutr	part
hlýða	obeying, suits
hlýði	listen
hnakka	neck
hnífskefti	knife-handle
hnigit	fallen
hnígr	fell
hœgri	other
höfðingja	chieftains
höfðingjar	chieftains
höfðu	had
hófi	reasonable
höfuð	head
höfuðit	head
höfuðskáld	chief-poet
höggva	to-strike
höldnum	held
höllina	the-hall
höllinni	the-hall
hon	it, she
hönd	hand
höndum	hand
honum	he, he, him, his, his, of-him, to-him
horfa	turn
horfin	lost
hornspánu	horn-spoon
hóti	not
hótun	a-threat
hræddir	afraid
hraustliga	boldly
hríð	awhile
hring	the-ring
hringinn	the-ring
hringnum	the-ring
hringum	circles
hroðit	cleared
hróðr	fame
hrökkvi-skafls	shaken
hröng	roaring
hrópyrði	obscenities
hrygg	the-spine
hryggrinn	spine
húðar	hide
hug	mind
hugar	minds
hugða	thought
hugðu	thought
humrum	lobsters
hungrar	hungry
hús	a-house
hvaðan	from-where
hvar	where
hvárigum	neither
hvárn	each
hvárr	each
hvárt	each, whether
hvárttveggja	each-way
hvat	that, what
hvatt	encouraged
hvé	how
hverfr	turned
hvergi	nowhere
hverjar	that
hverju	what, which
hverjum	each
hverr	what, who
hvers	how-so
hversu	how-so
hvert	each, what, where
hveru	each, what, whom
hví	if, why
hygg	think

I, i

Old Norse	English
iðnar	trade
ilfat	sole-bucket
illa	bad, badly, evil
illan	evil
illt	ill
ilvegs	evil-ways
inn	in, of, then

Word List (Old Norse to English)

Old Norse	English
innan	in, inside
innanborðs	onboard
innar	in

Í, í

Old Norse	English
í	a, about, as, at, by, in, into, of, on, that, the, to, was, with
Ísland	Iceland (place)
Íslandi	Iceland (place)
Íslands	Iceland (place)
Íslands-fari	Iceland-voyage
íslendinga	Icelanders
íslendingar	Icelanders
íslenzka	Icelander
íslenzkan	Icelander
íslenzkr	an-Icelander, Icelander

J, j

Old Norse	English
jafnan	always, equally, usually
jafngreypiliga	equally-badly
jafnir	equal
jafnsleppt	equally-slip
jarl	an-earl, earl
jarls	the-earl's
járn	iron-weapon
járnsmiðr	ironsmith
jaxlar	molars
jöfnum	even
jóladag	Yule-day
jólin	Yule
jólum	Yule
jólunum	Yule
Jótlands	Jutland (place)
jötni	giant
jötun	the-giant

K, k

Old Norse	English
kæra	accuse, discuss
kærleikum	dear-friendship, friendship
kagtat	cast
kálf	a-calf
kálfinn	the-calf
kálfrinn	the-calf
kalla	to-call
kallaði	called, the-king
kallaðir	be-called
kallaðr	called
kann	can, can-it, knows
kanntú	know-you
karlmanni	a-man
kastaði	cast
katli	and
katlinum	the-kettle
kátr	cheerful
kaup	had
Kaupang	Kaupang (place)
Kaupangs	Kapuang (place)
kaupferð	trading-voyage
kaupmennirnir	merchant-men
kaupmönnum	the-trading-men, trading-men
kaupskipinu	merchant-ship, trading-ship
kem	come
kemr	came, come, comes
kendi	hands
kenn	know
kenna	know, teach
kenndi	felt
kennt	blame
keyptut	bought
kilju	the-binding
kjöts	flesh
klámyrði	obscene
klámyrðum	obscene-words
klappaði	rapped, struck
klappar	hammering
klukku	a-bell
kné	knee
kníf	knife
knífi	knife
knífinum	knife
knörru	knorrs

Word List (Old Norse to English)

Old Norse	English
knúskim	knocked-down
köllu	call
kölluðu	called
Kollu-vísur	cow-verses
kom	came, come
koma	come, come-forward
kominn	coming
komit	came, come, coming
komst	came
komu	came
komum	came
konung	the-king
konunga	kings
konungi	the-king, the-king's
konunginn	the-king
konunginum	the-king
konungr	him, king, king's, the-king, the-king's
konungrinn	the-king
konungs	the-king, the-king's
konungsgarð	the-king
konungsins	the-king
kostr	a-choice
kunna	know
kunnu	could
kurteiss	polite
kúrvaldi	folded
kvað	recited, said, spoke
kvaddi	called, greeted
kváðu	recited
kvæði	composed, poem, poems, recited
kvæðin	poems
kvæðinu	the-poem
kvæðisins	the-poem
kvæðis-launin	poem-reward
kvæðis-mynd	poem-image
kvæðit	poem, the-poem
kvæðunum	the-poetry
kveð	recite
kveð'k	say
kveða	compose, recite
kveðin	recited, worded
kveðinn	after
kveðit	spoken, worded
kveðju	greeting
kveðr	recited, words
kveðst	said
kveld	the-evening
kveldit	evening
kvenna	women
kviðlingr	short-poem
kyns	kin
kýr	cows
kyrrt	peace, peaceful

L, l

Old Norse	English
lá	lay
læt	have
læt'k	let
lagði	became, laid
lagðist	lay
lagin	assigned, songs
lágu	laid, lay
lágum	laid
land	land
landi	land, the-land
landinu	the-land
langa	long
langskip	longships
lát	had, have
láta	allow, have
látir	leave
látit	had, let
launa	reward
launaði	rewarded
launin	also
laus	lost
laut	bowed
leðr	skin
legg	lay
leggja	allow, lay
leggr	laid
leið	passed
leiða	lead
leiðar	on-way
leigðu	rented
leika	games, play
leista	of-footwear
leita	find, look-for, seeking

Word List (Old Norse to English)

Old Norse	English
leitaði	sought
leitaðir	seek
lendr	land
lengi	long
lér	leaned
lét	gave, had
létti	let-up
léttum	let-up
leys	repay
leyst	answered
liðs	company
líf	life
lífi	life
lífinu	his-life, your-life
liggja	lie
líkaði	liked
líkar	consider, like, liked
líklegr	likely
líkr	like
lít'k	coloured
lítast	looked
lítil	little, men
lítilla	little
lítilsvert	little
lítilþægir	easily-satisfied
lítilþægr	little-behaving
lítinn	little
litist	looked
lítit	bites, little
litlu	a-little
lítt	little
ljóst	light
ljótlimaðr	ugly-limbed
ljúgi	lie
loðir	of-your-hair
lof	permission, praise
lofa	promise
loft	praised
lofuðu	praised
lögðu	laid
lögskilum	legal-settlement
lokit	concluded, ended, finished
lönd	land, lands
lyftingunni	lifting
lýgr	lies, lying
lýk	end
lykkja	noose
lykkjan	the-noose
lysti	appetite
lýsu	the-whitings

M, m

Old Norse	English
má	may
maðr	a-man, man, the-man
maðrinn	the-man
mæl	speak
mæla	matter, matters, say, speak
mælti	spoke
mæltist	recited
Magnús	Magnus (name)
maka	equal
makligra	well-deserved
makligri	more-suitable
makligust	the-best
mál	matter
málefnum	matters
málit	the-matter
málsþörf	matter
málum	matter, matters
mann	becomes, man
manna	man, men, people
manni	man
mannsbarn	man's-son
marga	many
margir	many
margs	many, many-things
margt	many
mat	food
matar	food
matr	food
mátti	as-might, may
með	with
meðan	as-long-as, while
megin	side
megu	may
mein	harm, mean
meir	more
meira	more

Word List (Old Norse to English)

Old Norse	English
meiri	more
menn	men, people
menntr	educated
mér	because, for-me, I, intended, me, mine, my, to-me
merkr	marks
mest	high, most, there
mesta	most
mestu	most
mettir	finished-eating, satisfied
mettr	finished-eating, satisfied
mik	me
mikill	great, much
mikils	great
mikinn	much
mikit	great, much
mikla	great, greatest
Miklagarði	Byzantium (place)
miklu	much
miklum	much
milli	between
mína	mine, my
mínir	kinsman
minn	father, mine
minna	less, lesser, mine
míns	mine
mínu	mine
mínum	mine
mislíkaði	mis-liked
missa	lose, miss
mitt	mine, the-middle
mjök	much
mjöli	meal
mœttum	met
mönnum	the-people
morgininn	morning
mörk	a-mark, one-mark
mörkina	the-border
móti	against, meet
mun	could, shall, should, should-be, then, will, would, would-be
mun'k	will
muna	would
munaðr	little
munar	delight
munat	remembered
munda	remembered
mundi	could-be, should-be, would
mundir	would
mundu	could, could-be, would
muni	shall
munni	mouth
munt	must, should
muntú	shall-you, should, would-you
munu	shall, would

N, n

Old Norse	English
ná	obtain, take
naðri	serpent
næða	neared
nær	near
nærri	close-to, near
næst	near
næsta	next
nafn	named
nam	took
námu	took
nauðliga	necessarily
nauðsyn	necessary
nauðsynja	needs
nautaleðrs	ox-skin
neðan	below
neflangr	long-nosed
nefndr	named
nei	no
nema	but, except
níð	slander
níðit	the-slander
niðr	down
Njörðr	Njord (name)
njót	enjoy
njótum	benefit
nóg	enough

Word List (Old Norse to English)

Old Norse	English
nökkur	some, something
nökkura	any
nökkurr	something
nökkuru	one-of, some, somehow, somewhat
nökkurum	some
nökkut	anything, few, something, somewhat
norðr	north
norðrlönd	northern-lands
Noreg	Norway (place)
Noregi	Norway (place)
Noregs	Norway (place)
nótt	night, the-night
nóttum	nights
nú	no, not, now

O, o

Old Norse	English
oddviti	leader
of	of, off
ofan	over
offylli	gluttony
ofraun	too-much
oftar	again, more
og	and
ok	also, and, killed, this, yours
olli	cause
opit	open
orð	word
orða	words
orðaskil	words-separated
orðfátt	word-fallen
orðgreppr	word-bold
orðhákr	word-tall
orðhvass	sharp-tongued
orðinn	of-words
orðit	become, worded
orðum	words
orlofs	vacation
orm	the-serpent
ort	had, worded, words
orta	worded
orti	worded

Old Norse	English
oss	tell, to-us, us, we

Ó, ó

Old Norse	English
óðindælu	puzzle
óeyrðarmaðr	unreliable
ógrligr	terrible
óp	shouting
ór	about, from, of, out, out-of
órleysingr	over-praised
órlofs	vacation
ósiðblendnir	un-custom-mixing
óskerðan	the-whole
ótæpt	unsettled
óþökk	un-thanks
ótíginna	un-ranking
ótrúligir	un-truthful
óvirðuligt	unworthy

Ö, ö

Old Norse	English
öðru	the-other
öðrum	eachother, other, others
öðruvísi	other-knowing
öfigt	reversed
öfundsjúkr	un-infatuated
öll	all, of-all
öllu	all
öndvert	upside-down
öngan	no
öngvan	none
önnur	another
ösku	ashes
öxarinnar	the-axe
öxi	an-axe, axe
öxina	the-axe

Œ, œ

Old Norse	English
œpir	cried-out
œptu	called-out

Word List (Old Norse to English)

Old Norse	English
œrit	greatly
œrr	awed

P, p

Old Norse	English
penningar	money
penningum	payment
prettr	trick
prettum	trickery
prófa	prove
prúða	Elegant (name)
prýði	finery

R, r

Old Norse	English
ráð	advice, plan
ráða	decided
ráðar	decide
ráði	advised
ráðigastr	well-advising
ráðinn	appointed
ráðleitinn	cunning
ráðs	agreement
ræð'k	speak
ræsi	the-ruler
rán	robbery
rana	the-trunk
Ránar	Ran (name)
randa	round
rangt	wrong
rannsóknar	a-search
Rauð	Raud (name)
rauðan	the-red
rauðar	red
Rauðr	Raud (name)
rauðum	red
réð	ruled
reðr	beam
reðra	genitals
réðst	appointed, took
réðust	decided
reiðasti	most-angry
reiði	anger
Rein	Reine (place)
rétti	extended
réttr	upright
reyndar	actually
reyndust	proved
reynt	tested
ríkari	richer
ritat	written
röru	rowing
rúghleifa	rye-loaf
rúms	rooms
runa	row
ryðja	cleared
rymskyndir	quickly-cleared

S, s

Old Norse	English
sá	looked, saw, so
sá's	so
sæhafa	sea-scattered
sæsjúkr	seasick
sæti	sit
sætis	seat
sættir	settlements
sættust	settled
sagða	said
sagði	said, told, told-of
sagðir	said, said
sagðist	said
sagt	said, said, told, told-to
sakir	sake
saklausa	sake-less
sama	same
saman	together
sami	same
sannmæli	true-words
sarð	wounded
sásk	with-footwear
satt	true, truth
satt?	TRUE
sátu	sat, were
sáu	saw
saurigt	filthy
sé	see, so
sé'k	see
seg	tell

Word List (Old Norse to English)

Old Norse	English
seggja	said
seggr	said
segi	say
segir	said
segit	tell
segja	Einar (name), say, to-tell
seinþreyttr	persistent
séit	look
selda'k	that
selja	barter, to-sell
sem	as, same-as, where, which
send	send
sendi	sent
sendingum	delivery
senn	but
sennur	chatter
sér	for-him, him, himself, his, saw, sees, themselves, to
serðast	to-get-hurt
serðr	wounder
sessunaut	bench-companion
sessunautr	bench-companion
sét	seen
setit	sat
setja	set
settist	sat, settled
settliga	sedately
settu	set
sezt	sat
síð	long
síðan	after, afterwards, since, then
síðar	afterwards, later
síðast	the-last
siðr	a-custom, the-custom
síðu	side
síður	since
sigldi	sailed
sigldu	sailed
Sigurð	Sigurd (name)
Sigurðarson	Sigurdson (name)
Sigurði	Sigurd (name)
Sigurðr	Sigurd (name)
sik	he, him, himself
silfr	silver
silfrhólkr	silver-band
silfri	silver
silfrinu	the-silver
silfrs	of-silver
silfrvafit	silver-wound
sín	his, themselves
sína	his
sinina	tendon
sinn	father's-killer, his, occasion, theirs, then
sinna	his
sinnar	his, their
sinni	himself, these
síns	father, his
sínu	his
sínum	his, theirs
sit	sit
sit'k	one, sit
sitja	settle, sit
sitr	sat
sitt	himself, his, their, this
síu	sift
siz'k	about
sízt	least
sjá	see
sjaldan	seldom
sjálfr	himself, yourself
sjálfs	self's
sjálfum	himself
sjóða	boil
sjóði	purse
sjóðnum	the-purse
sjúkr	sick
skaði	harm
skaftit	the-shaft
skal	shall, should
skál	shall
skáld	a-poet, poet, poets, the-poet
skálda	poets
skáldi	the-poet
skáldskap	poetry
skáldskapar	a-poet
skall	hit, rattled

Word List (Old Norse to English)

Old Norse	English
skalt	shall
skaltú	shall-you
skapdreki	mood-dragon
skapi	mind, mood
skarlatsklæðum	scarlet
skemt	entertainment
skemta	entertain
skerði	cuts
skift	exchange
skilat	settled
skinna	of-skins
skip	ship, the-ship
skipin	the-ships
skipinu	the-ship
skipit	ship, the-ship
skipsmiðir	ship-smiths
skipuðu	ships
skjöld	shield
skjótt	quickly, rapidly
skó	shoes
skömm	disgrace, scandal
skreið	crawled
skreppa	bag
skreppu-skrúði	bag-tackle
skrýfði	scrawled
skuld	debt
skulu	should
skulum	shall
skulut	should
skylda	would
skyldara	should
skyldi	should, would
skyldu	should, should-be, would
skylt	should
skyrkaupum	cow-buying
sleggju	the-hammer
slíðrar	sheathed
slík	such
slíka	such
slíkir	such
slíkt	such
smiðbelgja	smith-bellows
smiðju	of-the-smith
smjörvan	buttered
snætt	dined
snák	snake
snaraði	rushed
Sneglu-Halla	Sarcastic-Halli (name)
Sneglu-Halli	Sarcastic-Halli (name)
snöri	turned
snúa	return
snúit	turned
sœkir	sought
sofa	sleep
sögðu	announced, told
sögðuzt	said
sögu	the-story
sómir	common
son	son
Sorptrogs-vísur	food-trough-verses
sótt	not
spán	a-spoon
spara	withhold
sprengja	burst
sprungit	burst
spryngi	burst
spurði	asked, asking, learned
spurðu	asked
spurt	heard, questions
spyrr	asked
Stað	Stad (place), the-place
staðar	place
staddr	to
standa	standing
standit	standing
steiktr	roasted
steinn	a-stone
stendr	standing, stands
stígandi	ascending
stillir	heading
stóð	place, stood
stœrri	greater
stórlyndr	large-repaying (generous)
stórmannliga	big-man-like
stórra	great
stórum	great, stone-kettle

Word List (Old Norse to English)

Old Norse	English
stræti	the-street
stríði	battles
ströndu	the-shore
stund	awhile
stundu	awhile
stykki	piece
stýrimaðr	steersman
stýrir	steers
styrk	strong
sú	the-one
suðr	south
suðrmenn	southern-men, the-southerners
sufli	with-bread
sumar	summer
sumargamlan	one-summer-old
sumir	some
sumt	some
sútari	tanner
svá	coming, so, then
svangir	hungry
svara	answer, to-answer
svaraði	answered
svarar	answered
svarat	answered
Svarfaðardal	Svarfadardal (place)
svefni	sleep
sveini	this-lad
sveltir	starving
sverð	sword
sverði	a-sword, sword
sverðit	sword
svífst	shrinks-from
svíni	swine
sýlt	sleek
sýn	I
sýna	showed
sýndi	showed
sýndisk	seems
sýndist	thought
sýnir	show
sýnist	seems
synjuðu	refused
sýnna	appear
sýr	sow

Old Norse	English
sýslu	business, stewardship
systkinum	siblings

T, t

Old Norse	English
tak	take
taka	take
taki	takes
takist	take
takit	take
tala	speak, speaking
talaði	talked
talast	speak
talat	talking
tangar	tongs
taumi	leash
taums-endanum	the-leash
taumsins	the-leash
tekit	taken
tekizt	taken
tíðinda	news
tíðindi	news
tignari	nobler
tiguligr	dignified
til	about, as, for, into, that, to, towards, until, up-to
tíma	time
tíu	ten
tjöru	tar
tœki	take
tók	received, took
tóku	and, took
tókum	took
töluðu	spoke
torf	turf
trog	trough
trúa	believe
túngarði	hayfield-wall
Túta	Tuta (name)
Tútu	Tuta (name)
tvá	two
tveggja	both
tveir	two

64

Word List (Old Norse to English)

Old Norse	English
tví	tut
tvíræð	ambiguous
tvíræðis-orð	ambiguous
tvöföld	two-fold

Þ, þ

Old Norse	English
þá	in, now, then, though
það	that
þaðan	from-there
þær	there
þagna	silence
þagnaði	silenced
þakkaði	thanked, thanked
þangað	from-there
þangat	from-there, from-there
þann	that, that, then
þar	that, there, they, they
þar's	there
þari	intestines
þat	is, it, it, than, that, the, this, though, to-me, which
þau	there
þegar	already, as-soon-as, early, from-there, straight-away, then
þegnar	men
þeim	for-them, them, they
þeir	the, them, they
þeira	theirs, them
þeiri	of-them, theirs
þenna	then, this
þér	to-you, you, yours
þess	this
þessa	this
þessarrar	this
þessi	repay, these, this
þessu	this
þetta	it, that, these, this
þiggi	receives
þik	you
þing	assembly
þinga	assemble
þinginn	the-assembly
þingit	the-assembly
þings	the-assembly
þingsins	the-assembly
Þingvalla	Thingvellir (place)
þinn	yours
þíns	yours
þínu	yours
þit	you-two
þitt	yours
Þjóðólf	Thjodolf (name)
Þjóðólfi	Thjodolf (name)
Þjóðólfr	Thjodolf (name)
Þjóðólfs	Thjodolf's (name)
þjófr	thief
þjón	servant
þjóna	serve
þjónusta	service
þjónustu	service
þjónustumenn	the-servants
Þjóttu	Thjotta (place)
þó	shall, then, though
þœtti	seems
þœttist	thought
þögnuðu	silenced
þökk	thanks
þola	enduring
þoldi	endured
þolir	endures
þöngul	there
Þór	Thor (name)
Þóra	Thora (name)
Þórbergs	Thorberg's (name)
þori	dare
Þórleifi	Thorleif (name)
Þórleifr	Thorleif (name)
Þórljóti	Thorljot (name)
Þórljótr	Thorljot (name)
þorpi	village
Þórr	Thor (name)
Þóru	Thora (name)
þótt	though, though
þótti	seemed, thought
þóttir	thought
þóttist	thought
þóttu	thought

Word List (Old Norse to English)

Old Norse	English
þóttumst	seemed, thought
þóttust	thought
þræta	argued
þrætu	threatening
Þrándheim	Trondheim (place)
Þrándheims	Trondheim (place)
þrevett	three-winters-old
þriðja	a-third, third
þrjár	three
þrjú	three
þú	you
þula	thula (poem)
þunga	heavy-cargo
þurfti	needed
þverliga	crossly
því	accordingly, because, before, since, that, then, therefore
þykki	seems, think
þykkir	consider, considered, seems, that, think
þykkja	seemed
þyrði	dared

U, u

Old Norse	English
um	about, at, if
und	up
undan	out-from, under
undarligt	scandalous
undir	under
undr	wonder
undrskapaðr	wonder-created
unnit	won
unz	until
upp	up, upped, up-to, we-are
upphaf	beginning
ut	out

Ú, ú

Old Norse	English
út	about, out, outside
útan	out, without
útar	out
úthlaupi	out-running
úti	extended-out, out
útivist	out-journey
útróðr	out-rowing (fishing)

V, v

Old Norse	English
vændis	wicked
vænstr	promising
vænti	expected
væri	being, was, were, would, would-be
vakit	awake
vaknaða	awoke
váligrar	wretched
ván	expected
vandi	difficult
vánligt	expected
vanr	custom
vápnast	armed
var	have, mine, that, was, were, who
varð	became, came, was, were
varði	were
varðist	guarded
várit	spring
várkunn	understandable
varla	hardly
varlega	warily
varliga	warily
varp	threw
várr	our
váru	our, was, were, where
várum	were
veðja	wager
veðjanin	the-wager
veðjanina	wager
veg	way
vegar	way
veginn	was
veik	turned
veit	know, known
veita	grant

Word List (Old Norse to English)

Old Norse	English
veitt	given
vekja	awaken
vel	good, had, well
veltr	hung
ver	be
vér	are-we, we
vera	be, become, being, one, to-be, was, wished
verða	be, becomes, being, have-been, worth
verðr	money-bribe, worthy
verit	become, been
verk	work
verkmanns	workman's
verkum	actions
verr	worse
verra	was, worse, worst
verri	worse
vert	worth
vetr	winter
vetri	winter
vetrinn	winter
vetrvistar	winter-lodgings, winter-provisions
við	about, against, at, from, of, to, with
víg	slaying
vil	will, wish
vilda	wished
vildi	wanted, willed, wished
vilit	wish
vilja	to-be, wished
vilju	wish
viljum	we-wish, wish
vill	will, wish, wishes
vilt	will
viltú	will-you
vinskapr	friendship
virði	before, worthied
vísan	the-verse, verse
víss	certain
vissi	knew
vissu	knew
vist	provisions
víst	certainly
vistaðist	found-a-place
vistar	lodgings
vistin	the-supply
vistina	the-provisions
vísu	a-verse
vit	know, we, wit, with
vita	knew, know, to-know
vitit	know
vitrastr	the-wisest
vitsmuna	intellect
vöru	were

Y, y

Old Norse	English
yðar	you
yðarr	of-you
yðart	your, yours
yðr	you
yðrum	yours
yfir	over, sitting
ykkr	you
ynni	won
yrði	became, should, was
yrk	compose, write
yrkisefnin	the-themes
yrkis-efnin	compose
yrkja	compose, to-compose

Ý, ý

Old Norse	English
ýmsu	about
ýttu	pushed
ýttum	pushed

Word List *(English to Old Norse)*

English	Old Norse
A, a	
about	á, á, á, á, á, á, á, á, á, á'k
an	á
at	á, á, á, á, á
after	áðr, áðr, áðr, aðra
another	aðra, ætlat, ætluðu, ætt, ættaðr, ætti, ættsmár, af
Agdanes (place)	Agðanes, Agðaness
Agdi (name)	Agði, Agði
a-child	aldri
all	allir, allir, allr, allr, allra, allreiðr, allt, allt, allvel
all-angry	allreiðr
all-well	allvel
all-year	ári
a	at, at
am-I	at
and	at, at, at, at, at, at, at, at
as	at, at, at, at, at, at
ate	át, át
always	ávallt, bað
asked	bað, bað, bað, báðir, bæði
a-better	betri
ask	biðja
at-table	borðum
away	brott, brynju, brynju, brynjuna
a-plate	diskr
a-drapa (poem)	drápu
a-dream	draumr
alone	einn
am	em
age	er
are	er, er, er, er
are-you	ertú
are-we	eru, eru
a-few	fám
accomplished	fœrr
ahead	fram
agreeable	gæfr
a-delight	gaman
amusement	gamans
a-gold-ring	gullhring
autumn	haustit, haustum
avenge	hefna
avenged	hefnt
a-horse	hest
a-lot-of	hlaut
a-hearing	hljóð
a-thing	hluti
a-threat	hótun
afraid	hræddir
awhile	hríð, hringum, hroðit
a-house	hús
an-Icelander	íslenzkr
an-earl	jarl
accuse	kæra
a-calf	kálf
a-man	karlmanni, kastaði
a-bell	klukku
a-choice	kostr
assigned	lagin
allow	láta, láta
also	launin, laus
answered	leyst, liðs, líf, lífi
a-little	litlu
appetite	lysti
as-might	mátti
as-long-as	meðan
a-mark	mörk
against	móti, móti
any	nökkura
anything	nökkut
awed	œrr
again	oftar
ashes	ösku
an-axe	öxi
axe	öxi
advice	ráð
advised	ráði
appointed	ráðinn, ráðleitinn
agreement	ráðs

Word List (English to Old Norse)

a-search	rannsóknar	better	betr, betra
anger	reiði	best	bezt
actually	reyndar	bite	bitar
afterwards	síðan, síðar	biting	bitit
a-custom	siðr	bigger-men	bokkar
a-poet	skáld, skáldskapar	Bolli (name)	Bolla
announced	sögðu	boards	borð
a-spoon	spán	brought	borin, borinn, bótunum, brá, brákar, brauði, brenndan
asking	spurði		
a-stone	steinn		
ascending	stígandi	breaker	brákar
answer	svara	bread	brauði
a-sword	sverði	burnt	brenndan
appear	sýnna	brother	bróðir, bróður
already	þegar	boys	drengi
as-soon-as	þegar	but	eða, eðr, eðr, ef, eftir
assembly	þing	back-from	eftir
assemble	þinga	brow	enni
argued	þræta	bring	fœra
a-third	þriðja	because-of	fyrir
accordingly	því	became	gerðist, gerðu, gerðu, geri
ambiguous	tvíræð, tvíræðis-orð		
awake	vakit	beguile	gilja?, giljum
awoke	vaknaða	beside	hjá
armed	vápnast	be-heard	hljóðs
awaken	vekja	boldly	hraustliga
actions	verkum	bad	illa
a-verse	vísu	badly	illa
		be-called	kallaðir
		blame	kennt

B, b

		bought	keyptut
		bowed	laut
be	á, á, á, á, á	bites	lítit
by	á, á, á, á	becomes	mann, mann
back	áðr, áðr, aðra, ætlat, ætluðu	because	mér, mér
		Byzantium (place)	Miklagarði
before	áðr, aðra, ætlat, ætluðu, ætt, ættaðr, ætti, ættsmár, af	between	milli
		below	neðan
		benefit	njótum
being	annan, annarr, annarr, annars	become	orðit, ort, ösku
		beam	reðr
bid	bað	barter	selja
both	báðir, bæði, bafði, baki	bench-companion	sessunaut, sessunautr
bears	bar	boil	sjóða
bore	bar	bag	skreppa
Bard (name)	Bárð, Bárðr	bag-tackle	skreppu-skrúði
belt	belti	buttered	smjörvan

69

Word List (English to Old Norse)

burst	sprengja, sprungit, spryngi
big-man-like	stórmannliga
battles	stríði
business	sýslu
believe	trúa
beginning	upphaf
been	verit

C, c

completely	alla, allir
carried	bar, Bárð, Bárðr
child	barn
children	barna
compensation	bœta, bœti, bœtti
compensate	bœti
compensated	bœtti
cunning	brögðóttan, brosti
chain-mail	brynju
coat-of-mail	brynju, brynjuna
command	býð
can	fæ, fær
carry-out	fær
companion	félagi
composed	fémúta, fengu, fénu
caught	fengu
called	hann, hann, hann, hann, hans
commotion	háreysti
call	heita, heitir
court	hirðarinnar
care	hirði
courtiers	hirðin
court-man	hirðmaðr
court-men	hirðmanna
calm	hljóða
chieftains	höfðingja, höfðingjar
chief-poet	höfuðskáld
circles	hringum
cleared	hroðit, hróðr
cast	kagtat, kálf
can-it	kann
cheerful	kátr
come	kem, kemr, kemr, kemr, kendi
came	kemr, kemr, kemr, kendi, kenn, kenna, kenndi
comes	kemr
cow-verses	Kollu-vísur
come-forward	koma
coming	kominn, komit, komit
could	kunnu, kúrvaldi, kvaddi
compose	kveða, kveðinn, kveðju, kveldit
cows	kýr
company	lið s
consider	líkar, líkar
coloured	lít'k
concluded	lokit
could-be	mundi, mundu
close-to	nærri
cried-out	œpir
called-out	œptu
cause	olli
chatter	sennur
cuts	skerði
crawled	skreið
cow-buying	skyrkaupum
common	sómir
crossly	þverliga
considered	þykkir
custom	vanr
certain	víss
certainly	víst

D, d

descent	ætt
descended	ættaðr
disrespected	af
dead	andaðr, andróða, annan
difficulty	andróða
death-sentence	bana-sök
death	bani, bann
drew	brá, brákar, brauði
day	dag, dagana
Denmark	danmerkr
Denmark (place)	Danmerkr
daring	djarfan

Word List (English to Old Norse)

daughter	dóttur	ended	enda, Englandi
drapa (poem)	drápu	England (place)	Englandi, Englands
dream	draum, draumr	errand	erindi
draws	dregr	eating	eta
draw	dregst	extremely	furðanliga
dragon	dreki	enjoyment	gaman
drinking	drekka	entertaining	gaman
dreamed	dreymt	equipped	gyrði
drink	drykk, drykkjar	Earl-of-Lade (name)	Hlaðajarli
denied	duldu	each	hvárn, hvárr, hvárt, hvárttveggja, hvatt, hvé
dwarf	dvergr		
delivered	flutt		
delight	gaman, gaman	each-way	hvárttveggja
do	ger, ger, gera, gera	encouraged	hvatt
does	ger, gera	evil	illa, illan
doing	gera	evil-ways	ilvegs
done	gera, gera, gera	equally	jafnan
did	gerði, gerði, gerðist	equally-badly	jafngreypiliga
deception	ginning	equal	jafnir, jafnsleppt
dug	grafit	equally-slip	jafnsleppt
deep-red	gruntrauðustum	earl	jarl
danger	hættu	even	jöfnum
discuss	kæra	evening	kveldit
dear-friendship	kærleikum	easily-satisfied	lítilþægir
down	niðr	end	lýk
decided	ráða, ráðar	educated	menntr
decide	ráðar	except	nema
delivery	sendingum	enjoy	njót
disgrace	skömm	enough	nóg
debt	skuld	eachother	öðrum
dined	snætt	Elegant (name)	prúða
dare	þori	extended	rétti
dared	þyrði	entertainment	skemt
dignified	tiguligr	entertain	skemta
difficult	vandi	exchange	skift
		early	þegar
		enduring	þola
		endured	þoldi
		endures	þolir
		extended-out	úti
		expected	vænti, væri, vakit

E, e

excellent	ágætr
eat	át, átt
estate	búi
examples	dœmi
Einar (name)	Einar, Einari, Einarr, Einars, Einars
Einar's (name)	Einars
elderly	elliligt
Emma (name)	Emmu

F, f

for	á, á, á, á, á'k, áðr, áðr
from	á, á, á, á'k, áðr, áðr, áðr, aðra

Word List (English to Old Norse)

family-small	ættsmár	flesh	kjöts
farmers	bœndr, bœta	folded	kúrvaldi
farmer	bóndi	finished	lokit
fair-wind	byr	food	mat, matar, matr
fire-house (kitchen)	eldahús	for-me	mér
fire	eldi, eldingum	finished-eating	mettir, mettr
fine	enn	few	nökkut
forehead	enni	finery	prýði
father	faðir, fæ, fær, Fáfni	filthy	saurigt
Fafnir (name)	Fáfni	for-him	sér
found	fann, far, fara	father's-killer	sinn
fare	fara	food-trough-verses	Sorptrogs-vísur
fee-taken	fátœkr	for-them	þeim
fee-servant	féhirði, féhirðinn	found-a-place	vistaðist
fell	fell, fellt, fémúta		
five	fimm		
find	finna, finna, Finnferð		
Finland-voyages (place)	Finnferð		

G, g

fishermen	fiskimenn	grinned	brosti
fee	fjár	get	fá, fá, faðir
followers	fjölmennt, fjóra	give	fá, faðir, fæ, fær
four	fjóra, fjórar	go	far, fara, fara, fara, fara
fourth	fjórðung	goes	fara, fara
fourteen	fjórtán	going	fara, farit, fátœkr, fátt, fé
Fljot (place)	Fljótum	gone	farit
fleeing	flœr-at	got	fekk, fekk
Fly (name)	fluga, flugu	guarded	gætti, gaf
flew	flugust	gave	gaf, gakk, galdra
fore-knowing	forvitnar	gaping	gap
feet	fótum	garden	garðinn
forwards	fram	Gasir (place)	Gásum
from-saying	frásagnar	granted	gefa
Frisian (name)	Frísa	given	gefin, gefit, Geirrauð
Frisian	frískr	Geirrod (name)	Geirrauð, Geirrauðr
full	fullr, fullt	guest	gista
follow	fylgja	gladly	gjarna
first	fyrst, fyrstu	glad	glaðr
fun	gaman	gnawing	gnauða
famine	hallæri	good	góð, góða, góðan, góðr, góðum, gott, grafit
from-there	héðan, hefði, hefðim, hefðir, hefir, hefir		
force	hér	grasped	greppr
fallen	hnigit	Godwinson (name)	Guðinason
fame	hróðr	good-rightly	guðréttligast
from-where	hvaðan	Gula-assembly (name)	Gulaþing, Gulaþings
friendship	kærleikum, kagtat		
felt	kenndi		

Word List (English to Old Norse)

English	Old Norse
gold-band	gullhlað
gold-ring	gullhring
gold-inlaid	gullrekin
goat	hafra
giant	jötni
greeted	kvaddi
greeting	kveðju
games	leika
great	mikill, mikill, mikils, mikinn, mikit, mikit
greatest	mikla
greatly	œrit
gluttony	offylli
genitals	reðra
greater	stœrri
grant	veita

H, h

English	Old Norse
had	ætti, ættsmár, af, af, af, af, af, aftr, aftrábak, ágætr, Agðanes, Agðaness, Agði, Agði, aldri, alla, allir, allir, allr, allr, allra
having	átt, átti
hat	átti
he	bann, bar, bar, bar, Bárð, Bárðr, barn, barn, barna
Halli (name)	ek, ek, ek, eldahús
his	föður, föðurbana, fœra, fœra, fœrðr, fœrr, föll, fór, fór, för, förum, forvitnar, fót, fótum, frá, frændi
higher	hærra, hærri
have	haf, hafa, hafa, hafa, hafa, hafa, hafða, hafði, hafðir
has	hafa, hafa, hafa
Hakon (name)	Hákon, Hákoni
hold	halda
held	haldit, hálfa, Halla
half	hálfa
Halli's (name)	Halla
Halogaland (place)	Hálogaland, Hálogalandi
her	hana
hand-washing	handlaugar
him	hann, hans, hans, hans, hanu, hár
high	hár, Haraldi
Harald (name)	Haraldi, Haraldi, Haraldr
Harald's (name)	Haraldi, Haraldr, Haraldr
Harald's-poem	Haralds-drápu
Harek's (name)	Háreks
hair	hárinu
high-seat	hásætit
has-been	hefir
health	heill
home	heim
hone	hein
honing-grease	heinar-sufl
hung	hekk, helt
hand	hendi, hendr, hér, hér
here	hér
hostel	herbergi
horse	hestr, hestrinn
hear	heyra
heard	heyra, heyrða, heyrði, heyrðu, heyrt, hilmis
helmsman's	hilmis
Hitra (place)	Hítrar
helmet	hjálm
head	höfuð, höfuðit
horn-spoon	hornspánu
hide	húðar
hungry	hungrar, hús
how	hvé
how-so	hvers, hversu
hands	kendi
hammering	klappar
his-life	lífinu
harm	mein, mein
himself	sér, sér, sessunaut, sessunautr, síð, síðan
hit	skall
heading	stillir
heavy-cargo	þunga
hayfield-wall	túngarði
hardly	varla
have-been	verða

I, i

Word List (English to Old Norse)

English	Old Norse
in	á, á, á'k, áðr, áðr, áðr, aðra, ætlat, ætluðu, ætt
it	á, á'k, áðr, áðr, áðr, aðra
I	á'k, áðr, áðr, áðr, aðra, ætlat
intended	ætlat, ætluðu, ætt
invited	bað, báðir
if	ef, eftir, eftir
in-the-end	enn
is	er, erindi, erindi, ert
islands	eyja, eyjar
is-named	heitir
into	í, illa
ill	illt
inside	innan
Iceland (place)	Ísland, Íslandi, Íslands
Iceland-voyage	Íslands-fari
Icelanders	íslendinga, íslendingar
Icelander	íslenzka, íslenzkan, íslenzkr
iron-weapon	járn
ironsmith	járnsmiðr
intestines	þari
intellect	vitsmuna

J, j

English	Old Norse
journey	förum
jumped	hljóp
Jutland (place)	Jótlands

K, k

English	Old Norse
killed	drap, drápu, drápu, draum, draumr
kill	drepa, drepit
kinsman	frændi, frændunum
kinsmen	frændunum
knife-handle	hnífskefti
knows	kann
know-you	kanntú
Kaupang (place)	Kaupang
Kapuang (place)	Kaupangs
know	kenn, kenna, kenndi, kennt, keyptut, kjöts, klappar
knee	kné
knife	kníf, knífi, knífinum
knorrs	knörru
knocked-down	knúskim
kings	konunga
king	konungr
king's	konungr
kin	kyns
known	veit
knew	vissi, vissu, víst

L, l

English	Old Norse
lived	bjó
laughed	brosti
lodgings	búð, bú-Finna
lightning	eldingum
loved	elskaði
life	es, eta, eta
little	fátt, fé, fébœtr, féhirði, féhirðinn, fekk, fekk, fekk
lost	firrst, fiskimenn, fjár
leg	fót
last	fyrra
look-to	gera
long-neck	hálslangr
long-armed	handsiðr
lord	herra
ladened	hlaðna
listen	hlýði
lobsters	humrum
lay	lá, læt, læt'k, lagði, lagði
let	læt'k, lagði
laid	lagði, lagðist, lagin, lágu, lágu
land	land, landi, langa, langskip
long	langa, langskip, lát
longships	langskip
leave	látir
lead	leiða
look-for	leita
leaned	lér

74

Word List (English to Old Norse)

let-up	létti, léttum	make	gera
lie	liggja, líkaði	moustache	grön
liked	líkaði, líkar	mocking	háðyrðum
like	líkar, líkar	most-hardy	herðamestr
likely	líklegr	mind	hug, hugar
looked	lítast, lítil, lítil	minds	hugar
little-behaving	lítilþægr	molars	jaxlar
light	ljóst	merchant-men	kaupmennirnir
legal-settlement	lögskilum	merchant-ship	kaupskipinu
lands	lönd	men	lítil, lítilla, lítilsvert, lítilþægir
lifting	lyftingunni	may	má, maðr, maðr
lies	lýgr	matter	mæla, mæla, Magnús, maka
lying	lýgr		
less	minna	matters	mæla, Magnús, maka
lesser	minna	Magnus (name)	Magnús
lose	missa	more-suitable	makligri
long-nosed	neflangr	man's-son	mannsbarn
leader	oddviti	many-things	margs
look	séit	mean	mein
later	síðar	mine	mér, mér, merkr, mest, mest, mesta, mestu, mettir, mettr
least	sízt		
learned	spurði		
large-repaying (generous)	stórlyndr	my	mér, merkr
		marks	merkr
leash	taumi	much	mikill, mikils, mikinn, mikit, mikit, mikla

M, m

		mis-liked	mislíkaði
		miss	missa
man	af, aftr, aftrábak, ágætr, Agðanes	meal	mjöli
		morning	morgininn
married	átti	meet	móti
master	bóndi, borð	mouth	munni
mockery	dáruskapr, dauðan	must	munt
me	ek, eldahús, eldi, eldingum	most-angry	reiðasti
		mood-dragon	skapdreki
message	erindi	mood	skapi
money	fé, fébœtr, féhirði	money-bribe	verðr
many	fjölda, fjöldi, fjölmennt, fjóra, fjórar, fjórðung		
more	fleira, fleiri, flesta, Fljótum, flœr-at, fluga	# N, n	
most	flesta, Fljótum, flœr-at, fluga	never	aldrei, aldrigi
		not	eiga, eiga, eigi, eign, eina, einarr, einhugi
mistakes	föll		
met	fundumst, furðanliga	nothing	einkis, einmælt
magic	galdra	nonsense	endileysu
made	gera, gera, gerast, gerði	no	engan, engan, engi, engi, engu, engum

75

Word List (English to Old Norse)

none	engan, engi, engi, engu	*own*	eiga
neck	háls, hann	*ownership*	eign
named	heita, heitan, heitir, held, heldr, hella	*one-minded*	einhugi
		one-meal	einmælt
narrow-shouldered	herðalítill	*one-decision*	einráðir
nearby	hjá	*once*	eitt
neither	hvárigum	*or-else*	ella
nowhere	hvergi	*over*	fyrir, fyrr, gamall
noose	lykkja	*old*	gamall
neared	næða	*of-the-floor*	gólfið
near	nær, nærri, næst	*of-porridge*	grautar
next	næsta	*obeying*	hlýða
necessarily	nauðliga	*of-him*	honum
necessary	nauðsyn	*obscenities*	hrópyrði
needs	nauðsynja	*onboard*	innanborðs
Njord (name)	Njörðr	*obscene*	klámyrði
north	norðr	*obscene-words*	klámyrðum
northern-lands	norðrlönd	*on-way*	leiðar
Norway (place)	Noreg, Noregi, Noregs	*of-footwear*	leista
		of-your-hair	loðir
night	nótt	*one-mark*	mörk
nights	nóttum	*obtain*	ná
now	nú, óðindælu	*ox-skin*	nautaleðrs
needed	þurfti	*one-of*	nökkuru
news	tíðinda, tíðindi	*other-knowing*	öðruvísi
nobler	tignari	*open*	opit
		out	ór, ór, orð, orða, orðaskil, orðfátt

O, o

of	á, á, á, á, á, á, ábyrgst, aðra, aðra, aðrir	*out-of*	ór
		of-words	orðinn
		over-praised	órleysingr
		of-silver	silfrs
on	á, á	*occasion*	sinn
other	aðra, aðra, aðrir, ætla, ætla, ætlat, af	*of-skins*	skinna
		of-the-smith	smiðju
others	aðra, aðrir	*one-summer-old*	sumargamlan
off	af, af	*of-them*	þeiri
of-all	allra, allskammr	*out-from*	undan
one	annan, annan, annarr, annarra, annars, annat, Árnasonar, at	*outside*	út
		out-running	úthlaupi
		out-journey	útivist
		out-rowing (fishing)	útróðr
otherwise	annarr	*our*	várr, váru
ordered	bað	*of-you*	yðarr
order	bið, biðja		
offence	brot		
offered	býðr		
or	eðr		

Word List (English to Old Norse)

P, p

power	afli
pale	blakkir, bleikr
prepared	búinn, búinn
plate	disk
provoke	etja
passage	far
poor	fátœka
payment	fé, féit
pierced	festi
performed	fœrði
people	fólk, föng, fór
procession	för
pay	gjalda
porridge	graut, grautar, grauti, grautinn
peace	grið, griðníðingr
possessions	gripi
possession	gripr
pig	grís, gríss
pour	hella
poured	hella
part	hlotizt, hlut, hlut
polite	kurteiss
poem	kvæði, kvæði
poems	kvæði, kvæði
poem-reward	kvæðis-launin
poem-image	kvæðis-mynd
peaceful	kyrrt
passed	leið
play	leika
permission	lof
praise	lof
promise	lofa
praised	loft, lofuðu
puzzle	óðindælu
prove	prófa
plan	ráð
proved	reyndust
persistent	seinþreyttr
purse	sjóði
poet	skáld
poets	skáld, skáld
poetry	skáldskap
place	staðar, staddr
piece	stykki
promising	vænstr
provisions	vist
pushed	ýttu, ýttum

Q, q

queen	drottning
quickly	flýta, fœra
quickly-cleared	rymskyndir
questions	spurt

R, r

responsible	ábyrgst
returning	aftr
related-to	átta
ring-land	bauglands
ready	búnir
room	deild
remembered	dýran, eðr, ef
received	fekkst, fengum
rhymes	föng
ready-made	görr
revenge	hefnt
rather	heilt, heita, heitan
running	hlaupi, Hleyp'k
ran	hleypr, hljóð
reasonable	hófi
roaring	hröng
rapped	klappaði
recited	kvað, kvað, kvað, kváðu, kvæði, kvæði
recite	kveð, kveð'k
reward	launa
rewarded	launaði
rented	leigðu
repay	leys, lífinu
reversed	öfigt
robbery	rán
Ran (name)	Ránar
round	randa
Raud (name)	Rauð, rauðan
red	rauðar, Rauðr
ruled	réð
Reine (place)	Rein
richer	ríkari

Word List (English to Old Norse)

rowing	röru	*spine*	hryggrinn
rye-loaf	rúghleifa	*sole-bucket*	ilfat
rooms	rúms	*struck*	klappaði
row	runa	*spoke*	kvað, kváðu, kvæði
rattled	skall	*say*	kveð'k, kveða, kveðin, kveðin
rapidly	skjótt		
rushed	snaraði	*spoken*	kveðit
return	snúa	*short-poem*	kviðlingr
roasted	steiktr	*songs*	lagin
refused	synjuðu	*skin*	leðr
receives	þiggi	*seeking*	leita
		sought	leitaði, leitaðir
		speak	mæl, mæla, mæla, mælti, mæltist

S, s

		side	megin, menn
suppose	ætla	*satisfied*	mettir, mettr
supposed	ætla	*shall*	mun, mun, mun, mun, mun, mun, mun, mun'k
Son-of-Arni (name)	Árnasonar		
said	at, at, at, at, at, at, at, at, at, at, at, at, átta, bað	*should*	mun, mun, mun, mun, mun, mun, mun'k, muna, munat, munda, mundi
settled	bjó, blakkir, bleikr, boði, bœjar, bœnum	*should-be*	mun, mun, mun
soon	brátt	*shall-you*	muntú, muntú
smiled	brosti	*serpent*	naðri
shop-keeping	búðarvörð	*slander*	níð
spears	dörrum	*some*	nökkur, nökkur, nökkurr, nökkuru, nökkuru
seek	em, en		
so	eru, eru, etit, etja, eyddust	*something*	nökkur, nökkurr, nökkuru
spent	eyddust	*somehow*	nökkuru
Slayer-of-Fafnir (name)	Fáfnis-bana	*somewhat*	nökkuru, nökkurum
stout	feitr	*shouting*	óp
Sami-goods	finnskrepp	*sharp-tongued*	orðhvass
since	fjörs, flenna, flest, flýta	*saw*	sá, sá, sá's
sent-for	fœra	*sea-scattered*	sæhafa
stories	frásagnir	*seasick*	sæsjúkr
stopped	hætti	*sit*	sæti, sætis, sættir, sættust
sound-advice	heilræði	*seat*	sætis
sleeping-quarters	herbergjum	*settlements*	sættir
silence	hljóð, hljóðgreipum, hljóðit	*sake*	sakir
sound-grippers (ears)	hljóðgreipum	*sake-less*	saklausa
share	hlut	*same*	sama, saman
suits	hlýða	*sat*	sátu, sátu, sáu, sé, sé
she	hon	*see*	sé, sé, sé'k
shaken	hrökkvi-skafls	*same-as*	sem

Word List (English to Old Norse)

send	send	shrinks-from	svífst
sent	sendi	swine	svíni
sees	sér	sleek	sýlt
seen	sét	showed	sýna, sýndi
set	setja, settist	seems	sýndisk, sýndist, sýnir, sýnist, synjuðu
sedately	settliga		
sailed	sigldi, sigldu	show	sýnir
Sigurd (name)	Sigurð, Sigurðarson, Sigurði	sow	sýr
		stewardship	sýslu
Sigurdson (name)	Sigurðarson	siblings	systkinum
silver	silfr, silfrhólkr	speaking	tala
silver-band	silfrhólkr	silenced	þagnaði, þakkaði
silver-wound	silfrvafit	straight-away	þegar
settle	sitja	servant	þjón
sift	síu	serve	þjóna
seldom	sjaldan	service	þjónusta, þjónustu
self's	sjálfs	seemed	þótti, þótti, þóttir
sick	sjúkr	scandalous	undarligt
scarlet	skarlatsklæðum	spring	várit
ship	skip, skip	slaying	víg
ship-smiths	skipsmiðir	sitting	yfir
ships	skipuðu		
shield	skjöld		
shoes	skó		

T, t

that	á, á, á, á, ábyrgst, aðra, aðra, aðrir, ætla, ætla, ætlat, af, af, af, af, afli, aftr, akta, aldrei, aldrigi, allra
to	á, á, á, ábyrgst, aðra, aðra, aðrir, ætla, ætla
taxes	akta
talked	ámælisverðr, annan
the-next	annan
than	at, at, at, at
the	at, at, at, at, at, at, at, at, átta, bað, báti, báti
this	at, at, at, at, at, at, átta, bað, báti, báti, bátnum
the-boat	báti, báti
the-ship's-boat	báti
the-bench	bekkinn
the-best	bezt, bið
to-ask	biðja
the-town	bœjar
town	bœnum
table	borði, borði

scandal	skömm
scrawled	skrýfði
sheathed	slíðrar
such	slík, slíka, slíkir, slíkt
smith-bellows	smiðbelgja
snake	snák
Sarcastic-Halli (name)	Sneglu-Halla, Sneglu-Halli
sleep	sofa, sögðu
son	son
Stad (place)	Stað
standing	standa, standit, steiktr
stands	stendr
stood	stóð
stone-kettle	stórum
steersman	stýrimaðr
steers	stýrir
strong	styrk
south	suðr
southern-men	suðrmenn
summer	sumar
Svarfadardal (place)	Svarfaðardal
starving	sveltir
sword	sverð, sverði, sverðit

Word List (English to Old Norse)

English	Old Norse
the-table	borði, borðin
tables	borðin
the-city	börg
the-children	börnin
transformed	brást
the-day	daginn
thick-set	digrastr
the-plate	diskinum
the-Danes (name)	Dönum
the-killing	drápi
the-drapa (poem)	drápuna
this-dream	draum
the-dragon-ship	drekanum
the-boy	drengrinn
the-lord	dróttinn
the-queen	drottning, drottningu
the-dwarf	dverg, dverginn
then	ef, eggjaði, eiga, eiga, eigi, eign, eina, einarr, einhugi, einkis, einmælt, einn, einráðir, einu, eitt
the-fire	eld
the-end	enda
they-are	eru
to-eat	etit
thought	fannst, far, far, fara, fara, farit, fars, fátœka, fátœkra, fé, féit
travel	far, fara, fara, farit
travelled	farit, fars
the-poor	fátœkra
the-money	féit
the-Sami (name)	Finna
the-fjord	firðinum
to-extend	flenna
the-most	flest
the-legs	fœtrnir
took	frændr, frásagnir, fund, fúss, fyrir, fyrr, gamall
to-meet	fund
to-delight	gaman
the-house	garðinn
the-wall	garðinn, garðinum, garðrinn, garðsins
teach	gefa, gefa
to-give	gefa
told	getit, gjalda, gólf, gólfið
the-floor	gólf, gólfið
the-porridge	grautinn
the-poor-thing	greyit
truce-breaker	griðníðingr
the-trinkets	gripanna, gripi
things	gripi
treasure	gripi
the-handle	haddan
the-lid	haddan
to-have	hafa
traded	hafa
to-hold	halda
Thjodolf (name)	hann, hárinu, hávan, hefnt
the-hairs	hárinu
the harbour	hávan
the-heath	heiði
threat	heitan
think	held, heldr, hella, hella
to-hand	hendi
the-horse	hestinn
to-hear	heyra
the-court	hirð, hirðinni
the-court-men	hirðinni
the-helmet	hjálmfaldinn
to-strike	höggva
the-hall	höllina, höllinni
to-him	honum
turn	horfa
the-ring	hring, hringinn, hringnum
the-spine	hrygg
turned	hverfr, hvergi, hverjar, hverju
trade	iðnar
the-earl's	jarls
the-giant	jötun
the-calf	kálfinn, kálfrinn
to-call	kalla
the-king	kallaði, katlinum, kaupferð, kaupmönnum, kaupmönnum, kaupskipinu, kenna, kilju, klámyrði, klámyrðum

Word List (English to Old Norse)

English	Old Norse
the-kettle	katlinum
trading-voyage	kaupferð
the-trading-men	kaupmönnum
trading-men	kaupmönnum
trading-ship	kaupskipinu
the-binding	kilju
the-king's	konungi, konunginn, konunginum
the-poem	kvæðinu, kvæðisins, kvæðis-launin
the-poetry	kvæðunum
the-evening	kveld
the-land	landi, landinu
the-noose	lykkjan
the-whitings	lýsu
the-man	maðr, maðrinn
the-matter	málit
to-me	mér, mest
there	mest, mettir, mettr, mitt, mönnum, mörk
the-middle	mitt
the-people	mönnum
the-border	mörkina
take	ná, naðri, næða, nær, nærri, næst
the-slander	níðit
the-night	nótt
the-other	öðru
too-much	ofraun
terrible	ógrligr
the-serpent	orm
the-whole	óskerðan
tell	oss, oss, oss
to-us	oss
the-axe	öxarinnar, öxina
trick	prettr
trickery	prettum
the-ruler	ræsi
the-trunk	rana
the-red	rauðan
tested	reynt
told-of	sagði
told-to	sagt
together	saman
true-words	sannmæli
true	
truth	satt
true	
to-tell	segja
to-sell	selja
themselves	sér, sér
to-get-hurt	serðast
the-last	síðast
the-custom	siðr
the-silver	silfrinu
tendon	sinina
theirs	sinn, sinn, sinnar, sinni
their	sinnar, sinni
these	sinni, sínum, sit
the-purse	sjóðnum
the-shaft	skaftit
the-poet	skáld, skálda
the-ship	skip, skipin, skipinu
the-ships	skipin
the-hammer	sleggju
the-story	sögu
the-place	stað
the-street	stræti
the-shore	ströndu
the-one	sú
the-southerners	suðrmenn
tanner	sútari
to-answer	svara
this-lad	sveini
takes	taki
talking	talat
tongs	tangar
the-leash	taums-endanum, taumsins
taken	tekit, tekizt
though	þá, það, þær, þagna, þagnaði
thanked	þakkaði, þakkaði
they	þar, þar, þar's, þat
them	þeim, þeim, þeir
to-you	þér
the-assembly	þinginn, þingit, þings, þingsins
Thingvellir (place)	Þingvalla
Thjodolf's (name)	Þjóðólfs
thief	þjófr
the-servants	þjónustumenn
Thjotta (place)	Þjóttu
thanks	þökk
Thor (name)	Þór, Þóra

Word List (English to Old Norse)

Thora (name)	Þóra, Þórbergs	unsettled	ótæpt
Thorberg's (name)	Þórbergs	un-thanks	óþökk
Thorleif (name)	Þórleifi, Þórleifr	un-ranking	ótíginna
Thorljot (name)	Þórljóti, Þórljótr	un-truthful	ótrúligir
threatening	þrætu	unworthy	óvirðuligt
Trondheim (place)	Þrándheim, Þrándheims	upright	réttr
		until	til, til
three-winters-old	þrevett	up-to	til, tíma
third	þriðja	under	undan, undarligt
three	þrjár, þrjú	upped	upp
thula (poem)	þula	understandable	várkunn
therefore	því		
towards	til		
time	tíma		

V, v

very-short	allskammr
vacation	orlofs, órlofs
village	þorpi
verse	vísan

ten	tíu
tar	tjöru
turf	torf
trough	trog
Tuta (name)	Túta, Tútu
two	tvá, tveir
tut	tví
two-fold	tvöföld
threw	varp
the-wager	veðjanin
to-be	vera, vera
the-verse	vísan
the-supply	vistin
the-provisions	vistina
to-know	vita
the-wisest	vitrastr
the-themes	yrkisefnin
to-compose	yrkja

W, w

was	á, á, ábyrgst, aðra, aðra, aðrir, ætla, ætla, ætlat, af, af, af
with	á, ábyrgst, aðra, aðra, aðrir, ætla, ætla
waited	beið
were	er, er, er, er, er, er, eru, eru, etit
what	er, er, er, er, er, eru
when	er, er
where	er, er, er, eru, eru
which	er, er, eru, eru
who	er, eru, eru
welcomed	fagnar
went	fara, farit, fars, fátœka, fátœkra, fé, féit
went-you	fórtu
willing	fúss
went-before	fyrr
walking	gengi
we-are-going	göngum
well	hafa, halda
was-named	hét
whether	hvárt
whom	hveru

U, u

up	at, at, at
use	brúki
urged	eggjaði
us	einarr, einhugi
undertaking	fær
upper-shaft	forskeftinn
usually	jafnan
ugly-limbed	ljótlimaðr
unreliable	óeyrðarmaðr
un-infatuated	öfundsjúkr
upside-down	öndvert
un-custom-mixing	ósiðblendnir

Word List (English to Old Norse)

English	Old Norse
why	hví
worded	kveðin, kveðit, kveðit, kveðr, kveðr, kveðst
words	kveðr, kveðst, kveld, kvenna
women	kvenna
well-deserved	makligra
while	meðan
will	mun, mun, mun, mun'k, muna
would	mun, mun, mun'k, muna, munat, munda, mundi, mundi, mundir, mundu
would-be	mun, mun'k
would-you	muntú
word	orð
words-separated	orðaskil
word-fallen	orðfátt
word-bold	orðgreppr
word-tall	orðhákr
we	oss, ótæpt, óþökk
well-advising	ráðigastr
wrong	rangt
written	ritat
wounded	sarð
with-footwear	sásk
wounder	serðr
withhold	spara
with-bread	sufli
wonder	undr
wonder-created	undrskapaðr
won	unnit, unz
we-are	upp
without	útan
wicked	vændis
wretched	váligrar
warily	varlega, varliga
wager	veðja, veðjanin
way	veg, vegar
wished	vera, verða, verðr, verk
worth	verða, verðr
worthy	verðr
work	verk
workman's	verkmanns
worse	verr, verra, verra
worst	verra
winter	vetr, vetri, vetrinn
winter-lodgings	vetrvistar
winter-provisions	vetrvistar
wish	vil, vilda, vildi, vildi, vildi
wanted	vildi
willed	vildi
we-wish	viljum
wishes	vill
will-you	viltú
worthied	virði
wit	vit
write	yrk

Y, y

English	Old Norse
yet	enn
Yule-day	jóladag
Yule	jólin, jólum, jólunum
your-life	lífinu
yours	ok, öll, öndvert, öngan, öngvan, óp, opit, ór
yourself	sjálfr
you	þér, þér, þess, þessa, þessarrar, þessi
you-two	þit
your	yðart

The Tale of Sarcastic Halli (*Old Icelandic*)

Old Icelandic	Literal	English
1	**1**	**1**
Það er upphaf þessar frásagnar að Haraldur konungur Sigurðarson réð fyrir Noregi.	It is beginning this from-saying of Harald the-king Sigurdson ruled over Norway.	The beginning is to say that King Harald Sigurdson ruled Norway.
Það var í þann tíma er Magnús konungur frændi hans var andaður.	It was in that time that Magnus the-king's kinsman his was dead.	It was in that time that Magnus the king's kinsman was dead.
Svo er sagt að Haraldur konungur var allra manna vitrastur og ráðugastur.	So is said that Harald the-king was of-all men the-wisest and well-advising.	So it is said that King Harald was the wisest of all men and of advice.
Varð það og flest að ráði er hann lagði til.	Was it also the-most that advised that he became to.	Also most of what he had counselled had become good.
Hann var skáld gott	He was a-poet good	He was a good poet
og jafnan kastaði hann háðyrðum að þeim mönnum er honum sýndist.	and equally cast he mocking to they the-people as he thought.	and also mocked whoever he thought to.
Þoldi hann og allra manna best þótt að honum væri kastað klámyrðum þá er honum var gott í skapi.	Endured he also all men best though that he was cast obscene-words then that he was good of mood.	And when he was in a good mood, he endured most men even though obscenities were cast at him.
Hann átti þá Þóru dóttur Þorbergs Árnasonar.	He married then Thora daughter Thorberg's Son-of-Arni.	He was then married to Thora, daughter of Thorberg, Arni's son.
Honum þótti mikið gaman að skáldskap og hafði jafnan þá með sér er kveða kunnu.	He thought much delight in poetry and had always then with him that compose could.	He took much delight in poetry and always had people about him who could compose poetry.
Þjóðólfur hét maður.	Thjodolf was-named a-man.	There was a man named Thjodolf.
Hann var íslenskur og ættaður úr Svarfaðardal, kurteis maður og skáld mikið.	He was an-Icelander and descended from Svarfadardal, polite man and poet great.	He was an Icelander whose family came from Svarfadardal, a polite man and a great poet.

The Tale of Sarcastic Halli (Old Icelandic)

Old Icelandic	Literal	English
Hann var með Haraldi konungi í hinum mestum kærleikum.	He was with Harald the-king in the most dear-friendship.	He had great friendship with King Harald.
Kallaði konungur hann höfuðskáld sitt og virti hann mest allra skálda.	Called the-king him chief-poet his and worthied him most of-all poets.	The king called him his chief poet, and valued him most of all the poets.
Hann var ættsmár og menntur vel, öfundsjúkur við þá er til komu.	He was family-small and educated well, un-infatuated with then who to came.	He was from a humble family and well educated, he was envious of newcomers.
Haraldur konungur elskaði mjög Íslendinga.	Harald the-king loved much Icelanders.	King Harald loved Icelanders very much.
Gaf hann til Íslands marga góða hluti, klukku góða til Þingvallar.	Gave he to Iceland many good things, a-bell good for Thingvellir.	He gave many good things to Iceland, including a good bell for Thingvellir.
Og þá er hallæri það hið mikla kom á Ísland er ekki hefir slíkt komið annað þá sendi hann út til Íslands fjóra knörru hlaðna með mjöl, sinn í hvern fjórðung, og lét flytja í brott fátæka menn sem flesta af landinu.	And then when famine that the greatest came to Iceland that not had such come another then sent he out to Iceland four knorrs ladened with meal, then to each fourth, and had carried to brought poor men which most off the-land.	And when the greatest famine came to Iceland, which was like no other, he then sent four knorrs loaded with flour, one to each quarter, and had brought over many of the poorest men from the land.

2

Old Icelandic	Literal	English
Bárður hét maður og var hirðmaður Haralds konungs.	Bard was-named a-man and was court-man Harald's the-king's.	There was a man named Bard who was a court man of King Harald's.
Hann sigldi til Íslands og kom út að Gásum og vistaðist þar um veturinn.	He sailed to Iceland and came out to Gasir and found-a-place there about winter.	He sailed to Iceland and came out to Gasir and found a place there for the winter.
Sá maður tók sér far með honum er Halli hét og var kallaður Sneglu-Halli.	So a-man took himself passage with him was Halli named and was called Sarcastic-Halli.	So a man took passage with him who was named Halli, and he was called Sarcastic Halli.
Hann var skáld gott og orðgreppur mikill.	He was a-poet good and word-bold much.	He was a good poet and very bold with words.
Halli var hár maður og hálslangur, herðilítill og handsíður og ljótlimaður.	Halli was high man and long-neck, narrow-shouldered and long-armed and ugly-limbed.	Halli was a tall man with a long neck, narrow shoulders, long arms, and ill-proportioned limbs.

The Tale of Sarcastic Halli (Old Icelandic)

Old Icelandic	Literal	English
Hann var ættaður úr Fljótum.	He was descended out-of Fljot.	His descendants were from Fljot.
Þeir sigldu þegar þeir voru búnir og höfðu langa útivist, tóku Noreg um haustið norður við Þrándheim við eyjar þær er Hítrar heita og sigldu síðan inn til Agðaness og lágu þar um nótt.	They sailed as-soon-as they were prepared and had long out-journey, took Norway about autumn north with Trondheim with islands there which Hitra named and sailed since then to Agdanes and lay there about the-night.	They sailed as soon as they were ready and had a long passage, they reached Norway in the autumn north of Trondheim at the islands there which are called Hitra, and then sailed to Agdanes and laid up there for the night.
En um morguninn sigldu þeir inn eftir firðinum lítinn byr.	Then about morning sailed they then back-from the-fjord little fair-wind.	Then in the morning they sailed afterwards into the fjord with a light fair wind.
Og er þeir komu inn um Rein sáu þeir að langskip þrjú reru innan eftir firðinum.	And when they came of about Reine saw they of longships three rowing in after the-fjord.	And when they came to Reine they saw three longships rowing back from the fjord.
Dreki var hið þriðja skipið.	Dragon was the third ship.	The third ship was a dragon ship.
Og er skipin reru hjá kaupskipinu þá gekk maður fram úr lyftingunni á drekanum í rauðum skarlatsklæðum og hafði gullhlað um enni, bæði mikill og tigulegur.	And when the-ships rowing beside trading-ship then got a-man from out lifting from the-dragon-ship in red scarlet and had gold-band about forehead, both great and dignified.	And when the ships were rowing beside the trading ship, a man came up out of the dragon ship in red scarlet with a gold band about his forehead, both great and dignified.
Þessi maður tók til orða:	This man took to words:	This man spoke:
"Hver stýrir skipinu eða hvar voruð þér í vetur eða hvar tókuð þér fyrst land eða hvar láguð þér í nótt?"	"Who steers the-ship and where were you in winter and where took you first land and where laid you in the-night?"	"Who steers the ship, and where were you in winter, and where did you first take land, and where did you lay up last night?"
Þeim varð næsta orðfall kaupmönnum er svo var margs spurt en	They were next word-fallen the-trading-men as so were many questions but	The trading men were lost for words because there were so many questions, but
Halli svarar þá:	Halli answered then:	Halli answered them.

The Tale of Sarcastic Halli (Old Icelandic)

Old Icelandic	Literal	English
"Vér vorum í vetur á Íslandi en ýttum af Gásum en Bárður heitir stýrimaður en tókum land við Hítrar en lágum í nótt við Agðanes".	"We were in winter in Iceland and pushed from Gasir and Bard is-named steersman and took land at Hitra and laid about the-night at Agdanes".	"We were in Iceland for the winter, and we pushed on from Gasir, and Bard is the name of the steersman, we took land at Hitra, and we laid up for the night at Agdanes".
Þessi maður spurði, er reyndar var Haraldur konungur Sigurðarson:	This man asking, which actually was Harald the-king Sigurdson:	This man who was asking, was actually King Harald Sigurdson.
"Sarð hann yður ei Agði?"	"Wounded he you not Agdi	"Did Agdi not wound you?"
"Eigi enna", segir Halli.	"Not yet", said Halli.	"Not yet", said Halli.
Konungurinn brosti að og mælti:	The-king laughed and also spoke:	The king laughed and also spoke:
"Er nokkur til ráðs um að hann muni enn síðar meir veita yður þessa þjónustu?"	"Is something to agreement about that he shall but afterwards more grant you this service?"	"Is there some agreement that he shall do you this service sometime later?"
Ekki, sagði hann Halli, "og bar þó einn hlutur þar mest til þess er vér fórum enga skömm af honum".	Not, told he Halli, "and bears though one part there most to this that we travel not disgrace of him".	Halli told him not, "and so it bears most in one part that we travel without suffering disgrace by him".
"Hvað var það?"	"What was that?"	"What was that?"
segir konungur.	said the-king.	said the king.
Halli vissi gjörla við hvern hann talaði.	Halli knew completely with whom he talked.	Halli knew completely who he was talking to.
"Það herra",	"That lord",	"That, lord",
segir hann, "ef yður forvitnar að vita að hann Agði beið að þessu oss tignari manna og vætti yðvar þangað í kveld og mun hann þá gjalda af höndum þessa skuld ótæpt".	said he, "if you fore-knowing to know that he Agdi waited for this us nobler men and expected you from-there in the-evening and shall he then pay of hand this debt unsettled".	he said, "if you are curious to know, that Agdi was waiting for nobler men than us, and expected your arrival there this evening, and he shall pay you this debt fully".
"Þú munt vera orðhákur mikill",	"You must be word-tall much",	"You must be very brave of words",
segir konungur.	said the-king.	said the king.

The Tale of Sarcastic Halli (Old Icelandic)

Old Icelandic	Literal	English
Ei er getið orða þeirra fleiri að sinni.	Not is told words theirs more than these.	It is not told what more their words were than this.
Sigldu þeir kaupmennirnir inn til Kaupangs og skipuðu þar upp og leigðu sér hús í bænum.	Sailed they merchant-men then to Kapuang and ships there upped and rented themselves a-house in town.	The merchants then sailed to Kaupang, upped their ships and rented themselves a house in town.
Fám nóttum síðar kom konungur inn aftur til bæjar og hafði hann farið í eyjar út að skemmta sér.	A-few nights afterwards came the-king then returning to the-town and had he travelled to islands out to entertain himself.	After a few nights the king came returning to the town, as he had gone out to the islands to entertain himself.
Halli bað Bárð fylgja sér til konungsins og kveðst vilja biðja hann veturvistar.	Halli asked Bard follow him to the-king and said wished to-ask him winter-provisions.	Halli asked Bard to lead him to the king and said that he wished to ask him for winter lodgings.
En Bárður bauð honum með sér að vera.	But Bard invited him with himself to be.	But Bard invited him to stay with him.
Halli bað hann hafa þökk fyrir en kveðst með konunginum vilja vera ef þess væri kostur.	Halli bid him having thanks for but said with the-king wished to-be if this was a-choice.	Halli thanked him but said that he wished to stay with the king if that was a choice.

3

Einn dag gekk Bárður til konungs og Halli með honum.	One day went Bard to the-king and Halli with him.	One day Bard went to meet the king and Halli went with him.
Bárður kvaddi konung.	Bard greeted the-king.	Bard greeted the king.
Konungur tók vel kveðju hans og spurði margs af Íslandi eða hvort hann hefði flutt utan nokkra íslenska menn.	The-king received well greeting his and asked many-things of Iceland and whether he had brought out any Icelander men.	The king received his greeting well and asked many things of Iceland and whether he had brought any men from Iceland.
Bárður sagðist flutt hafa einn íslenskan mann	Bard said brought had one Icelander man	Bard said that he had brought one Icelander man
"og heitir hann Halli og er nú hér herra og vill biðja yður veturvistar".	"and named he Halli and is now here lord and wishes to-ask you winter-lodgings".	"and he is named Halli, and he is now here lord, and wishes to ask you for winter lodgings".
Halli gekk þá fyrir konunginn og kvaddi hann.	Halli went then before the-king and greeted him.	Halli then went before the king and greeted him.

The Tale of Sarcastic Halli (Old Icelandic)

Old Icelandic	Literal	English
Konungurinn tók honum vel og spurði hvort hann hefði svaraði honum á firðinum "er vér fundumst".	The-king received him well and asked whether he had answered him in the-fjord "when we met".	The king received him well and asked whether he had answered him in the fjord "when we met".
"Sjá hinn sami",	"So the same",	"I am the same",
segir Halli.	said Halli.	said Halli.
Konungurinn sagðist ei spara mundu mat við hann og bað vera að búi sínu nokkru.	The-king said not withhold would food from him and invited to-be to estate his one-of.	The king said he would not withhold food from him and invited him to be on one of his estates.
Halli kveðst með hirðinni vera vilja eða leita sér annars ella.	Halli said with the-court to-be wished or find himself another or-else.	Halli said that he wished to be at court or to find somewhere else.
Konungurinn kvað svo fara jafnan "að mér er um kennt ef vor vinskapur fer ei vel af hendi þó að mér þyki varla svo vera.	The-king said so goes always "that to-me is about blame if our friendship goes not well of to-hand though that to-me seems hardly so being.	The king said that it always goes "that I am to blame if our friendship does not go well, though that seems to me hardly to be.
Eruð þér einráðir Íslendingar og ósiðblandnir.	They-are you one-decision Icelanders and un-custom-mixing.	You are single-minded, you Icelanders, and unsociable.
Nú ver ef þú vilt og ábyrgst þig sjálfur hvað sem í kann gerast".	Now be if you wish and responsible you yourself what which about can be".	Now be here if you wish, and you are responsible for yourself whatever will be".
Halli kvað svo vera skyldu og þakkaði konunginum.	Halli said so being would and thanked the-king.	Halli said that it would be so, and thanked the king.
Var hann nú með hirðinni og líkaði hverjum manni vel til hans.	Was he now with the-court-men and liked each man well to him.	He was now with the court men and he was liked by each of them.
Sigurður hét sessunautur Halla, gamall hirðmaður og gæfur.	Sigurd was-named bench-companion Halli, old court-man and agreeable.	Halli's bench companion was named Sigurd, an old court man and agreeable.
Sá var siður Haralds konungs að eta einmælt.	So was the-custom Harald's the-king's to eat one-meal.	It was Harald's custom to eat one meal a day.

The Tale of Sarcastic Halli (Old Icelandic)

Old Icelandic	Literal	English
Var fyrst borin vist fyrir konung, sem von var, og var hann þá jafnan mjög mettur er vistin kom fyrir aðra.	Were first brought provisions for the-king, as expected was, and was he then usually much satisfied when the-supply came before others.	First the food was brought before the king, as was expected, and he was usually very much satisfied when the food was brought to the others.
En þá er hann var mettur klappaði hann með hnífskafti sínu á borðið og skyldi þá þegar ryðja borðin og voru margir þá hvergi nærri mettir.	But then when he was satisfied rapped he with knife-handle his on the-table and would then straight-away cleared tables and were many then nowhere near satisfied.	But then when he was satisfied, he rapped his knife handle on the table, and then straight away the tables were cleared, and many people were then nowhere near satisfied.
Það bar við eitt sinn er konungur gekk úti um stræti og fylgdin með honum og voru margir þá hvergi nærri mettir.	It bore to once then that the-king went out about the-street and followers with him and were many then none near satisfied.	It happened once that the king went out in the street with his followers, and many of them were nowhere near satisfied.
Þeir heyrðu í eitt herbergi deild mikla.	They heard in one hostel room great.	They heard something great in an inn.
Þar voru að sútari og járnsmiður og þar næst flugust þeir á.	They were a tanner and ironsmith and there near flew they to.	It was a tanner and an ironsmith, and they nearly flew towards eachother.
Konungurinn nam staðar og sá á um stund.	The-king took place and saw for about awhile.	The king took his place and watched for a while.
Síðan mælti hann:	Afterwards spoke he:	Afterwards he spoke:
"Göngum brott.	"We-are-going away.	"Let us go away.
Hér vil eg öngvan hlut að eiga	Here wish I none part to own	I do not wish to be a part of this here,
en þú Þjóðólfur yrk um þá vísu".	but you Thjodolf write about then a-verse".	but you Thjodolf write a verse about it".
Herra, segir Þjóðólfur, "ei samir það þar sem eg er kallaður höfuðskáld yðvart".	Lord, said Thjodolf, "not common that there as I am called chief-poet yours".	"Lord", said Thjodolf, "I don't agree there, since I am called your chief poet".
Konungur svarar:	The-king answered:	The king answered:
"Þetta er meiri vandi en þú munt ætla.	"This is more difficult than you should suppose.	"This is more difficult than you think.

The Tale of Sarcastic Halli (Old Icelandic)

Old Icelandic	Literal	English
Þú skalt gera af þeim alla menn aðra en þeir eru.	You shall make of them completely men other than they are.	You shall make the men completely other than they are.
Lát annan vera Sigurð Fáfnisbana en annan Fáfni og kenn þó hvern til sinnar iðnar".	Have one be Sigurd Slayer-of-Fafnir and another Fafnir also know though each to his trade".	Have one be Sigurd the Slayer of Fafnir, and another Fafnir, and also identify each one's trade".
Þjóðólfur kvað þá vísu:	Thjodolf recited then a-verse:	Thjodolf then recited a verse:
Sigurðr eggjaði sleggju snák válegrar brákar en skapdreki skinna skreið af leista heiði.	Sigurd urged the-hammer snake wretched breaker, but mood-dragon of-skins crawled off of-footwear the-heath.	Sigurd urged the-hammer snake wretched breaker, but mood-dragon of-skins crawled off of-footwear the-heath.
Mönnum leist ormr áðr ynni ilvegs búinn kilju, nautaleðrs á naðri neflangr konungr tangar.	People with-footwear the-serpent before won evil-ways prepared the-binding, ox-skin of serpent long-nosed king's tongs.	People with-footwear the-serpent before won evil-ways prepared the-binding, ox-skin of serpent long-nosed king's tongs.
"Þetta er vel kveðið",	"That is well worded",	"That is well composed",
segir konungur, "og kveð nú aðra og lát nú vera annan Þór en annan Geirröð jötun og kenn þó hvern til sinnar iðnar".	said the-king, "and recite now another and have now being one Thor and another Geirrod the-giant and know though each to their trade".	said the king, "and now recite another and have one being Thor and another Geirrod the Giant, and identify each with their trade".
Þá kvað Þjóðólfur vísu:	Then recited Thjodolf a-verse:	Then Thjodolf recited a verse:
Varp úr þrætu þorpi Þórr smiðbelgja stórra hvofteldingum höldnu hafra kjöts að jötni. Hljóðgreipum tók húðar	Threw from threatening village Thor smith-bellows great encouraged-lightning held goat flesh the giant. Sound-grippers (ears) took hide	Threw from threatening village Thor smith-bellows great lightning held goat flesh the giant. Sound-grippers (ears) took hide
hrökkviskafls af afli glaðr við galdra smiðju Geirröðr síu þeirri.	shaken of power glad with magic of-the-smith Geirrod sift of-them.	shaken of power glad with magic of-the-smith Geirrod sift of-them.
"Ekki ertu mæltur um það",	"Not are-you talked about that",	"You are not over talked about",
segir konungur, "að þú ert úrleysingur til skáldskapar".	said the-king, "that you are over-praised as a-poet".	said the king, "when you are praised as a poet".

The Tale of Sarcastic Halli (Old Icelandic)

Old Icelandic	Literal	English
Og lofuðu allir að vel væri ort.	And praised all to well being worded.	And all praised him on how well it had been composed.
Ekki var Halli við þetta.	Not was Halli with this.	Halli was not present with them.
Og um kveldið er menn sátu við drykk kváðu þeir fyrir Halla og sögðu hann ei mundu svo yrkja þótt hann þættist skáld mikið.	And about evening when men sat with drink recited they for Halli and told him not would so compose though he thought a-poet great.	And that evening when men sat drinking they recited the poem for Halli and told him that he could not compose such a poem even though he thought of himself as a great poet.
Halli kveðst vita að hann orti verr en Þjóðólfur	Halli said knew that he worded worse than Thjodolf	Halli said that he knew he composed worse poetry than Thjodolf
"enda mun þá firrst um fara ef eg leita ekki við að yrkja enda sé eg ekki við",	"in-the-end shall then lost about going if I seek not with to compose and am I not with",	"in the end I shall lose if I do not try to compose a verse, and if I am not present",
segir Halli.	said Halli.	said Halli.
Þetta var þegar sagt konungi og snúið svo að hann þættist ei minna skáld en Þjóðólfur.	This was then told-to the-king and turned so that he thought not less a-poet than Thjodolf.	This was then told to the king and turned around to say that he thought himself no less of a poet than Thjodolf.
Konungur kvað honum ei að því verða mundu "en vera kann að vér fáum þetta reynt af stundu".	The-king said him not that therefore be would "but be can-it that we get that tested in awhile".	The king said that he would not be that, "but it can be that we can test him in a while".

4

Það var einn dag er menn sátu yfir borðum að þar gekk inn í höllina dvergur einn er Túta hét.	It was one day when people were sitting at-table that there went then into the-hall dwarf one who Tuta named.	It was one day when people were sitting at the table that a dwarf named Tuta went into the hall.
Hann var frískur að ætt.	He was Frisian by descent.	He was Frisian by descent.
Hann hafði lengi verið með Haraldi konungi.	He had long been with Harald the-king.	He had been with King Harald a long time.

The Tale of Sarcastic Halli (Old Icelandic)

Old Icelandic	Literal	English
Hann var ei hærri en þrevett barn en allra manna digrastur og herðimestur, höfuðið mikið og eldilegt, hryggurinn ei allskammur en sýlt í neðan þar sem fæturnir voru.	He was not higher than three-winters-old child but of-all men thick-set and most-hardy, head great and elderly, spine not very-short but sleek of below there where the-legs were.	He was no taller than a child of three years old, but he was the most thick set and hardy of all men, he had a large and elderly looking head, and his back was not very short, but sleek below where his legs were.
Haraldur konungur átti brynju þá er hann kallaði Emmu.	Harald the-king hat coat-of-mail then which he called Emma.	King Harald had a coat of mail which he called Emma.
Hann hafði látið gera hana í Miklagarði.	He had had made her in Byzantium.	He had had it made in Byzantium.
Hún var svo síð að hún tók niður á skó Haraldi konungi þá er hann stóð réttur.	She was so long that she took down to shoes Harald's the-king then when he stood upright.	It was so long that it reached down to King Harald's shoes when he stood upright.
Var hún öll tveföld og svo styrk að aldrei festi járn á.	Was she all two-fold and so strong that never pierced iron-weapon an.	It was all double-thickness and so strong that it was never pierced by an iron weapon.
Konungurinn hafði látið fara dverginn í brynjuna og setja hjálm á höfuð honum og gyrti hann sverði.	The-king had had sent-for the-dwarf in coat-of-mail and set helmet on head his and equipped him a-sword.	The king had ordered the dwarf to be in the coat of mail with a helmet set on his head and equipped with a sword.
Síðan gekk hann í höllina sem fyrr var ritað og þótti maðurinn vera undurskapaður.	After went he into the-hall as before was written and thought the-man was wonder-created.	After he went into the hall as was written before, and the man was thought to be a wonder.
Konungur kvaddi sér hljóðs og mælti:	The-king called to be-heard and spoke:	The king called to be heard and spoke:
"Sá maður er kveður um dverginn vísu svo að mér þyki vel kveðin þiggi að mér hníf þenna og belti"	"So the-man who words about the-dwarf a-verse so that to-me seems well worded receives of me knife this and belt"	"So the man who composes a verse about the dwarf, so that I think it is a good verse, will accept of me this knife and a belt",
og lagði fram á borðið fyrir sig gripina	and laid from to table before him the-trinkets,	and he put the trinkets on the table for him,

The Tale of Sarcastic Halli (Old Icelandic)

Old Icelandic	Literal	English
"en vitið það víst ef mér þykir ei vel kveðin að hann skal hafa óþökk mína en missa gripanna beggja".	"but know that certainly if to-me seems not well worded that he shall have un-thanks mine and miss the-trinkets both".	"but know for certain that if I don't think it is a good poem, he will have my displeasure and lose the trinkets both".
Og þegar er konungur hafði flutt erindi sitt kveður maður vísu utar á bekkinn og var það Sneglu-Halli:	And as-soon-as when the-king had delivered message his recited a-man a-verse out from the-bench and was that Sarcastic-Halli:	And as soon as the king had delivered his speech, a man recited a verse outside of the bench, and it was Sarcastic-Halli:
Færðr sýnist mér frændi Frísa kyns í brynju. Gengr fyrir hirð í hringum hjálmfaldinn kurfaldi. Flærat eld í ári úthlaupi vanr Túta. Sé eg á síðu leika sverð rúghleifa skerði.	Brought seems to-me kinsman Frisian kin in chain-mail. Going before the-court in circles the-helmet folded. Fleeing the-fire in all-year out-running custom Tuta. See I of side games sword rye-loaf cuts.	Brought seems to-me kinsman Frisian kin in chain-mail. Going before the-court in circles the-helmet folded. Fleeing the-fire in all-year out-running custom Tuta. See I of side games sword rye-loaf cuts.
Konungur bað færa honum gripuna	The-king ordered brought to-him the-trinkets	The king ordered the trinkets to be brought to him
"og skaltu ná hér á sannmæli því að vísan er vel kveðin".	"and shall-you obtain here in true-words because it the-verse is well worded".	"and you will find the truth here, because the verse is well recited".
Það var einn dag er konungurinn var mettur að konungur klappaði hnífi á borðið og bað ryðja.	It was one day when the-king was finished-eating that the-king struck knife on the-table and ordered cleared.	One day when the king had finished eating he struck his knife on the table and ordered the tables to be cleared.
Þjónustumenn gerðu svo.	The-servants did so.	The servants did so.
Þá var Halli hvergi nærri mettur.	Then was Halli nowhere near satisfied.	Then Halli was nowhere near satisfied.
Tók hann þá stykki eitt af diskinum og hélt eftir og kvað þetta:	Took he then piece one off the-plate and held back and recited this:	He then took a piece of food from the place and held it back and recited this:
Hirði eg ei hvað Haraldr klappar. Læt eg gnadda grön. Geng eg fullur að sofa.	Care I not that Harald's hammering. Have I gnawing moustache. Going I full to sleep.	Care I not that Harald's hammering. Have I gnawing moustache. Going I full to sleep.

The Tale of Sarcastic Halli (Old Icelandic)

Old Icelandic	Literal	English
Um morguninn eftir er konungur var kominn í sæti sitt og hirðin gekk Halli í höllina og fyrir konunginn.	About morning after when the-king was coming to sit himself and courtiers went Halli into the-hall and before the-king.	About morning when the king had come to sit with his courtiers, Halli went into the hall and went before the king.
Hann hafði skjöld sinn og sverð á baki sér.	He had shield his and sword about back his.	He had his shield and sword on his back.
Hann kvað vísu:	He spoke a-verse:	He spoke a verse:
Selja mun eg við sufli *sverð mitt, konungr, verða,* *og rymskyndir randa* *rauðan skjöld við brauði.* *Hungrar hilmis drengi.* *Heldr göngum vér svangir.* *Mér dregr hrygg, að hvoru,* *Haraldr sveltir mig, belti.*	Barter will I of with-bread sword mine, the-king, becomes, and quickly-cleared round the-red shield with bread. Hungry helmsman's boys. Rather going are-we hungry. To-me draws the-spine, that which, Harald starving me, belt.	Barter will I of with-bread sword mine, the-king, becomes, and quickly-cleared round the-red shield with bread. Hungry helmsman's boys. Rather going are-we hungry. To-me draws the-spine, that which, Harald starving me, belt.
Engu svarar konungur og lét sem hann heyrði ei	None answered the-king and had as he heard not	The king gave no answer and acted as though he had not heard,
en þó vissu allir menn að honum mislíkaði.	but though knew all people that he mis-liked.	but all the people knew that he disliked this.
Litlu síðar var það einn dag er konungurinn gekk úti um stræti og fylgdin með honum.	A-little afterwards was it one day that the-king went out about the-street and followers with him.	A little while afterwards one day the king went out into the street and had his followers with him.
Þar var og Halli í för.	There was also Halli with going.	And there was also Halli going with them.
Hann snaraði fram hjá konunginum.	He rushed ahead nearby the-king.	He rushed ahead to be near the king.
Konungurinn kvað þetta:	The-king spoke this:	The king spoke this:
"Hvert stillir þú Halli?"	"Where heading you Halli?"	"Where are you heading Halli?"
Halli svarar:	Halli answered:	Halli answered:
"Hleyp eg fram að kýrkaupi".	"Running I forwards to cow-buying".	"I am running to buy a cow".

The Tale of Sarcastic Halli (Old Icelandic)

Old Icelandic	Literal	English
"Graut muntu gervan láta?"	"Porridge would-you look-to have?"	"Will you look to have porridge?"
segir konungur.	said the-king.	said the king.
"Gjör matr er það, smjörvan",	"Ready-made food is that, buttered",	"It is a ready made meal, when buttered",
segir Halli.	said Halli.	said Halli.
Hleypur hann Halli þá upp í garðinn og þangað sem var eldahús.	Ran he Halli then up to garden and from-there as was fire-house (kitchen).	Then Halli ran up to a house where there was a kitchen.
Þar hafði hann látið gera graut í steinkatli og settist til og etur grautinn.	There had he had made porridge in stone-kettle and sat to and eat the-porridge.	There he had made porridge in a stone kettle, and sat there to eat the porridge.
Konungurinn sér að Halli hverfur upp í garðinn.	The-king saw that Halli turned up-to the garden.	The king saw that Halli had gone into the house.
Hann kvaddi til Þjóðólf og tvo menn aðra að leita Halla.	He called to Thjodolf and two men other to look-for Halli.	He called to Thjodolf and two other men to look for Halli.
Konungur veik og upp í garðinn.	The-king turned also up to the-house.	The king also arrived at the house.
Þeir finna hann þar sem hann át grautinn.	They found him there as he ate porridge.	They found him there as he ate the porridge.
Konungurinn kom þá að og sá hvað Halli hafðist að.	The-king came then to and saw what Halli had to.	The king came to him and saw what Halli was doing.
Konungurinn var hinn reiðasti og spurði Halla því hann fór af Íslandi til höfðingja til þess að gera af sér skömm og gabb.	The-king was the most-angry and asked Halli if he travelled from Iceland to chieftains to this that make of himself scandal and mockery.	The king was very angry and asked Halli if he had travelled from Iceland to visit chieftains and make scandal and mockery.
"Látið eigi svo herra",	"Let not so lord",	"Let it not be so",
segir Halli,	said Halli,	said Halli,
"jafnan sé eg yður ei drepa hendi við góðum sendingum".	"always see I you not kill hands with good delivery".	"always I see that you do not kill hands that deliver good food".

The Tale of Sarcastic Halli (Old Icelandic)

Old Icelandic	Literal	English
Halli stóð þá upp og kastaði niður katlinum og skall við haddan.	Halli stood then up and cast down the-kettle and hit against the-lid.	Halli then stood up and threw down the kettle, and hit against the lid.
Þjóðólfur kvað þá þetta:	Thjodolf recited then this:	Thjodolf then recited this:
Haddan skall en Halli hlaut offylli grautar. Hornspónu kveð eg honum hlýða betr en prýði.	The-handle rattled and Halli a-lot-of gluttony of-porridge. Horn-spoon say I to-him suits better than finery.	The-handle rattled and Halli a-lot-of gluttony of-porridge. Horn-spoon say I to-him suits better than finery.
Konungurinn gekk þá brottu og var allreiður.	The-king went then away and was all-angry.	The king then went away and was very angry.
Og um kveldið kom engi matur fyrir Halla sem fyrir aðra menn.	And about evening came no food before Halli as before other people.	And about evening there came no food for Halli as there had been for the other people.
Og er menn höfðu snætt um stund komu enn tveir menn og báru í milli sín trog mikið, fullt grautar, og með spón og settu fyrir Halla.	And when people had dined about awhile came then two men and carried in between themselves trough great, full of-porridge, and with a-spoon and set before Halli.	And when people had dined for a while, then came two men carrying between themselves a great through, full of porridge, and with a spoon set it before Halli.
Hann tók til og át sem hann lysti og hætti síðan.	He took to and ate as he appetite and stopped afterwards.	He took it and ate as much as his appetite would allow, and then stopped.
Konungur bað Halla eta meira.	The-king ordered Halli eat more.	The king ordered Halli to eat more.
Hann kveðst ei mundu eta meira að sinni.	He said not would eat more for himself.	He said he himself would not eat any more.
Haraldur konungur brá þá sverði og bað Halla eta grautinn þar til er hann spryngi af.	Harald the-king drew then a-sword and ordered Halli eat porridge there until that he burst of.	King Harald then drew a sword and ordered Halli to eat the porridge until he burst.
Halli kveðst ei mundu sprengja sig á grauti en segir konung ná mundu lífi sínu ef hann væri á það einhugi.	Halli said not would burst himself with porridge but told the-king take could life his if he would-be of that one-minded.	Halli said that he would not burst himself with porridge, but told the king that he could take his life if he was of a mind to do so.
Konungur sest þá niður og slíðrar sverðið.	The-king sat then down and sheathed sword.	The king then sat down and sheathed his sword.

The Tale of Sarcastic Halli (Old Icelandic)

Old Icelandic	Literal	English
# 5	# 5	# 5
Nokkru síðar var það einn dag að konungur tók disk einn af borði sínu og var á steiktur grís og bað Tútu dverg færa Halla	Somewhat later was it one day that the-king took plate one off table his and was it roasted pig and ordered Tuta the-dwarf bring Halli	One day somewhat later, the king took a plate off his table, and on it was a roasted pig, he ordered Tuta the dwarf to bring it to Halli
"og bið hann yrkja vísu ef hann vill halda lífinu og hafa kveðið áður þú kemur fyrir hann og seg honum ei fyrr en þú kemur á mitt gólf"	"and order him to-compose a-verse if he wishes to-hold his-life and have spoken after you come before him and tell him not before that you come to the-middle the-floor	"and order him to compose a verse if he wishes to hold his life, and recite it after you come before him, and tell him not before you are in the middle of the floor".
"Ekki er eg þess fús",	"Not am I this willing",	"I am not willing to do this",
segir Túta, "því að mér líkar vel við Halla".	said Tuta, "because that I like well with Halli".	said Tuta, "because I like Halli".
"Sé eg",	"See I",	"I see",
sagði konungur,	said the-king,	said the king,
"að þér þykir góð vísan sú er hann orti um þig og muntu gjörla heyra kunna.	"that you consider good verse yours that he worded about you and shall-you completely hear know.	that you consider his verse good that he composed about you, and you know how to listen carefully.
Nú far í burt í stað og ger sem eg býð".	Now go to away to the-place and do as I command".	Now to away and do as I command".
Túta tók nú við diskinum og gekk á mitt gólfið og mælti:	Tuta took now with the-plate and went to the-middle of-the-floor and spoke:	Tuta now took the place and went to the middle of the floor and spoke:
"Þú Halli yrk vísu að boði konungs og haf ort áður eg kem fyrir þig ef þú vilt halda lífinu".	"You Halli compose a-verse to order the-king's and have worded before I come before you if you wish to-hold your-life".	"You Halli are ordered by the king to compose a verse and have it composed before I come before you if you wish to hold your life".
Halli stóð þá upp og rétti hendur í móti diskinum og kvað vísu:	Halli stood then up and extended hand to meet the-plate and recited a-verse:	Halli then stood up and extended a hand to meet the plate and recited a verse:
Grís þá greppr að ræsi gruntrauðustum dauðan.	Pig then grasped of the-ruler deep-red death.	Pig then grasped of the-ruler deep-red death.

The Tale of Sarcastic Halli (Old Icelandic)

Old Icelandic	Literal	English
Njörðr sér börg á borði bauglands fyrir standa. Runa síðr lít eg rauðar. Ræð eg skjótt gera kvæði. Rana hefir seggr af svíni, send heill konungr, brenndan.	Njord sees the-city on the-table ring-land before standing. Row since coloured I red. Speak I rapidly made poem. The-trunk has said man swine, send health king, burnt.	Njord sees the-city on the-table ring-land before standing. Row since coloured I red. Speak I rapidly made poem. The-trunk has said man swine, send health king, burnt.
Konungur mælti þá:	The-king spoke then:	The king then spoke:
"Nú skal gefa þér upp reiði mína Halli því að vísan er vel kveðin svo skjótt sem til var tekið".	"Now shall give you up anger mine Halli because that verse is well recited so quickly as to was taken".	"Now I will give up my anger for you, Halli, because the sentence is well recited as soon as it was taken".

6

Frá því er sagt einn dag að Halli gekk fyrir konunginn þá er hann var glaður og kátur.	From then is said one day that Halli went before the-king then as he was glad and cheerful.	From then it is said that one day Halli went before the king as he was glad and cheerful.
Þar var þá Þjóðólfur og margt annarra manna.	There was then Thjodolf and many other people.	Then Thjodolf and many other people were there.
Halli sagðist hafa ort drápu um konunginn og bað sér hljóðs.	Halli said had worded drapa about the-king and asked for-him be-heard.	Halli said that he had composed a drapa about the king and ask him for it to be heard.
Konungurinn spurði hvort Halli hefði nokkuð kvæði fyrri ort.	The-king asked whether Halli had anything composed before worded.	The king asked whether Halli had composed anything before.
Halli kveðst ekki hafa ort.	Halli said not had worded.	He said he had not composed anything.
"Það munu sumir menn mæla",	"It would some people say",	"Some people would say",
segir konungur, "að þú takist mikið á hendur, slík skáld sem ort hafa um mig áður eftir nokkrum málefnum.	said the-king, "that you take much in hand, such poets as worded have about me before after some matters.	said the king, "that you take much in hand, as such poets have composed poems about me for various reasons.
Eða hvað sýnist þér ráð Þjóðólfur?"	But what seems to-you advisable Thjodolf?"	But what seems advisable to you Thjodolf?"
"Ekki kann eg herra að gefa yður ráð",	"Not can I lord to give you advice",	"I can not give you advice, lord",

The Tale of Sarcastic Halli (Old Icelandic)

Old Icelandic	Literal	English
segir Þjóðólfur, "en hitt mun hóti nær að eg mun kunna að kenna Halla heilræði".	said Thjodolf, "but then could not near that I would know to teach Halli sound-advice".	said Thjodolf, "but then I could give Halli some sound advice".
"Hvert er það?"	"What is that?"	"What is that?"
segir konungur.	said the-king.	said the king.
"Það fyrst herra að hann ljúgi ekki að yður".	"That first lord that he lie not to you".	"First of all that he not lie to you".
"Hvað lýgur hann nú?"	"What lies he now?"	"What does he lie about now?"
segir konungur.	said the-king.	said the king.
"Það lýgur hann að hann sagðist ekki kvæði ort hafa",	"That lying he that he said not composed words had",	"He is lying when he says that he has not composed such words",
segir Þjóðólfur, "en eg segi hann ort hafa".	said Thjodolf, "but I say he words has".	said Thjodolf, "but I say that he has composed".
"Hvert er kvæði það",	"What is composed that",	"What has he composed?",
segir konungur, "eða um hvað er ort?"	said the-king, "and about what is worded?"	said the king, "and what is it composed about?"
Þjóðólfur svarar:	Thjodolf answered:	Thjodolf answered:
"Það köllum vér Kolluvísur er hann orti um kýr er hann gætti út á Íslandi".	"That call we Cow-verses which he worded about cows that he guarded out in Iceland".	"That which we call Cow-verses, which he composed about cows that he guarded out in Iceland".
"Er það satt Halli?"	"Is that true Halli?"	"Is that true Halli?"
segir konungur.	said the-king.	said the king.
"Satt er það",	"True is that",	"That is true",
segir Halli.	said Halli.	said Halli.
"Því sagðir þú að þú hefðir ekki kvæði ort?"	"Why said you that you had not composed words?"	"Why did you say that you had not composed such words?"
segir konungur.	said the-king.	said the king.

The Tale of Sarcastic Halli (Old Icelandic)

Old Icelandic	Literal	English
"Því", segir Halli, "að lítil kvæðismynd mundi á því þykja ef þetta skal heyra og lítt mun því verða á loft haldið".	"Because", said Halli, "that little poem-image would be therefore seemed if it should heard and little would therefore worth of praised held".	"Because", said Halli, "that such a little poem would seem if heard worth little praise".
"Það viljum vér fyrst heyra",	"That wish we first to-hear",	"We wish to hear that first",
segir konungur.	said the-king.	said the king.
"Skemmt mun þá fleira",	"Entertainment should then more",	"Then there should be more than one amusement",
segir Halli.	said Halli.	said Halli.
"Hverju þá?"	"What then?"	"What then?"
segir konungur.	said the-king.	said the king.
"Kveða mun Þjóðólfur þá skulu Soðtrogsvísur er hann orti út á Íslandi",	"Recite should Thjodolf then should Food-trough-verses which he worded out in Iceland",	"Thjodolf should then recite Food-trough-verses which he composed out in Iceland",
segir Halli, "og er það vel að Þjóðólfur leitaði á mig eða afvirti fyrir mér því að upp eru svo komnir í mér bitar og jaxlar að eg kann vel að svara honum jöfnum orðum".	said Halli, "and is that well that Thjodolf sought to me but disrespected before me because that up we-are so coming that my bite and molars that I can well to answer him even words".	said Halli, "and it is well that Thjodolf sought to disrespect me, but because my bite and molars are up I can answer him well with words".
Konungur brosti að og þótti honum gaman að etja þeim saman.	The-king smiled at and thought he enjoyment to provoke them together.	The king smiled and thought it was enjoyable to provoke them against eachother.
"Hvern veg er kvæði það eða um hvað er ort?"	"What way is composed that and about what are words?"	"What is it composed about and what are the words?"
segir konungur.	said the-king.	said the king.
Halli svarar:	Halli answered:	Halli answered:

The Tale of Sarcastic Halli (Old Icelandic)

Old Icelandic	Literal	English
"Það er ort um það er hann bar út ösku með öðrum systkinum sínum og þótti þá til einkis annars fær fyrir vitsmuna sakir og varð þó um að sjá að ei væri eldur í því að hann þurfti allt vit sitt í þann tíma".	"That is worded about that which he bore out ashes with other siblings his and thought then to nothing other accomplished before intellect sake and became though about to see that not would fire about because that he needed all wit his at that time".	"It is composed about carrying out ashes with his other siblings, and he was thought capable of accomplishing nothing more for the sake of his intellect, and it was necessary to see that there was no fire about because he needed all his wit at that time".
Konungur spyr ef þetta væri satt.	The-king asked if that was true.	The king asked if that was true.
"Satt er það herra",	"True is that lord",	"That is true, lord",
segir Þjóðólfur.	said Thjodolf.	said Thjodolf.
"Því hafðir þú svo óvirðulegt verk?"	"Why had you so unworthy work?"	"Why did you have such unworthy work?"
segir konungur.	said the-king.	said the king.
"Því herra",	"Because lord",	"Because lord",
segir Þjóðólfur,	said Thjodolf,	said Thjodolf,
"að eg vildi flýta oss til leika en ekki voru verk á mig lagin".	"that I wished quickly us to play and not was work to me assigned".	"that I wished to get us quickly out to play, and no work was assigned to me".
"Það olli því",	"That cause therefore",	"It caused",
segir Halli,	said Halli,	said Halli,
"að þú þóttir ei hafa verkmanns vit".	"that you thought not had workman's wit".	that you were thought not to have the sense of a worker".
"Ekki skuluð þið við talast",	"Not should you-two against speak",	"You must not argue",
segir konungur, "en heyra viljum vér kvæðin bæði".	said the-king, "but hear wish we poems both".	said the king, "but we want to hear both the poems".
Og svo varð að vera.	And so became to be.	And so it was.
Kvað þá hvor sitt kvæði.	Recited then each their poems.	Then each recited their poems.
Og er lokið var kvæðunum mælti konungurinn:	And when concluded was the-poetry spoke the-king:	And when the poems were finished, the king said:

The Tale of Sarcastic Halli (Old Icelandic)

Old Icelandic	Literal	English
"Lítið er kvæðið hvorttveggja enda munu lítil hafa verið yrkisefnin og er það þó enn minna er þú hefir ort Þjóðólfur".	"Little is poem each-way ended would little have been the-themes and is that though the lesser is you have worded Thjodolf".	"The poems are little on both sides, because the themes were small, and the lesser one is the one that you have composed Thjodolf".
"Svo er og herra",	"So is also lord",	"And so it is, lord",
segir Þjóðólfur, "og er Halli orðhvass mjög.	said Thjodolf, "and is Halli sharp-tongued much.	said Thjodolf, "and Halli is very sharp tongued.
En skyldara þætti mér honum að hefna föður síns en eiga sennur við mig hér í Noregi".	But should seems to-me of-him to avenge father his but not chatter with me here in Norway".	But I think it's more important for him to avenge his father than to have a fight with me here in Norway".
"Er það satt Halli?"	"Is that true Halli?"	"Is that true Halli?"
segir konungur.	said the-king.	said the king.
"Satt er það herra",	"True is that lord",	"That is true, lord",
segir hann.	said he.	he said.
"Hví fórstu af Íslandi til höfðingja við það að þú hafðir eigi hefnt föður þíns?"	"Why went-you from Iceland to chieftains with than that you have not avenged father yours?"	"Why did you go from Iceland to meet the chieftains when you had not avenged your father?"
segir konungur.	said the-king.	said the king.
"Því herra",	"Because lord",	"Because, lord",
segir Halli, "að eg var barn að aldri er faðir minn var veginn og tóku frændur málið og sættust á fyrir mína hönd.	said Halli, "that I was a-child in age when father mine was killed and took kinsman the-matter and settled it before my hand.	said Halli, "I was a child in age when my father was killed, and my cousins took the case and settled on my behalf.
En það þykir illt nafn á voru landi að heita griðníðingur".	But it considered ill named in our land to call truce-breaker".	But it is considered ill called in our land to be a truce-breaker".
Konungurinn svarar:	The-king answered:	The king answered:
"Það er nauðsyn að ganga ei á grið eða sættir og er úr þessu allvel leyst".	"It is necessary to go not to peace or settlements and that from this all-well answered".	"It is necessary to go to peace or reconciliation and this is well resolved".

The Tale of Sarcastic Halli (Old Icelandic)

Old Icelandic	Literal	English
"Svo hugði eg herra",	"So thought I lord",	"So I thought, lord",
segir Halli, "en vel má Þjóðólfur tala stórmannlega um slíka hluti því að öngvan veit eg jafngreypilega hefnt hafa síns föður sem hann".	said Halli, "and well may Thjodolf speak big-man-like about such a-thing since that none know I equally-badly revenge had his father as he".	said Halli, "and well may Thjodolf speak arrogantly about such a thing since no one I know has equally badly avenged his father as him".
"Víst er Þjóðólfur líklegur til að hafa það hraustlega gert",	"Certainly is Thjodolf likely to that have that boldly done",	"Certainly Thjodolf is like to have done that boldly",
segir konungur,	said the-king,	said the king,
"eða hvað verkum gert um það að hann hafi það framar gert en aðrir menn?"	"but what actions done about it that he has that from done than other people?"	but what actions did he take unlike other people?
"Það helst herra",	"That rather lord",	"Rather, lord",
segir Halli, "að hann át sinn föðurbana".	said Halli, "that he ate his father's-killer.	said Halli, "that he ate his father's killer".
Nú æptu menn upp og þóttust aldrei slík undur heyrt hafa.	Now called-out people up and thought never such wonder heard had.	Now people rose up and called out and thought they had never heard of such a wonder.
Konungurinn brosti að og bað menn vera hljóða.	The-king grinned at and ordered men to-be calm.	The king grinned and ordered people to be calm.
"Ger þetta satt er þú segir Halli",	"Does this true that you said Halli",	"Do so that what you say is true Halli",
segir konungur.	said the-king.	said the king.
Halli mælti:	Halli spoke:	Halli spoke:
"Það hygg eg að Þorljótur héti faðir Þjóðólfs.	"That think I that Thorljot named father Thjodolf's.	"I think that Thjodolf's father was named Thorljot.
Hann bjó í Svarfaðardal á Íslandi og var hann fátækur mjög en átti fjölda barna.	He lived in Svarfadardal in Iceland and was he fee-taken much and had many children.	He lived in Svarfadardal in Iceland and he was very poor and had many children.

The Tale of Sarcastic Halli (Old Icelandic)

Old Icelandic	Literal	English
En það er siður á Íslandi á haustum að bændur þinga til fátækra manna og var þá engi fyrri til nefndur en Þorljótur faðir Þjóðólfs	But it is a-custom in Iceland in autumn that farmers assemble to the-poor people and was then none before to named than Thorljot father Thjodolf's	But it is a custom in Iceland in the autumn for farmers to hold meetings for poor people, and there was no one better than Thorljot, Thjodolf's father,
og einn bóndi var svo stórlyndur að honum gaf sumargamlan kálf.	and one farmer was so large-repaying (generous) that he gave one-summer-old a-calf.	and one farmer was so generous that he gave him a summer-old calf.
Síðan sækir hann kálfinn og hafði á taum og var lykkja á enda taumsins.	Then sought he the-calf and had a leash and was noose at the-end the-leash.	Then he fetched the calf and had it on a leash and there was a loop at the end of the leash.
Og er hann kemur heim að túngarði sínum hefur hann kálfinn upp á garðinn og var furðulega hár garðurinn en	And when he came home to hayfield-wall his had he the-calf up on the-wall and was extremely high the-wall but	And when he came home to his yard wall he had the calf up on the wall, and it was extremely high,
þó var hærra fyrir innan því að þar hafði verið grafið torf til garðsins.	though was higher before inside because that there had been dug turf up-to the-wall.	but it was higher on the inside because the turf had been dug up to the wall.
Síðan fer hann inn yfir garðinn	Afterwards went he then over the-wall	Then he went into the yard,
en kálfurinn veltur út af garðinum.	but the-calf hung outside of the-wall.	but the calf tumbled out of the yard.
En lykkjan er á var taumsendanum brást um háls honum Þorljóti og kenndi hann ei niður fótum.	Then the-noose that about was the-leash transformed about neck his Thorljot and felt he not down feet.	But the loop that was on the end of the leash snapped around Thorljot's neck and he didn't fall to his feet.
Hékk nú sínumegin hvor og voru dauðir báðir er til var komið.	Hung now on-his-side each and were dead both then until who came.	Now each hung separately and both were dead by the time it was over.
Drógu börnin heim kálfinn og gerðu til matar og hygg eg að Þjóðólfur hefði óskert sinn hlut af honum".	Drew the-children home the-calf and made into food and think I that Thjodolf had the-whole his share of him".	The children brought the calf home and made it for dinner, and I think Thjodolf had his share of it intact".
"Nærri hófi mundi það",	"Close-to reasonable should-be that",	"That would be more reasonable",
segir konungur.	said the-king.	said the king.

The Tale of Sarcastic Halli (Old Icelandic)

Old Icelandic	Literal	English
Þjóðólfur brá sverði og vildi höggva til Halla.	Thjodolf drew sword and wished to-strike to Halli.	Thjodolf drew his sword and wanted to attack Halli.
Hljópu menn þá í milli þeirra.	Ran men then in between them.	Men ran in between them.
Konungur kvað hvorigum hlýða skyldu að gera öðrum mein:	The-king said neither obeying should to do eachother harm:	The king said that neither should do eachother harm if they obeyed him.
"Leitaðir þú Þjóðólfur fyrri á Halla".	"Seek you Thjodolf went-before to Halli".	"Thjodolf, you went for Halli first".
Varð nú svo að vera sem konungur vildi.	Was now so as being as the-king willed.	Then it was now as the king wished.
Færði Halli drápuna og mæltist hún vel fyrir og launaði konungur honum góðum peningum.	Performed Halli the-drapa (poem) and recited it well for and rewarded the-king him good payment.	Halli performed the drapa and it was well received, and the king paid him good money.
Leið nú á veturinn og var allt kyrrt.	Passed now to winter and was all peaceful.	It now passed to winter and everything was quiet.

7

Old Icelandic	Literal	English
Einar var maður nefndur og var kallaður fluga.	Einar was a-man named and was called Fly.	There was a man named Einar who was called Fly.
Hann var son Háreks úr Þjóttu.	He was son Harek's from Thjotta.	He was the son of Harek from Thjotta.
Hann var lendur maður og hafði sýslu á Hálogalandi og finnferð af konungi og var nú í kærleikum miklum við konung en þó eldi þar jafnan ýmsu á.	He was land man and had business in Halogaland and Finland-voyages of the-king's and was now in friendship much with the-king but though fire there equally about was.	He was a land owning man and had business in Halogaland and voyages to Finland, and was now in great friendship with the king, but there was always something going on there.
Einar var óeinarðarmaður mikill.	Einar was unreliable much.	Einar was very unreliable.
Drap hann menn ef ei gerðu allt sem hann vildi og bætti öngvan mann.	Killed he men if not did all as he wished and compensated no man.	He killed people if they didn't do everything he wanted and gave compensation to no man.
Einars var von til hirðarinnar að jólunum.	Einar was expected to court at Yule.	Einar was expected at court during Yule.

The Tale of Sarcastic Halli (Old Icelandic)

Old Icelandic	Literal	English
Þeim Halla og Sigurði sessunaut hans varð talað til Einars.	They Halli and Sigurd bench-companion his were talking about Einar.	Halli and his bench companion Sigurd were talking about Einar.
Sagði Sigurður Halla frá að engi maður þorði að mæla í móti Einari eða í aðra skál að leggja en hann vildi og hann bætti ekki fé fyrir víg eða rán.	Told Sigurd Halli from that no man dared to speak to against Einar or that other shall to allow but he wished and he compensated not payment for slaying or robbery.	Sigurd told Halli that no man dared to speak against Einar or to allow anything other than what he wished, and that he paid no compensation for slaying or robbery.
Halli svarar:	Halli answered:	Halli answered:
"Vændishöfðingjar mundu slíkt kallaðir á voru landi".	"Wicked-chieftain would such be-called in our land".	"Such a chieftain would be called wicked in our land".
"Mæl þú varlega félagi",	"Speak you warily companion",	"Speak carefully, friend",
segir Sigurður, "því að hann er lítilþægur að orðum ef honum er í móti skapi".	said Sigurd, "because that he is little-behaving that words if he is to against mind".	said Sigurd, "because he doesn't mix his words if he's in a bad mood".
"Þó að þér séuð allir svo hræddir",	"Though that you look all so afraid",	"Although you are all so afraid",
segir Halli, "að enginn yðvar þori að mæla eitt orð í móti honum þá segi eg þér það að eg skyldi kæra ef hann gerði mér rangt og þess get eg að hann bæti mér".	said Halli, "that none of-you dare to say one word to against him then say I to-you this that I would accuse if he did me wrong and this get I of him compensate me".	said Halli, "that none of you dare to say a word against him, I tell you that I would complain if he did me wrong and I expect him to make it up to me".
"Hví þér en öðrum?"	"Why to-you than others?"	"Why are you different from others?"
segir Sigurður.	said Sigurd.	said Sigurd.
"Það mundi honum sýnast",	"That would to-him appear",	"That shall become apparent to him",
segir Halli.	said Halli.	said Halli.
Þar til þræta þeir hér um að Halli býður Sigurði að veðja hér um.	They to argued them here about that Halli offered Sigurd to wager here about.	They argued amongst themselves until Halli offered to make a wager with Sigurd about it.

The Tale of Sarcastic Halli (Old Icelandic)

Old Icelandic	Literal	English
Leggur Sigurður hér við gullhring er stóð hálfa mörk en Halli leggur við höfuð sitt.	Laid Sigurd here with a-gold-ring in place half a-mark and Halli laid with head his.	Here, Sigurd placed a gold ring that stood at half a mark, but Halli placed his head.
Einar kemur að jólunum og situr hann á aðra hönd konungi og menn hans út frá honum.	Einar came at Yule and sat he by other hand the-king's and people his about from him.	Einar came at Yule and he sat by the king's hand with his people around him.
Var honum öll þjónusta veitt sem konungi sjálfum.	Was he all service given as the-king himself.	He was given every service as much as the king himself.
Og jóladag er menn voru mettir mælti konungurinn:	And Yule-day when people were finished-eating spoke the-king:	And on Yule day when people had finished eating the king spoke:
"Nú viljum vér hafa fleira til gamans en drekka.	"Now wish we to-have more to amusement than drinking.	"Now we wish to have more amusement than drinking.
Skaltu nú Einar segja oss hvað til tíðinda hefir orðið í förum yðrum".	Shall-you now Einar tell us what to news have worded on journey yours".	Einar, you shall now tell us what word you have of news on your journey.
Einar svarar:	Einar answered:	Einar answered:
"Ekki kann eg það í frásagnir að færa herra þó að vér hnúskum búfinna eða fiskimenn".	"Not can I that as stories to bring lord though that we knocked-down farmers and fishermen".	"I don't know how to tell stories, lord, even though we knocked down some farmers and fishermen".
Konungur svarar:	The-king answered:	The king answered:
"Segið settlega því að vér erum lítilþægir að og þykir oss gaman að því öllu þó að yður þyki lítils vert er jafnan standið í stríði".	"Tell sedately because that we are easily-satisfied by and seems to-us a-delight that therefore all though that you think little worth is always standing in battles".	"Tell us calmly because we are easily satisfied by it and it all seems to us a delight even though you think it is of little worth, and as you are constantly in battles".
"Það er þó herra helst að segja",	"It is though lord rather to say",	"However, lord, I prefer to say",
segir Einar, "að í fyrra sumar er vér komum norður á Mörkina mættum vér Íslandsfari einu og höfðu þeir orðið þangað sæhafa og setið þar um veturinn.	said Einar, "that of last summer when we came north of The-border met we Iceland-voyage one and had they become from-there sea-scattered and sat there about winter.	said Einar, "that last summer when we came north of the border we met a ship journeying from Iceland, and they had been sea-scattered and were there since winter.

The Tale of Sarcastic Halli (Old Icelandic)

Old Icelandic	Literal	English
Bar eg á hendur þeim að þeir mundu átt hafa kaup við Finna fyrir utan yðvart lof eða mitt	Bore I to hand them that they would had having traded with The-Sami for without your permission or mine	I put it to them that they had traded with the Sami people without your permission or mine,
en þeir duldu og gengu ei við	that the denied and went not with	which they denied and would not agree with,
en oss þóttu þeir ótrúlegir og beiddi eg þá rannsóknar	but we thought them un-truthful and asked I then a-search	but we thought they were untruthful, and I asked to search them,
en þeir synjuðu þverlega.	but they refused crossly.	but they flatly refused.
Eg sagði það þá að þeir skyldu hafa það er þeim væri verra og maklegra og bað eg mína menn vopnast og leggja að þeim.	I said that then that they should have it what for-them being worse and well-deserved and ordered I my men armed and lay at them.	I then said that they should have what was worse and more deserved for them, and I asked my men to arm themselves and attack them.
Eg hafði fimm langskip og lögðum vér að á bæði borð og léttum ei fyrr en hroðið var skipið.	I had five longships and laid we to at both boards and let-up not before that cleared was the-ship.	I had five longships and we anchored on both sides and did not let up until the ship was cleared.
Og einn íslenskur maður er þeir kölluðu Einar varðist svo vel að hans maka fann eg aldrei og víst var skaði að um þann mann og ei hefðum vér unnið skipið ef slíkir hefðu allir verið innanborðs".	And one Icelander man that they called Einar guarded so well that he equal found I never and certainly was harm to about that man and not have we won the-ship if such had all been onboard".	And one Icelander man, that they called Einar, guarded so well that I have never found his equal, and it was certainly a loss for that man, and we would not have won the ship if such men as him had all been aboard".
"Illa gerðir þú það Einar",	"Badly done you it Einar",	"You did badly, Einar",
segir konungur, "er þú drepur saklausa menn þó að ei geri allt sem þér líkar best".	said the-king, "when you killed sake-less people though that not did all as you liked best".	said the king, "you kill innocent people who don't do everything you like best".
"Mun eg ei",	"Would I not",	"I will not",
segir Einar, "sitja fyrir hættu þeirri.	said Einar, "settle for danger theirs.	said Einar, "sit before that danger.
En mæla það sumir menn herra að þér gerið ei allt sem guðréttilegast.	And say it some people lord that you do not all as good-rightly.	But some people say, sir, that you don't do everything in the most godly way.

The Tale of Sarcastic Halli (Old Icelandic)

Old Icelandic	Literal	English
En þeir reyndust illa og fundum vér mikinn finnskrepp í skipinu".	But they proved bad also found we much Sami-goods in the-ship".	But they turned out to be bad and we found a great amount of Sami goods in the ship".
Halli heyrði hvað þeir töluðu og kastaði hnífinum fram á borðið og hætti að eta.	Halli heard what they spoke and cast knife away from the-table and stopped of eating.	Halli heard what they were talking about and threw the knife on the table and stopped eating.
Sigurður spurði ef hann væri sjúkur.	Sigurd asked if he was sick.	Sigurd asked if he was sick.
Hann kvað það ei vera	He said that not was	He said it wasn't,
en kvað þetta þó sótt verra:	but said this though sickness worse:	but he said this was even worse:
"Einar fluga sagði lát Einars bróður míns er hann kveðst fellt hafa á kaupskipinu í fyrra sumar og má vera að nú gefi til að leita eftir bótunum við hann Einar".	"Einar Fly told-of had Einar brother mine that he said fell had on merchant-ship in before summer and may be that now give to of seeking after compensation with him Einar".	"Einar Fly told about the death of my brother Einar, who he claims to have killed on the merchant ship last summer, and it may be that he now seeks to give compensation for Einar".
"Tala ekki um félagi",	"Speak not about companion",	"Do not speak about it, companion",
segir Sigurður,	said Sigurd,	said Sigurd,
"sá mun vænstur".	"so would-be promising".	that would be the most promising.
Nei, sagði Halli, "ekki mundi hann svo við mig gera ef hann ætti eftir mig að mæla".	No, said Halli, "not would he so with me doing if he had after me the matter".	Halli said no, "he would not do that with me if it was my case he was dealing with".
Hljóp hann þá fram yfir borðið, gekk innar fyrir hásætið og mælti:	Jumped he then from over table, went in before high-seat and spoke:	He then jumped over the table, and went before the high seat and spoke:
"Tíðindi sögðuð þér Einar bóndi, þau mér akta ærið mjög, í drápi Einars bróður míns er þér sögðust felldan hafa á kaupskipinu í fyrra sumar.	"News announced you Einar master, that me taxes greatly much, by the-killing Einar's brother mine who you said killed had in merchant-ship about last summer.	"You announced news which concerns me greatly, the killing of Einar, my brother, who you said you killed in the merchant ship last summer.

The Tale of Sarcastic Halli (Old Icelandic)

Old Icelandic	Literal	English
Nú vil eg vita hvort þú vilt nokkru bæta mér Einar bróður minn".	Now wish I to-know whether you will some compensation to-me Einar brother mine".	Now I wish to know if you will pay me some compensation for my brother".
"Hefir þú ei spurt að eg bæti engan mann?"	"Have you not heard that I compensate no man?"	"Have you not heard that I compensate no one",
segir Einar.	said Einar.	said Einar.
"Eigi er mér skylt að trúa því",	"Not I me should to believe accordingly",	"I was not obliged to believe",
segir Halli, "að þér væri allt illa gefið þó að eg heyrði það sagt".	said Halli, "that you were all evil given though that I heard that said".	said Halli, "that you were all evil, though I heard it said".
"Gakk burt maður",	"Go away man",	"Go away man",
segir Einar, "annar mun verri".	said Einar, "otherwise should-be worse".	said Einar, "otherwise it shall be worse".
Halli gekk að sitja.	Halli went to sit.	Halli went to sit.
Sigurður spyr hve farist hefði.	Sigurd asked how gone had.	Sigurd asked how it had gone.
Hann svarar og kveðst hafa hótun fyrir fébætur.	He answered and said had a-threat for compensation.	He answered and said that he had been given a threat as compensation.
Sigurður bað hann ei oftar koma á þetta mál og sé laus veðjanin.	Sigurd asked him not more come that this matter and so lost the-wager.	Sigurd ask him not to persist in this matter any more, and the wager would be lost.
Halli kvað honum vel fara	Halli said he well went	Halli said it had gone well,
"en á skal koma oftar".	"but about shall come more".	but there is more to come.
Og annan dag eftir gekk Halli fyrir Einar og mælti:	And the-next day after went Halli before Einar and spoke:	And the next day Halli went before Einar and spoke:
"Það mál vil eg vekja Einar ef þú vilt nokkru bæta mér bróður minn".	"The matter wish I awaken Einar if you will some compensation to-me brother mine".	"I wish to raise the matter with you, Einar, whether you will give me some compensation for my brother".
Einar svarar:	Einar answered:	Einar answered:

The Tale of Sarcastic Halli (Old Icelandic)

Old Icelandic	Literal	English
"Þú ert seinþreyttur að og ef þú dregst ei brott þá muntu fara slíka för sem bróðir þinn eða verri".	"You are persistent this and if you draw not away then should fare such before as brother yours or worse".	"You are persistent in this, and if you do not back away, then it should go the same way as you brother did or worse".
Konungurinn bað hann ei svo svara	The-king ordered him not so to-answer	The king ordered him not to answer like that,
"og er það frændunum ofraun og veit ei hvers hugar hverjum lér.	"and was it kinsmen too-much and known not how-so minds each leaned.	and it is too-much for the kinsmen and not known how each mind goes.
En þú Halli kom ei aftur á þetta mál því að stærri bokkar verða að þola honum slíkt en þú ert".	But you Halli come not again of this matter because that greater bigger-men have-been that enduring him such than you are".	But you, Halli, do not raise this matter again because greater and bigger men have endured such as you are".
Halli svarar:	Halli answered:	Halli answered:
"Svo mun vera verða".	"So should be becomes".	"So it will have to be".
Gekk hann þá til rúms síns.	Went he then to rooms his.	Then he went to his rooms.
Sigurður fagnar honum vel og spurði hve farist hafði.	Sigurd welcomed him well and asked how gone had.	Sigurd welcomed him well and asked how it had gone.
Halli kveðst hafa heitan fyrir fébætur af Einari.	Halli said had threat for compensation of Einar.	Halli said that he had received a threat for compensation from Einar.
"Þótti mér það í hug",	"Thought me that in mind",	"I thought that in my mind",
segir Sigurður, "og sé laus veðjanin".	said Sigurd, "and so lost the-wager".	said Sigurd, "and so the wager is lost".
"Vel fer þér",	"Well go you",	"You behave well",
segir Halli, "en á skal eg koma þriðja sinn".	said Halli, "but for shall I come a-third occasion".	said Halli, "but I shall raise the matter a third time".
"Gefa vil eg þér nú til hringinn",	"Give will I you now to the-ring",	"I will now give you the ring",
sagði Sigurður, "að þú látir vera kyrrt er þetta hefir þó nokkuð af mér til hlotist í fyrstu".	said Sigurd, "that you leave be peace as this has though somewhat of me to part the first".	said Sigurd, "so that you will let there be peace, because I am responsible for part of this.

The Tale of Sarcastic Halli (Old Icelandic)

Old Icelandic	Literal	English
Halli svarar:	Halli answered:	Halli answered:
"Sýnir þú hver maður þú ert og ekki má þér um kenna hversu sem til vegar fer.	"Show you what man you are and not may you about know how-so as to way go.	"You show what kind of man you are and you can't be blamed no matter what happens.
En prófa skal enn um sinn".	But prove shall one about occasion".	But it must be tried one more time".
Og þegar um morguninn er konungur tók handlaugar og Einar fluga gekk Halli að honum og kvaddi konunginn.	And early about morning when the-king took hand-washing and Einar Fly went Halli to him and greeted the-king.	And early the next morning, when the king took to washing his hands along with Einar Fly, Halli went to him and greeted the king.
Konungurinn spyr hvað hann vildi.	The-king asked what he wanted.	The king asked what he wanted.
Herra,	"Lord",	"Lord",
segir Halli, "eg vil segja yður draum minn.	said Halli, "I wish to-tell you dream mine.	said Halli, "I wish to tell you about my dream.
Eg þóttist vera allur maður annar en eg er".	I seemed to-be all man another than I am".	I thought I was a completely different person than I am".
"Hvað manni þóttist þú vera?"	"What man thought you to-be?"	"Who did you think you were?"
segir konungur.	said the-king.	said the king.
"Eg þóttist vera Þorleifur skáld en hann Einar fluga þótti mér vera Hákon jarl Sigurðarson og þóttist eg hafa ort um hann níð og mundi eg sumt níðið er eg vaknaði".	"I thought being Thorleif the-poet but he Einar Fly seemed to-me to-be Hakon earl Sigurdson and thought I had worded about him slander and remembered I some the-slander when I awoke".	I thought I was Thorleif the poet, but Einar Fly was Earl Hakon Sigurdson, and I thought I had written about him, and I remembered some things when I woke up".
Sneri Halli þá utar eftir höllunni og kvað nokkuð fyrir munni sér og námu menn ei orðaskil.	Turned Halli then out after the-hall and spoke something before mouth his and took people not words-separated.	Halli then turned around outside the palace and said something in front of his mouth and the people did not understand any of it.
Konungur mælti:	The-king spoke:	The king spoke:

The Tale of Sarcastic Halli (Old Icelandic)

Old Icelandic	Literal	English
"Þetta var ekki draumur annar en hann dregur þessi dæmi saman.	"This was not a-dream another that he drew these examples together.	"This was not a dream, and he has drawn these examples together.
Og svo mun fara með ykkur sem fór með þeim Hákoni Hlaðajarli og Þorleifi skáldi og það sama gerir Halli.	And so should go with you as went with they Hakon Earl-of-Lade and Thorleif the-poet and that same does Halli.	And so it should go with you as it went with Earl Hakon of Lade and Thorleif the poet, and Halli is doing the same thing.
Hann svífst einkis og megum við sjá að bitið hefir níðið ríkari menn en svo sem þú ert Einar, sem var Hákon jarl, og mun það munað meðan Norðurlönd eru byggð og er verri einn kviðlingur, ef munaður verður eftir, en lítil fémúta, um dýran mann kveðinn	He shrinks-from nothing and may we see that biting has-been the-slander richer men than so as you are Einar, as was Hakon earl, and would-be that remembered as-long-as Northern-lands are settled and is worse one short-poem, if remembered becomes after, then little money-bribe, about fine men composed	He shrinks from nothing, and we may see how slander has bitten richer men than you are, Einar, as Earl Hakon was, and it would be remembered as long as the Northern Lands are settled, one short verse about powerful men, if it becomes remembered afterwards, is worse than paying a small bribe,
og ger svo vel og leys hann af með nokkru".	and do so well and repay him of with somehow".	and so it would do well to repay him somehow".
"Þér skuluð ráða herra",	"You should decide lord",	"You will decide, lord"
segir Einar, "og seg honum að hann taki þrjár merkur silfurs af féhirði mínum er eg fékk honum síðast í sjóði".	said Einar, "and tell him that he takes three marks of-silver of fee-servant mine that I give him the-last in purse".	said Einar, "and tell him that he may take three marks of silver from my fee-servant in the purse I just gave him".
Þetta var sagt Halla.	This was told Halli.	This was told to Halli.
Gekk hann að finna féhirðinn og sagði honum.	Went he to find fee-servant and told him.	He went to find the fee-servant and told him.
Hann kvað vera fjórar merkur silfurs í sjóðnum.	He said be four marks of-silver in the-purse.	He said there were four marks of silver in the purse.
Halli kveðst þrjár hafa skyldu.	Halli said three have should-be.	Halli said that he was to have three.
Halli gekk þá fyrir Einar og sagði honum.	Halli went then before Einar and told him.	Halli went before Einar and said to him:
"Hafa mundir þú það er í var sjóðnum",	"Have would you that which in was the-purse",	"Have you taken what was in the purse?",
segir Einar.	said Einar.	said Einar.

The Tale of Sarcastic Halli (Old Icelandic)

Old Icelandic	Literal	English
Nei, sagði Halli, "öðruvís skaltu ná lífi mínu en eg verði þjófur af fé þínu og sá eg að þú hafðir það ætlað mér".	No, said Halli, "other-knowing shall-you obtain life mine than I being thief of money yours and saw I that you have that intended to-me".	Halli said no, "you will have to find another way to take my life than me being a thief of your money, and I saw what you intended for me".
Og svo var að Einar hafði það ætlað Halla að hann mundi það er í var sjóðnum hafa og þótti honum það nóg banasök.	And so was that Einar had it intended Halli that he would that which in was the-purse have and thought him that enough death-sentence.	And so it was that Einar thought that Halli would have taken whatever was in the purse, which he thought would be enough of an offence for a death sentence.
Gekk Halli nú til sætis síns og sýndi Sigurði féð.	Went Halli no to seat his and showed Sigurd the-money.	Halli went now to his seat and showed Sigurd the money.
Sigurður tók hringinn og kvað Halla vel hafa til unnið.	Sigurd took the-ring and said Halli well had to won.	Sigurd took the ring and said that Halli had won it.
Hann svarar:	He answered:	He answered:
"Eigi erum við þá jafnir þegnar og tak hring þinn og njót manna best.	"Not are-we with then equal men and take the-ring yours and enjoy man the-best.	"We are not equally good men, keep the ring and enjoy it, best of men.
En þér satt að segja þá átti eg aldrei skylt við þenna mann er Einar hefir drepið og vildi eg vita ef eg næði fénu af honum".	But to-you truth to say then related-to I never should with this man which Einar had killed and wished I to-know if I neared money of him".	But to tell you the truth, I was never related to this man which Einar killed, and I wished to know if I could obtain money from him".
"Engum manni ertu líkur að prettum",	"No man are-you like in trickery",	"There is no one like you in trickery",
segir Sigurður.	said Sigurd.	said Sigurd.
Einar fór brott eftir jólin norður á Hálogaland.	Einar went away after Yule north to Halogaland.	Einar went away after Yule north to Halogaland.

8

Um vorið bað Halli konung orlofs að fara til Danmerkur í kaupferð.	About spring asked Halli the-king vacation to travel to Denmark on trading-voyage.	In the spring, King Halli asked for leave to go to Denmark on a trading voyage.

The Tale of Sarcastic Halli (Old Icelandic)

Old Icelandic	Literal	English
Konungur bað hann fara sem hann vildi "og kom aftur skjótt því oss þykir gaman að þér og far varlega fyrir Einari flugu.	The-king bid he travel as he wished "and come back quickly because we consider fun that to-you and travel warily because-of Einar Fly.	The king asked him to go as he wished "and come back quickly because we like you and be careful of Einar Fly.
Hann mun hafa illan hug á þér og sjaldan veit eg honum jafnsleppt tekist hafa".	He should have evil mind to you and seldom know I him equally-slip taken has".	He will have a bad opinion of you and I rarely know of him slipping up".
Halli tók sér far með kaupmönnum suður til Danmerkur og svo til Jótlands.	Halli took himself passage with trading-men south to Denmark and so to Jutland.	Halli took found passage with merchants south to Denmark and then to Jutland.
Rauður hét maður er þar hafði sýslu og réðst Halli þar til vistar.	Raud was-named a-man who there had stewardship and appointed Halli there to lodgings.	There was a man named Raud who had a stewardship there and appointed Halli there some lodgings.
Það bar til eitt sinn er hann skyldi hafa þing fjölmennt og er menn skyldu þar mæla lögskilum sínum þá var svo mikið háreysti og gap að engi maður mátti þar málum sínum fram koma	It bore to one occasion that he should have assembly followers and that men should there matters legal-settlement theirs then was so much commotion and gaping that no man may there matter his from come-forward	It happened day when he was supposed to have a large assembly and when people were supposed to discuss their legal issues there, there was so much shouting and gaping that no one was allowed to present their case there
og fóru menn við það heim um kveldið.	and went people with that home about evening.	and the people went home that evening.
Það var um kveldið er menn komu til drykkjar að Rauður mælti:	It was about evening that men came to drink that Raud spoke:	It was in the evening when people came to drink that Raud said:
"Það væri ráðleitinn maður er ráð fyndi til að fólk þetta allt þagnaði".	"It being cunning man who plan find to that people these all silenced".	"It would be a wise man who could find a way to keep all these people quiet".
Halli svarar:	Halli answered:	Halli answered:
"Það fæ eg gert þegar eg vil að hér skal hvert mannsbarn þagna".	"That can I do as-soon-as I wish that here shall each man's-son silence".	"I can do that when I want every human being to be silent".
"Það færð þú ei gert landi",	"That undertaking you not do the-land",	"You will not get that done in this land",
segir Rauður.	said Raud.	said Raud.

The Tale of Sarcastic Halli (Old Icelandic)

Old Icelandic	Literal	English
Um morguninn komu menn til þings og var nú slíkt óp og gap sem hinn fyrra dag og varð öngum málum skilað.	About morning came people to the-assembly and were now such shouting and gaping as the before day and were no matters settled.	In the morning, people came to the assembly and now there was such an uproar as the previous day and no issues were resolved.
Fóru menn við það heim.	Went men with that home.	The men then went home.
Þá mælti Rauður:	Then spoke Raud:	Then Raud spoke:
"Viltu veðja um Halli hvort þú færð hljóðið á þinginu eða ei?"	"Will-you wager about Halli each you carry-out silence to the-assembly or not?"	"Will you wager, Halli, that you will get silence at the assembly or not?".
Halli kveðst þess búinn.	Halli said this settled.	Halli said this would be done.
Rauður svarar:	Raud answered:	Raud answered:
"Legg við höfuð þitt en eg gullhring er stendur mörk".	"Lay with head yours and I gold-ring which stands one-mark".	"Lay down your head, and I will lay down a ring which is worth one mark".
"Það skal vera",	"That shall be",	"So it shall be",
segir Halli.	said Halli.	said Halli.
Um morguninn spurði Halli Rauð ef hann vildi veðjanina halda.	About morning asked Halli Raud if he wished wager to-hold.	In the morning, Halli asked Raud if he wanted to keep the wager.
Hann kveðst halda vilja.	He said hold wished.	He said that he wished to keep it.
Komu menn nú til þingsins og var nú slíkt óp eða meira sem hina fyrri dagana.	Came men now to the-assembly and were not such shouting and more than the before day.	Now people came to the assembly and there was as much shouting or more as the previous days.
Og er menn varði síst hleypur Halli upp og æpir sem hæst mátti hann:	And when people were least ran Halli up and cried-out as high as-might he:	And when the people were at their least, Halli ran up and shouted as loud as he could:
"Hlýði allir menn.	"Listen all people.	"Listen everyone.
Mér er máls þörf.	For-me is matter of-need.	For me this is a matter of need.

The Tale of Sarcastic Halli (Old Icelandic)

Old Icelandic	Literal	English
Mér er horfin hein og heinasmjör, skreppa og þar með allur skreppuskrúði sá er karlmanni er betra að hafa en að missa".	Mine is lost hone and honing-grease, bag and there with all bag-tackle so is a-man that better to have than to lose".	I have lost my hone and honing grease, and my bag with all its tackle, which is better for a man to have than lose".
Allir menn þögnuðu.	All people silenced.	All the people were silent.
Sumir hugðu að hann mundi ær orðinn en sumir hugðu að hann mundi tala konungs erindi nokkur.	Some thought that he could-be awed of-words and some thought that he could-be speaking the-king's errand some.	Some people thought that he was lost for words, and some thought that he could be speaking some message from the king.
Og er hljóð fékkst settist Halli niður og tók við hringinum.	And when silence received settled Halli down and took with the-ring.	And when there was a sound, Halli sat down and took the ring.
En þegar menn sáu að þetta var ekki nema dáruskapur þá var háreysti sem áður og komst Halli á hlaupi undan því að Rauður vildi hafa líf hans og þótti þetta verið hafa hin mesta ginning.	Then as-soon-as people saw that this was nothing but mockery then was commotion as before and came Halli to running out-from because that Rauð wished to-have life his and thought this become had the most deception.	But when people saw that this was nothing but a prank, Halli was as stubborn as before and ran away from Raud who wanted his head and thought that this was the greatest deception.
Létti hann eigi fyrr en hann kom til Englands.	Let-up he not before that he came to England.	He did not let up until he came to England.

9

Þá réð fyrir Englandi Haraldur Guðinason.	Then ruled for England Harald Godwinson.	Then Harald Godwinson ruled England.
Halli fer þegar á konungs fund og kveðst hafa ort um hann drápu og bað sér hljóðs.	Halli went straight-away to the-king to-meet and said had composed about him a-drapa (poem) and asked for-him be-heard.	Halli went straight away to the king and said that he had composed a drapa about him and asked that it be heard.
Konungur lét gefa honum hljóð.	The-king had granted him a-hearing.	The king granted him a hearing.
Sest Halli fyrir kné konungi og flutti fram kvæðið.	Sat Halli before knee the-king's and brought from the-poem.	Halli sat down before the king and recited the poem.

The Tale of Sarcastic Halli (Old Icelandic)

Old Icelandic	Literal	English
Og er lokið var kvæðinu spurði konungur skáld sitt er var með honum hvern veg væri kvæðið.	And when ended was the-poem asked the-king the-poet this that was with him each way being the-poem.	And when the poem was finished, the king asked his poet who was with him and what the poem was about.
Hann kveðst ætla að gott væri.	He said supposed that good was.	He said that he supposed it was good.
Konungur bauð Halla með sér að vera en Halli kveðst búinn vera til Noregs áður.	The-king invited Halli with him to be but Halli said prepared being to Norway back.	The king invited Halli to stay with him, but Halli said he has already prepared to return to Norway.
Konungur kvað þá þann veg fara mundu af hendi "um kvæðislaun við þig sem vér njótum kvæðisins því að enginn hróður verður oss að því kvæði er enginn kann.	The-king said then that way going would of hand "about poem-reward with you as we benefit the-poem because that none fame worthy to-us that before recited as none knows.	The king said then that it would go the same way "in rewarding you for the poem, as we benefit from the poem, because we get no fame's worth from a poem that no one knows.
Sit nú niður á gólfið en eg mun láta hella silfri í höfuð þér og haf þá það er í hárinu loðir og þykir mér þá hvort horfa eftir öðru er vér skulum eigi ná að nema kvæðið".	Sit now down on the-floor then I will have poured silver on head yours and have then it which in the-hairs of-your-hair and seems to-me then each turn after the-other that we shall not obtain to but the-poem".	Now sit down on the floor, and I will have silver poured over your head, and keep whatever sticks to your hair, and it seems to me that it looks the same on both sides because we will not get to learn the poem".
Halli svarar:	Halli answered:	Halli answered:
"Bæði mun vera að lítilla launa mun vert vera enda munu þessi launin og lítil vera.	"Both should be that little reward should worth become and shall this repay also little being.	"Both are small rewards due and that the rewards will be small.
Lofa munuð þér herra að eg gangi út nauðsynja minna".	Promise shall you lord that I go out needs mine".	Will you promise me that I may go outside to attend to my needs".
"Gakk sem þú vilt",	"Go as you wish",	"Go as you wish",
segir konungur.	said the-king.	said the king.
Halli gekk þar til er skipsmiðir voru og bar í höfuð sér tjöru og gerði sem diskur væri	Halli went there to where ship-smiths were and bore on head his tar and made as a-plate being	Halli walked to where the shipbuilders were and carried tar on his head and fashioned into the shape of a plate

The Tale of Sarcastic Halli (Old Icelandic)

Old Icelandic	Literal	English
og gekk síðan inn og bað hella silfrinu yfir sig.	and went afterwards in and asked pour the-silver over him.	and then went back inside and asked for the silver to be poured over him.
Konungur kvað hann vera brögðóttan	The-king said he was cunning	The king said that he was cunning,
og var nú hellt yfir hann og var það mikið silfur er hann fékk.	and was now rather over him and was it much silver that he got.	and now the silver was poured over him, and it was a lot of silver that he got.
Fór hann síðan þangað er skip þau voru er til Noregs ætluðu og voru öll burtu nema eitt og var þar ráðinn fjöldi manna með miklum þunga.	Went he afterwards from-there to ship there where that to Norway intended and were all away except one and was that appointed many men with much heavy-cargo.	He then went to where the ships were that were going to Norway, and they were all gone, except one that had many men with much heavy cargo.
En Halli hafði of fjár og vildi gjarna í burt því að hann hafði ekki kvæði ort um konung annað en kveðið endilausu og mátti hann því ekki kenna það.	But Halli had of fee and wished gladly to away because that he had not composed words about the-king other than reciting nonsense and may he therefore not teach it.	Halli had plenty of money and wished very much to travel away, because he had not composed words about the king other than reciting nonsense, and therefore could not teach it.
Stýrimaður bað hann fá til ráð að suðurmenn gengju úr skipinu og kveðst þá vilja gjarna taka við honum.	Steersman bid him get to advice that southern-men walking out-of the-ship and said then wished gladly take with him.	The steersman told him to find a scheme so that the southern men would leave the ship, then he would gladly take him.
En þá var komið að vetri.	But then was coming the winter.	But then winter was coming.
Halli var hjá þeim í herbergjum um hríð.	Halli was beside them in sleeping-quarters about awhile.	Halli stayed with them in sleeping quarters for a while.
Eina nótt lét Halli illa í svefni og var lengi áður þeir fengu vakið hann.	One night had Halli badly in sleep and was long before they caught awake him.	One night, Halli felt sick in his sleep and it was a long time before they could wake him up.
Þeir spurðu hvað hann hefði dreymt.	They asked what he had dreamed.	They asked what he had dreamed.
Halli kvað lokið því að hann mundi biðja þá fars héðan frá,	Halli said finished therefore that he would ask then travel from-there from,	Halli said that he was finished with asking for passage from there,

The Tale of Sarcastic Halli (Old Icelandic)

Old Icelandic	Literal	English
"mér þótti maður koma að mér ógurlegur og kvað þetta:"	"to-me seemed a-man come that to-me terrible and recited this:	It seemed to me that a terrible looking man came to me and recited this:
Hröng er þars hafnan þöngul	Roaring is there the harbour there	Roaring is there the harbour there
held eg um, síð er eg fjör seldag.	think me about, since that I life sold.	think me about, since that I life sold.
Hverft er sitk að Ránar.	Disappeared am-I one to Ran.	Disappeared am-I one to Ran.
Sumir eru í búð með humrum.	Some are in lodgings with lobsters.	Some are in lodgings with lobsters.
Ljóst er lýsu að gista.	Light is the-whitings with guest.	Light is the-whitings with guest.
Lendi eg út við ströndu.	Lands I out from the-shore.	Lands I out from the-shore.
Því sit eg bleikr í brúki.	Because sit I pale in use.	Because sit I pale in use.
Blakir mér þarmr um hnakka,	Pale mine intestines about neck,	Pale mine intestines about neck,
blakir mér fyrir þínum hnakka.	pale mine intestines about neck.	pale mine intestines about neck.
Og er suðurmenn vissu draum þenna réðust þeir úr skipinu og þótti bani sinn ef þeir færu þar í.	And when the-southerners knew this-dream then decided they out-of the-ship and thought death theirs if they went there in.	And when the southerners knew this dream, they got out of the ship and thought it would be their death if they went there.
Halli réðst þegar í skip og sagði að þetta var prettur hans en engi draumur.	Halli took straight-away in the-ship and said that this was trick his and no dream.	Halli took passage in the ship straight away, and said that it was a trick, and not a dream.
Og tóku þeir út þegar þeir voru búnir og tóku Noreg um haustið	And took they out from-there they were ready and took Norway about autumn	And they went out when they were ready and took to Norway in the autumn,
og fór Halli þegar til Haralds konungs.	and went Halli then to Harald the-king.	and Halli immediately went to King Harald.
Hann tók vel við Halla og spurði hvort hann hefði þá ort um aðra konunga.	He received well with Halli and asked whether he had then words about other kings.	He welcomed Halli and asked if he had written about other kings.
Halli kvað þetta:	Halli said this:	Halli said this:
Orti eg eina um jarl	"Worded I one about an-earl	Worded I one about an earl
þulu.	a-thula (poem).	a-'thula' (poem).
Verðrat drápa	Worthy-that drapa (poem)	Poorer drapa
með Dönum verri.	with The-Danes worse.	with The-Danes worse.

The Tale of Sarcastic Halli (Old Icelandic)

Old Icelandic	Literal	English
Föll eru fjórtán og föng tíu. Opið er og öndvert, öfugt stígandi. Svo skal yrkja sá er illa kann.	Mistakes are fourteen and rhymes ten. Open is and upside-down, reversed ascending. Then shall compose so who badly knows.	Mistakes are fourteen and rhymes ten. Open is and upside-down, reversed ascending. Then shall compose so who badly knows.
Konungur brosti að og þótti honum jafnan gaman að Halla.	The-king smiled that and thought him always entertaining of Halli.	The king smiled an thought he always found Halli entertaining.

10

Haraldur konungur fór um vorið til Gulaþings.	Harald the-king went about spring to Gula-assembly.	In the spring Harald went to the Gulathing Assembly.
Og um daginn spurði konungur Halla hversu honum yrði til kvenna um þingið.	And about the-day asked the-king Halli how-so he became to women at the-assembly.	And one day the king asked Halli how he was with women at the assembly.
Halli svarar:	Halli answered:	Halli answered:
Gott er Gulaþing þetta, giljum við hvað er viljum.	Good is Gula-assembly this, beguile we that as we-wish.	Good is Gulathing this, beguile we that as we-wish.
Konungurinn fór þaðan norður til Þrándheims.	The-king went from-there north to Trondheim.	The king went north from there to Trondheim.
Og er þeir sigldu fyrir Stað áttu þeir Þjóðólfur og Halli búðarvörð að halda og var Halli sæsjúkur mjög og lá undir báti en Þjóðólfur varð að þjóna einn.	And when they sailed for Stad had they Thjodolf and Halli shop-keeping to hold and was Halli seasick much and lay under the-ship's-boat and Thjodolf came to serve alone.	And when they sailed for Stad, Thjodolf and Halli were assigned the cooking and serving, and Halli was very seasick and lay under the ship's boat, and Thjodolf had to serve alone.
Og er hann bar vistina féll hann um fót Halla er stóð út undan bátinum.	And when he carried the-provisions fell he about leg Halli's which stood out under the-boat.	And when he was carrying the provisions, he fell on Halli's leg, which was standing out from under the boat.
Þjóðólfur kvað þetta:	Thjodolf spoke this:	Thjodolf spoke this:
Út stendr undan báti ilfat. Muntu nú gilja?	Out standing under the-boat sole-bucket. Shall-you now beguile?"	"Out standing under the-boat sole-bucket. Shall-you now beguile?"

The Tale of Sarcastic Halli (Old Icelandic)

Old Icelandic	Literal	English
Halli svarar:	Halli answered:	Halli answered:
Þjón geri eg þann að sveini, Þjóðólf læt eg mat sjóða.	Servant made I then to this-lad, Thjodolf let I food boil.	Servant made I then to this-lad, Thjodolf let I food boil.
Fór konungurinn nú leiðar sinnar uns hann kom í Kaupangur.	For the-king now on-way his until he came to Kaupang.	The king now went on his way until he came to Kaupang.
Þóra drottning var nú með honum og var hún lítt til Halla	Thora the-queen was not with him and was she little towards Halli	Queen Thora was now with him and she did not like Halli,
en konungur var vel til hans og þótti gaman að Halla jafnan.	but the-king was well towards him and seemed to-delight in Halli always.	but the king liked him and always delighted in Halli.
Þess er getið einn dag að konungurinn gekk út um stræti og fylgdin með honum.	This is told one day that the-king went out about the-street and followers with him.	It is said that one day the king went out into the street and his follower with him.
Halli var þar í för.	Halli was there in procession.	Halli was there in the procession.
Konungurinn hafði öxi í hendi og öll gullrekin en silfurvafið skaftið og silfurhólkur mikill á forskeftinu og þar í ofan steinn góður.	The-king had an-axe in hand and all gold-inlaid and silver-wound the-shaft and silver-band great in upper-shaft and there in over a-stone good.	The king had an axe in his hand and all the shafts were gold, but the shaft was wrapped in silver, and a large silver cylinder on the foreshaft, and above it a good stone.
Það var ágætur gripur.	It was excellent possession.	It was excellent possession.
Halli sá jafnan til öxarinnar.	Halli looked always to the-axe.	Halli kept looking towards the axe.
Konungur fann það brátt og spurði hvort Halla litist vel á öxina.	The-king found that soon and asked whether Halli looked well of the-axe.	The king soon found out and asked if Halla had a good look at the axe.
Honum kveðst vel á lítast.	He said well it looked.	He said it looked good.
"Hefir þú séð betri öxi?"	"Have you seen a-better axe?"	"Have you seen a-better axe?"
"Eigi ætla eg", segir Halli.	"Not suppose I", said Halli.	"I suppose not", said Halli.

The Tale of Sarcastic Halli (Old Icelandic)

Old Icelandic	Literal	English
"Viltu láta serðast til öxarinnar?"	"Will-you allow to-get-hurt for the-axe?"	"Do you want to be hurt by the axe?"
segir konungur.	said the-king.	said the king.
Eigi, segir Halli,	Not, said Halli,	Halli said not,
"en vorkunn þykir mér yður að þér viljið svo selja sem þér keyptuð".	"but understandable seems to-me you that you wish so to-sell same-as you bought".	"but it's understandable to me that you would wish to sell it for the same as you bought it".
"Svo skal vera Halli",	"So shall be Halli",	"So it shall be Halli",
segir konungur,	said the-king,	said the king,
"tak með og njót manna best,	"take with and enjoy man the-best,	take it with you and enjoy it, best man,
gefin var mér enda skal svo selja".	given was to-me and shall so to-sell".	it was given to me, and now shall it be given to you.
Halli þakkaði konungi.	Halli thanked the-king.	Halli thanked the king.
Um kveldið er menn komu til drykkjar talaði drottning við konung að það væri undarlegt	About evening when men came to drink talked the-queen with the-king that it was scandalous	In the evening, when the men came to drink, the queen spoke to the king that it was strange
"og ei vel til skipt að gefa Halla þá gripi er varla er ótiginna manna eiga fyrir klámyrði sín	"and not well to exchange to give Halli then treasure that hardly was un-ranking man not before obscene his	and it is not a good idea to give Halli the those things to a lowly man hardly has for his obscenities,
en þá fá sumir lítið fyrir góða þjónustu".	that then give some little before good service".	but then some people get little for good service".
Konungur kveðst því ráða vilja hverjum hann gæfi gripi sína,	The-king said therefore decided wished each he gave possessions his,	The king said that he would decide who he would give his possessions to,
"vil eg ei snúa orðum Halla til hins verra þeim er tvíræði eru".	"wish I not return words Halli to his worst they are ambiguous are".	for I do not wish to turn Halli's words to the worse, which are ambiguous in a bad sense".
Konungur bað kalla Halla og svo var gert.	The-king asked to-call Halli and so was done.	The king asked to call Halli, and it was done.
Halli laut honum.	Halli bowed to-him.	Halli bowed to him.

The Tale of Sarcastic Halli (Old Icelandic)

Old Icelandic	Literal	English
Konungur bað Halla mæla nokkur tvíræðisorð við Þóru drottningu	The-king ordered Halli speak something ambiguous about Thora the-queen	The king asked Halli to say some ambiguous words to Queen Thora
"og vit hversu hún þolir".	"and know how-so she endures".	and know how she endures it.
Halli laut þá að Þóru og kvað:	Halli bowed then to Thora and said:	Halli bowed then to Thora and said:
Þú ert maklegust miklu, munar stórum það, Þóra, flenna upp að enni allt leðr Haralds reðri.	You are the-best much, delight great that, Thora, to-extend up to brow all skin Harald's genitals.	You are the-best much, delight great that, Thora, to-extend up to brow all the skin of Harald's genitals.
"Takið hann og drepið",	"Take him and kill",	"Take him and kill him",
segir drottning.	said the-queen.	said the queen.
"Vil eg eigi hafa hrópyrði hans".	"Will I not have obscenities his".	"I will not have his obscenities".
Konungur bað öngvan svo djarfan vera að á Halla tæki hér fyrir:	The-king ordered none so daring be that to Halli take force for:	The king ordered that no one should dare take Halli by force:
"En að því má gera ef þér þykir önnur maklegri til að liggja hjá mér og vera drottning og kanntu varla að heyra lof þitt".	"But that then may done if you think another more-suitable that to lie beside me and be queen and know-you hardly to hear praise yours".	"But then it may be done if you think another is more suitable to lie beside me and be queen, and you hardly know how to hear your praise".
Þjóðólfur skáld hafði farið til Íslands meðan Halli var í burtu frá konungi.	Thjodolf poet had travelled to Iceland while Halli was to away from the-king.	The poet Thjodolf had gone to Iceland while Halli was away from the king.
Þjóðólfur hafði flutt utan af Íslandi hest góðan og vildi gefa konungi og lét Þjóðólfur leiða hestinn í konungsgarð og sýna konungi.	Thjodolf had brought out from Iceland a-horse good and wished to-give the-king and had Thjodolf lead the-horse to the-king and showed the-king.	Thjodolf had brought a good horse from Iceland and wanted to give it to the king, and he had Thjodolf lead the horse to the king's garden and show it to the king.
Konungurinn gekk að sjá hestinn og var mikill og feitur.	The-king went to see the-horse and was great and stout.	The king went to see the horse and it was big and fat.

The Tale of Sarcastic Halli (Old Icelandic)

Old Icelandic	Literal	English
Halli var þar hjá er hesturinn hafði úti sinina.	Halli was there beside when horse had extended-out tendon.	Halli was there when the horse extended its tendon.
Halli kvað þá:	Halli spoke then:	Halli then spoke:
Sýr er ávallt, hefir saurugt allt hestr Þjóðólfs erðr, hann er drottinserðr.	Sow as always, has filthy all horse Thjodolf's beam, he is master-wounder.	Sow as always, has filthy all horse Thjodolf's beam, he is master-wounder.
"Tví, tví",	"Tut, tut",	"Tut tut",
segir konungur, "hann kemur aldrei í mína eigu að þessu".	said the-king, "he comes never in mine ownership at this".	said the king, "he will not come into my ownership at this rate".
Halli gerðist hirðmaður konungs og bað sér orlofs til Íslands.	Halli became court-man the-king's and asked him vacation to Iceland.	Halli became the king's court man and asked him for leave to vacate to Iceland.
Konungur bað hann fara varlega fyrir Einar flugu.	The-king bid him travel warily because-of Einar Fly.	The king asked that he travel carefully because of Einar Fly.
Halli fór til Íslands og bjó þar.	Halli went to Iceland and settled there.	Halli went to Iceland and settled there.
Eyddust honum peningar og lagðist hann í útróður	Spent his money and lay he to out-rowing (fishing)	He spent his money and he took to fishing,
og eitt sinn fékk hann andróða svo mikinn að þeir tóku nauðulega land.	and one occasion had he difficulty so much that they took necessarily land.	and on one occasion he had so much difficulty rowing back that they just reached land.
Og um kveldið var borinn fyrir Halla grautur	And about evening was brought before Halli porridge	That evening porridge was brought before Halli,
og er hann hafði etið fá bita hnígur hann aftur og var þá dauður.	and as he had to-eat few bites fell he back and was then dead.	and when he had eaten a few bites, he fell back and was then dead.
Haraldur spurði lát tveggja hirðmanna sinna af Íslandi,	Harald learned had both court-men his from Iceland,	Harald learned of the death of both his court men from Iceland,
Bolla hins prúða og Sneglu-Halla.	Bolli the Elegant and Sarcastic-Halli.	Bolli the Elegant, and Sarcastic Halli.
Hann svaraði svo til Bolla:	He answered so to Bolli:	He said of Bolli:

The Tale of Sarcastic Halli (Old Icelandic)

Old Icelandic	Literal	English
"Fyrir dörrum mun drengurinn hnigið hafa".	"Before spears would the-boy fallen had".	"The boy must have fallen to spears".
En til Halla sagði hann svo:	And to Halli said he so:	And he said of Halli:
"Á grauti mundi greyið sprungið hafa".	"On porridge would the-poor-thing burst have".	"The poor thing must have burst eating porridge".
Lýk eg þar sögu frá Sneglu-Halla.	End I there the-story from Sarcastic-Halli.	And there I end the story of Sarcastic Halli.

Word List *(Old Icelandic to English)*

Old Icelandic	English
að	a, and, as, at, by, for, in, it, of, than, that, the, this, to, with
aðra	another, other, others
aðrir	other
af	from, from, in, man, of, of, off
afli	power
aftur	again, back, returning
afvirti	disrespected
Agðanes	Agdanes (place)
Agðaness	Agdanes (place)
Agði	Agdi (name), Agdi (name)
akta	taxes
aldrei	never, never
aldri	age
alla	completely
allir	all, all
allra	all, of-all, of-all
allreiður	all-angry
allskammur	very-short
allt	all
allur	all
allvel	all-well
andaður	dead
andróða	difficulty
annað	another, other
annan	another, one, the-next
annar	another, another, otherwise
annarra	other
annars	another, other

Á, á

Old Icelandic	English
á	a, about, an, at, be, by, for, from, in, it, of, on, that, to, was, with
ábyrgst	responsible
áðr	before
áður	after, back, before
ágætur	excellent
ári	all-year
Árnasonar	Son-of-Arni (name)
át	ate, ate
átt	had
átti	had, hat, married, related-to
áttu	had
ávallt	always

Æ, æ

Old Icelandic	English
æpir	cried-out
æptu	called-out
ær	awed
ærið	greatly
ætla	suppose, suppose, supposed
ætlað	intended
ætluðu	intended
ætt	descent
ættaður	descended
ætti	had
ættsmár	family-small

B, b

Old Icelandic	English
bað	asked, bid, invited, ordered
báðir	both
bæði	both
bæjar	the-town
bændur	farmers

Word List (Old Icelandic to English)

Old Icelandic	English
bænum	town
bæta	compensation
bæti	compensate
bætti	compensated
baki	back
banasök	death-sentence
bani	death
bar	bears, bore, carried
Bárð	Bard (name)
Bárður	Bard (name)
barn	a-child, child
barna	children
báru	carried
báti	the-boat, the-ship's-boat
bátinum	the-boat
bauð	invited
bauglands	ring-land
beggja	both
beið	waited
beiddi	asked
bekkinn	the-bench
belti	belt
best	best, the-best
betr	better
betra	better
betri	a-better
bið	order
biðja	ask, to-ask
bita	bites
bitar	bite
bitið	biting
bjó	lived, settled
blakir	pale
bleikr	pale
boði	order
bokkar	bigger-men
Bolla	Bolli (name)
bóndi	farmer, master
borð	boards
borði	table, the-table
borðið	table, the-table
borðin	tables
borðum	at-table
börg	the-city
borin	brought
borinn	brought
börnin	the-children
bótunum	compensation
brá	drew
brákar	breaker
brást	transformed
brátt	soon
brauði	bread
brenndan	burnt
bróðir	brother
bróður	brother
brögðóttan	cunning
brosti	grinned, laughed, smiled
brott	away, brought
brottu	away
brúki	use
brynju	chain-mail, coat-of-mail
brynjuna	coat-of-mail
búð	lodgings
búðarvörð	shop-keeping
búfinna	farmers
búi	estate
búinn	prepared, settled
búnir	prepared, ready
burt	away
burtu	away
býð	command
býður	offered
byggð	settled
byr	fair-wind

D, d

Old Icelandic	English
dæmi	examples
dag	day
dagana	day
daginn	the-day
Danmerkur	Denmark (place)
dáruskapur	mockery
dauðan	death
dauðir	dead
dauður	dead
deild	room

Word List (Old Icelandic to English)

Old Icelandic	English
digrastur	thick-set
disk	plate
diskinum	the-plate
diskur	a-plate
djarfan	daring
dönum	the-Danes (name)
dörrum	spears
dóttur	daughter
drap	killed
drápa	drapa (poem)
drápi	the-killing
drápu	a-drapa (poem), drapa
drápuna	the-drapa (poem)
draum	dream, this-dream
draumur	a-dream, dream
dregr	draws
dregst	draw
dregur	drew
drekanum	the-dragon-ship
dreki	dragon
drekka	drinking
drengi	boys
drengurinn	the-boy
drepa	kill
drepið	kill, killed
drepur	killed
dreymt	dreamed
drógu	drew
drottinserðr	master-wounder
drottning	queen, the-queen
drottningu	the-queen
drykk	drink
drykkjar	drink
duldu	denied
dverg	the-dwarf
dverginn	the-dwarf
dvergur	dwarf
dýran	fine

E, e

Old Icelandic	English
eða	and, but, or
ef	if
eftir	after, back, back-from
eg	I, me
eggjaði	urged
ei	not
eiga	not, own
eigi	not
eigu	ownership
eina	one
Einar	Einar (name)
Einari	Einar (name)
Einars	Einar (name), Einar's (name)
einhugi	one-minded
einkis	nothing
einmælt	one-meal
einn	alone, one
einráðir	one-decision
einu	one
eitt	once, one
ekki	not, nothing
eld	the-fire
eldahús	fire-house (kitchen)
eldi	fire
eldilegt	elderly
eldur	fire
ella	or-else
elskaði	loved
Emmu	Emma (name)
en	and, but, than, that, then
enda	and, ended, in-the-end, the-end
endilausu	nonsense
enga	not
engan	no
engi	no, none
enginn	none
Englandi	England (place)
Englands	England (place)
engu	none
engum	no
enn	but, one, the, then
enna	yet
enni	brow, forehead

Word List (Old Icelandic to English)

Old Icelandic	English
er	am, am-I, are, as, I, in, is, that, then, to, was, what, when, where, which, who
erðr	beam
erindi	errand, message
ert	are
ertu	are-you
eru	are, we-are
eruð	they-are
erum	are, are-we
eta	eat, eating
etið	to-eat
etja	provoke
etur	eat
eyddust	spent
eyjar	islands

F, f

Old Icelandic	English
fá	few, get, give
faðir	father
fæ	can
fær	accomplished
færa	bring, brought
færð	carry-out, undertaking
færði	performed
færðr	brought
færu	went
fæturnir	the-legs
Fáfni	Fafnir (name)
Fáfnisbana	Slayer-of-Fafnir (name)
fagnar	welcomed
fám	a-few
fann	found
far	go, passage, travel
fara	fare, go, goes, going, sent-for, travel, went
farið	travelled
farist	gone
fars	travel
fátæka	poor
fátækra	the-poor
fátækur	fee-taken
fáum	get
fé	money, payment
fébætur	compensation
féð	the-money
féhirði	fee-servant
féhirðinn	fee-servant
feitur	stout
fékk	give, got, had
fékkst	received
félagi	companion
féll	fell
felldan	killed
fellt	fell
fémúta	money-bribe
fengu	caught
fénu	money
fer	go, goes, went
festi	pierced
fimm	five
finna	find, found, the-Sami (name)
finnferð	Finland-voyages (place)
finnskrepp	Sami-goods
firðinum	the-fjord
firrst	lost
fiskimenn	fishermen
fjár	fee
fjölda	many
fjöldi	many
fjölmennt	followers
fjör	life
fjóra	four
fjórar	four
fjórðung	fourth
fjórtán	fourteen
flærat	fleeing
fleira	more
fleiri	more
flenna	to-extend
flest	the-most
flesta	most
Fljótum	Fljot (place)
Fluga	Fly (name)
Flugu	Fly (name)
flugust	flew

Word List (Old Icelandic to English)

Old Icelandic	English
flutt	brought, delivered
flutti	brought
flýta	quickly
flytja	carried
föður	father
föðurbana	father's-killer
fólk	people
föll	mistakes
föng	rhymes
fór	for, travelled, went
för	before, going, procession
forskeftinu	upper-shaft
fórstu	went-you
fóru	went
fórum	travel
förum	journey
forvitnar	fore-knowing
fót	leg
fótum	feet
frá	from
frændi	kinsman
frændunum	kinsmen
frændur	kinsman
fram	ahead, away, forwards, from
framar	from
frásagnar	from-saying
frásagnir	stories
frísa	Frisian (name)
frískur	Frisian
fullt	full
fullur	full
fund	to-meet
fundum	found
fundumst	met
furðulega	extremely
fús	willing
fylgdin	followers
fylgja	follow
fyndi	find
fyrir	because-of, before, for, intestines, over
fyrr	before
fyrra	before, last
fyrri	before, went-before
fyrst	first
fyrstu	first

G, g

Old Icelandic	English
gabb	mockery
gæfi	gave
gæfur	agreeable
gætti	guarded
gaf	gave
gakk	go
galdra	magic
gamall	old
gaman	a-delight, delight, enjoyment, entertaining, fun, to-delight
gamans	amusement
ganga	go
gangi	go
gap	gaping
garðinn	garden, the-house, the-wall
garðinum	the-wall
garðsins	the-wall
garðurinn	the-wall
Gásum	Gasir (place)
gefa	give, granted, to-give
gefi	give
gefið	given
gefin	given
Geirröð	Geirrod (name)
Geirröðr	Geirrod (name)
gekk	got, went
geng	going
gengju	walking
gengr	going
gengu	went
ger	do, does
gera	do, doing, done, made, make
gerast	be
gerði	did, made
gerðir	done
gerðist	became

Word List (Old Icelandic to English)

Old Icelandic	English
gerðu	did, made
geri	did, made
gerið	do
gerir	does
gert	do, done
gervan	look-to
get	get
getið	told
gilja	beguile
giljum	beguile
ginning	deception
gista	guest
gjalda	pay
gjarna	gladly
gjör	ready-made
gjörla	completely
glaðr	glad
glaður	glad
gnadda	gnawing
góð	good
góða	good
góðan	good
góðum	good
góður	good
gólf	the-floor
gólfið	of-the-floor, the-floor
göngum	going, we-are-going
gott	good
grafið	dug
graut	porridge
grautar	of-porridge
grauti	porridge
grautinn	porridge, the-porridge
grautur	porridge
greppr	grasped
greyið	the-poor-thing
grið	peace
griðníðingur	truce-breaker
gripanna	the-trinkets
gripi	possessions, treasure
gripina	the-trinkets
gripuna	the-trinkets
gripur	possession
grís	pig
grön	moustache
gruntrauðustum	deep-red
Guðinason	Godwinson (name)
guðréttilegast	good-rightly
gulaþing	Gula-assembly (name)
gulaþings	Gula-assembly (name)
gullhlað	gold-band
gullhring	a-gold-ring, gold-ring
gullrekin	gold-inlaid
gyrti	equipped

H, h

Old Icelandic	English
haddan	the-handle, the-lid
háðyrðum	mocking
hærra	higher
hærri	higher
hæst	high
hætti	stopped
hættu	danger
haf	have
hafa	had, has, have, having, to-have
hafði	had
hafðir	had, have
hafðist	had
hafi	has
hafnan	the harbour
hafra	goat
Hákon	Hakon (name)
Hákoni	Hakon (name)
halda	hold, to-hold
haldið	held
hálfa	half
Halla	Halli (name), Halli's (name)
hallæri	famine
Halli	Halli (name)
Hálogaland	Halogaland (place)
Hálogalandi	Halogaland (place)
háls	neck
hálslangur	long-neck
hana	her

Word List (Old Icelandic to English)

Old Icelandic	English
handlaugar	hand-washing
handsíður	long-armed
hann	he, him
hans	he, him, his
hár	high
Haraldi	Harald (name), Harald's (name)
haraldr	Harald (name), Harald's (name)
Haralds	Harald (name), Harald's (name)
Haraldur	Harald (name)
Háreks	Harek's (name)
háreysti	commotion
hárinu	the-hairs
hásætið	high-seat
haustið	autumn
haustum	autumn
héðan	from-there
hefði	had
hefðir	had
hefðu	had
hefðum	have
hefir	had, has, has-been, have
hefna	avenge
hefnt	avenged, revenge
hefur	had
heiði	the-heath
heill	health
heilræði	sound-advice
heim	home
hein	hone
heinasmjör	honing-grease
heita	call, named
heitan	threat
heitir	is-named, named
hékk	hung
held	think
heldr	rather
hella	pour, poured
hellt	rather
helst	rather
hélt	held
hendi	hand, hands, to-hand
hendur	hand
hér	force, here
herbergi	hostel
herbergjum	sleeping-quarters
herðilítill	narrow-shouldered
herðimestur	most-hardy
herra	lord
hest	a-horse
hestinn	the-horse
hestr	horse
hesturinn	horse
hét	named, was-named
héti	named
heyra	hear, heard, to-hear
heyrði	heard
heyrðu	heard
heyrt	heard
hið	the
hilmis	helmsman's
hin	the
hina	the
hinn	the
hins	his, the
hinum	the
hirð	the-court
hirðarinnar	court
hirði	care
hirðin	courtiers
hirðinni	the-court, the-court-men
hirðmaður	court-man
hirðmanna	court-men
Hítrar	Hitra (place)
hitt	then
hjá	beside, nearby
hjálm	helmet
hjálmfaldinn	the-helmet
Hlaðajarli	Earl-of-Lade (name)
hlaðna	ladened
hlaupi	running
hlaut	a-lot-of
hleyp	running
hleypur	ran
hljóð	a-hearing, silence
hljóða	calm
hljóðgreipum	sound-grippers (ears)

Word List (Old Icelandic to English)

Old Icelandic	English
hljóðið	silence
hljóðs	be-heard
hljóp	jumped
hljópu	ran
hlotist	part
hlut	part, share
hluti	a-thing, things
hlutur	part
hlýða	obeying, suits
hlýði	listen
hnakka	neck
hníf	knife
hnífi	knife
hnífinum	knife
hnífskafti	knife-handle
hnigið	fallen
hnígur	fell
hnúskum	knocked-down
höfðingja	chieftains
höfðu	had
hófi	reasonable
höfuð	head
höfuðið	head
höfuðskáld	chief-poet
höggva	to-strike
höldnu	held
höllina	the-hall
höllunni	the-hall
hönd	hand
höndum	hand
honum	he, him, his, of-him, to-him
horfa	turn
horfin	lost
hornspónu	horn-spoon
hóti	not
hótun	a-threat
hræddir	afraid
hraustlega	boldly
hríð	awhile
hring	the-ring
hringinn	the-ring
hringinum	the-ring
hringum	circles
hroðið	cleared
hróður	fame
hrökkviskafls	shaken
hröng	roaring
hrópyrði	obscenities
hrygg	the-spine
hryggurinn	spine
húðar	hide
hug	mind
hugar	minds
hugði	thought
hugðu	thought
humrum	lobsters
hún	it, she
hungrar	hungry
hús	a-house
hvað	that, what
hvar	where
hve	how
hver	what, who
hverft	disappeared
hverfur	turned
hvergi	none, nowhere
hverju	what
hverjum	each
hvern	each, what, whom
hvers	how-so
hversu	how-so
hvert	each, what, where
hví	why
hvofteldingum	encouraged-lightning
hvor	each
hvorigum	neither
hvort	each, whether
hvorttveggja	each-way
hvoru	which
hygg	think

I, i

Old Icelandic	English
iðnar	trade
ilfat	sole-bucket
illa	bad, badly, evil
illan	evil
illt	ill
ilvegs	evil-ways
inn	in, of, then

Word List (Old Icelandic to English)

Old Icelandic	English
innan	in, inside
innanborðs	onboard
innar	in

Í, í

í	about, as, at, by, in, into, of, on, that, the, to, with
Ísland	Iceland (place)
Íslandi	Iceland (place)
Íslands	Iceland (place)
íslandsfari	Iceland-voyage
íslendinga	Icelanders
íslendingar	Icelanders
íslenska	Icelander
íslenskan	Icelander
íslenskur	an-Icelander, Icelander

J, j

jafnan	always, equally, usually
jafngreypilega	equally-badly
jafnir	equal
jafnsleppt	equally-slip
jarl	an-earl, earl
járn	iron-weapon
járnsmiður	ironsmith
jaxlar	molars
jöfnum	even
jóladag	Yule-day
jólin	Yule
jólunum	Yule
Jótlands	Jutland (place)
jötni	giant
jötun	the-giant

K, k

kæra	accuse
kærleikum	dear-friendship, friendship
kálf	a-calf
kálfinn	the-calf
kálfurinn	the-calf
kalla	to-call
kallaði	called
kallaðir	be-called
kallaður	called
kann	can, can-it, knows
kanntu	know-you
karlmanni	a-man
kastað	cast
kastaði	cast
katlinum	the-kettle
kátur	cheerful
kaup	traded
Kaupangs	Kapuang (place)
Kaupangur	Kaupang (place)
kaupferð	trading-voyage
kaupmennirnir	merchant-men
kaupmönnum	the-trading-men, trading-men
kaupskipinu	merchant-ship, trading-ship
kem	come
kemur	came, come, comes
kenn	know
kenna	know, teach
kenndi	felt
kennt	blame
keyptuð	bought
kilju	the-binding
kjöts	flesh
klámyrði	obscene
klámyrðum	obscene-words
klappaði	rapped, struck
klappar	hammering
klukku	a-bell
kné	knee
knörru	knorrs
kölluðu	called
köllum	call
kolluvísur	cow-verses
kom	came, come
koma	come, come-forward
komið	came, come, coming
kominn	coming

Word List (Old Icelandic to English)

Old Icelandic	English
komnir	coming
komst	came
komu	came
komum	came
konung	the-king
konunga	kings
konungi	the-king, the-king's
konunginn	the-king
konunginum	the-king
konungr	king, king's, the-king
konungs	the-king, the-king's
konungsgarð	the-king
konungsins	the-king
konungur	the-king, the-king's
konungurinn	the-king
kostur	a-choice
kunna	know
kunnu	could
kurfaldi	folded
kurteis	polite
kvað	recited, said, spoke
kvaddi	called, greeted
kváðu	recited
kvæði	composed, poem, poems, recited
kvæðið	poem, the-poem
kvæðin	poems
kvæðinu	the-poem
kvæðisins	the-poem
kvæðislaun	poem-reward
kvæðismynd	poem-image
kvæðunum	the-poetry
kveð	recite, say
kveða	compose, recite
kveðið	reciting, spoken, worded
kveðin	recited, worded
kveðinn	composed
kveðju	greeting
kveðst	said
kveður	recited, words
kveld	the-evening
kveldið	evening
kvenna	women
kviðlingur	short-poem
kyns	kin

Old Icelandic	English
kýr	cows
kýrkaupi	cow-buying
kyrrt	peace, peaceful

L, l

Old Icelandic	English
lá	lay
læt	have, let
lagði	became, laid
lagðist	lay
lagin	assigned
lágu	lay
láguð	laid
lágum	laid
land	land
landi	land, the-land
landinu	the-land
langa	long
langskip	longships
lát	had, have, have
láta	allow, have
látið	had, let
látir	leave
launa	reward
launaði	rewarded
launin	repay
laus	lost
laut	bowed
leðr	skin
legg	lay
leggja	allow, lay
leggur	laid
leið	passed
leiða	lead
leiðar	on-way
leigðu	rented
leika	games, play
leist	with-footwear
leista	of-footwear
leita	find, look-for, seek, seeking
leitaði	sought
leitaðir	seek
lendi	lands
lendur	land

Word List (Old Icelandic to English)

Old Icelandic	English
lengi	long
lér	leaned
lét	had
létti	let-up
léttum	let-up
leys	repay
leyst	answered
líf	life
lífi	life
lífinu	his-life, your-life
liggja	lie
líkaði	liked
líkar	like, liked
líklegur	likely
líkur	like
lít	coloured
lítast	looked
lítið	little
lítil	little
lítilla	little
lítils	little
lítilþægir	easily-satisfied
lítilþægur	little-behaving
lítinn	little
litist	looked
litlu	a-little
lítt	little
ljóst	light
ljótlimaður	ugly-limbed
ljúgi	lie
loðir	of-your-hair
lof	permission, praise
lofa	promise
loft	praised
lofuðu	praised
lögðum	laid
lögskilum	legal-settlement
lokið	concluded, ended, finished
lyftingunni	lifting
lýgur	lies, lying
lýk	end
lykkja	noose
lykkjan	the-noose
lysti	appetite
lýsu	the-whitings

M, m

Old Icelandic	English
má	may
maður	a-man, man, the-man
maðurinn	the-man
mæl	speak
mæla	matter, matters, say, speak
mælti	spoke
mæltist	recited
mæltur	talked
mættum	met
Magnús	Magnus (name)
maka	equal
maklegra	well-deserved
maklegri	more-suitable
maklegust	the-best
mál	matter
málefnum	matters
málið	the-matter
máls	matter
málum	matter, matters
mann	man, men
manna	man, men, people
manni	man
mannsbarn	man's-son
marga	many
margir	many
margs	many, many-things
margt	many
mat	food
matar	food
matr	food
mátti	as-might, may
matur	food
með	with
meðan	as-long-as, while
megum	may
mein	harm
meir	more
meira	more
meiri	more
menn	men, people

Word List (Old Icelandic to English)

Old Icelandic	English
menntur	educated
mér	for-me, I, me, mine, my, to-me
merkur	marks
mest	most
mesta	most
mestum	most
mettir	finished-eating, satisfied
mettur	finished-eating, satisfied
mig	me
mikið	great, much
mikill	great, much
mikinn	much
mikla	great, greatest
miklagarði	Byzantium (place)
miklu	much
miklum	much
milli	between
mína	mine, my
minn	mine
minna	less, lesser, mine
míns	mine
mínu	mine
mínum	mine
mislíkaði	mis-liked
missa	lose, miss
mitt	mine, the-middle
mjög	much
mjöl	meal
mönnum	people, the-people
morguninn	morning
mörk	a-mark, one-mark
mörkina	the-border
móti	against, meet
mun	could, shall, should, should-be, will, would, would-be
munað	remembered
munaður	remembered
munar	delight
mundi	could-be, remembered, should-be, would
mundir	would
mundu	could, would

Old Icelandic	English
muni	shall
munni	mouth
munt	must, should
muntu	shall-you, should, would-you
munu	shall, would
munuð	shall

N, n

Old Icelandic	English
ná	obtain, take
naðri	serpent
næði	neared
nær	near
nærri	close-to, near
næst	near
næsta	next
nafn	named
nam	took
námu	took
nauðsyn	necessary
nauðsynja	needs
nauðulega	necessarily
nautaleðrs	ox-skin
neðan	below
neflangr	long-nosed
nefndur	named
nei	no
nema	but, except
níð	slander
níðið	the-slander
niður	down
Njörðr	Njord (name)
njót	enjoy
njótum	benefit
nóg	enough
nokkra	any
nokkru	one-of, some, somehow, somewhat
nokkrum	some
nokkuð	anything, something, somewhat
nokkur	some, something
norður	north
norðurlönd	northern-lands

Word List (Old Icelandic to English)

Old Icelandic	English
Noreg	Norway (place)
Noregi	Norway (place)
Noregs	Norway (place)
nótt	night, the-night
nóttum	nights
nú	no, not, now

O, o

Old Icelandic	English
of	of
ofan	over
offylli	gluttony
ofraun	too-much
oftar	more
og	also, and
olli	cause
opið	open
orð	word
orða	words
orðaskil	words-separated
orðfall	word-fallen
orðgreppur	word-bold
orðhákur	word-tall
orðhvass	sharp-tongued
orðið	become, worded
orðinn	of-words
orðum	words
orlofs	vacation
ormr	the-serpent
ort	composed, worded, words
orti	worded
oss	to-us, us, we

Ó, ó

Old Icelandic	English
óeinarðarmaður	unreliable
ógurlegur	terrible
óp	shouting
ósiðblandnir	un-custom-mixing
óskert	the-whole
ótæpt	unsettled
óþökk	un-thanks
ótiginna	un-ranking
ótrúlegir	un-truthful
óvirðulegt	unworthy

Ö, ö

Old Icelandic	English
öðru	the-other
öðrum	eachother, other, others
öðruvís	other-knowing
öfugt	reversed
öfundsjúkur	un-infatuated
öll	all
öllu	all
öndvert	upside-down
öngum	no
öngvan	no, none
önnur	another
ösku	ashes
öxarinnar	the-axe
öxi	an-axe, axe
öxina	the-axe

P, p

Old Icelandic	English
peningar	money
peningum	payment
prettum	trickery
prettur	trick
prófa	prove
Prúða	Elegant (name)
prýði	finery

R, r

Old Icelandic	English
ráð	advice, advisable, plan
ráða	decide, decided
ráði	advised
ráðinn	appointed
ráðleitinn	cunning
ráðs	agreement
ráðugastur	well-advising
ræð	speak

Word List (Old Icelandic to English)

Old Icelandic	English
ræsi	the-ruler
rán	robbery
rana	the-trunk
Ránar	Ran (name)
randa	round
rangt	wrong
rannsóknar	a-search
Rauð	Raud (name)
rauðan	the-red
rauðar	red
rauðum	red
Rauður	Raud (name)
réð	ruled
reðri	genitals
réðst	appointed, took
réðust	decided
reiðasti	most-angry
reiði	anger
Rein	Reine (place)
reru	rowing
rétti	extended
réttur	upright
reyndar	actually
reyndust	proved
reynt	tested
ríkari	richer
ritað	written
rúghleifa	rye-loaf
rúms	rooms
runa	row
ryðja	cleared
rymskyndir	quickly-cleared

S, s

Old Icelandic	English
sá	looked, saw, so
sæhafa	sea-scattered
sækir	sought
sæsjúkur	seasick
sæti	sit
sætis	seat
sættir	settlements
sættust	settled
sagði	said, said, told, told-of
sagðir	said
sagðist	said
sagt	said, said, told, told-to
sakir	sake
saklausa	sake-less
sama	same
saman	together
sami	same
samir	common
sannmæli	true-words
sarð	wounded
satt	true, truth
sátu	sat, were
sáu	saw
saurugt	filthy
sé	am, see, so
séð	seen
seen	so
seg	tell
seggr	said
segi	say
segið	tell
segir	said, told
segja	say, tell, to-tell
seinþreyttur	persistent
seldag	sold
selja	barter, to-sell
sem	as, same-as, than, where, which
send	send
sendi	sent
sendingum	delivery
sennur	chatter
sér	for-him, him, himself, his, saw, sees, themselves, to
serðast	to-get-hurt
sessunaut	bench-companion
sessunautur	bench-companion
sest	sat
setið	sat
setja	set
settist	sat, settled
settlega	sedately
settu	set

Word List (Old Icelandic to English)

Old Icelandic	English
séuð	look
síð	long, since
síðan	after, afterwards, since, then
síðar	afterwards, later
síðast	the-last
síðr	since
síðu	side
siður	a-custom, the-custom
sig	him, himself
sigldi	sailed
sigldu	sailed
Sigurð	Sigurd (name)
Sigurðarson	Sigurdson (name)
Sigurði	Sigurd (name)
Sigurðr	Sigurd (name)
Sigurður	Sigurd (name)
silfri	silver
silfrinu	the-silver
silfur	silver
silfurhólkur	silver-band
silfurs	of-silver
silfurvafið	silver-wound
sín	his, themselves
sína	his
sinina	tendon
sinn	his, occasion, theirs, then
sinna	his
sinnar	his, their
sinni	himself, these
síns	his
sínu	his
sínum	his, theirs
sínumegin	on-his-side
síst	least
sit	sit
sitja	settle, sit
sitk	one
sitt	himself, his, their, this
situr	sat
síu	sift
sjá	see
sjaldan	seldom
sjálfum	himself
sjálfur	yourself
sjóða	boil
sjóði	purse
sjóðnum	the-purse
sjúkur	sick
skaði	harm
skaftið	the-shaft
skal	shall, should
skál	shall
skáld	a-poet, poet, poets, the-poet
skálda	poets
skáldi	the-poet
skáldskap	poetry
skáldskapar	a-poet
skall	hit, rattled
skalt	shall
skaltu	shall-you
skapdreki	mood-dragon
skapi	mind, mood
skarlatsklæðum	scarlet
skemmt	entertainment
skemmta	entertain
skerði	cuts
skilað	settled
skinna	of-skins
skip	ship, the-ship
skipið	ship, the-ship
skipin	the-ships
skipinu	the-ship
skipsmiðir	ship-smiths
skipt	exchange
skipuðu	ships
skjöld	shield
skjótt	quickly, rapidly
skó	shoes
skömm	disgrace, scandal
skreið	crawled
skreppa	bag
skreppuskrúði	bag-tackle
skuld	debt
skulu	should
skuluð	should
skulum	shall
skyldara	should

Word List (Old Icelandic to English)

Old Icelandic	English
skyldi	should, would
skyldu	should, should-be, would
skylt	should
sleggju	the-hammer
slíðrar	sheathed
slík	such
slíka	such
slíkir	such
slíkt	such
smiðbelgja	smith-bellows
smiðju	of-the-smith
smjörvan	buttered
snætt	dined
snák	snake
snaraði	rushed
Sneglu-Halla	Sarcastic-Halli (name)
Sneglu-Halli	Sarcastic-Halli (name)
sneri	turned
snúa	return
snúið	turned
soðtrogsvísur	food-trough-verses
sofa	sleep
sögðu	told
sögðuð	announced
sögðust	said
sögu	the-story
son	son
sótt	sickness
spara	withhold
spón	a-spoon
sprengja	burst
sprungið	burst
spryngi	burst
spurði	asked, asking, learned
spurðu	asked
spurt	heard, questions
spyr	asked
Stað	Stad (place), the-place
staðar	place
stærri	greater
standa	standing
standið	standing
steiktur	roasted
steinkatli	stone-kettle
steinn	a-stone
stendr	standing
stendur	stands
stígandi	ascending
stillir	heading
stóð	place, stood
stórlyndur	large-repaying (generous)
stórmannlega	big-man-like
stórra	great
stórum	great
stræti	the-street
stríði	battles
ströndu	the-shore
stund	awhile
stund	awhile
stundu	awhile
stykki	piece
stýrimaður	steersman
stýrir	steers
styrk	strong
sú	yours
suður	south
suðurmenn	southern-men, the-southerners
sufli	with-bread
sumar	summer
sumargamlan	one-summer-old
sumir	some
sumt	some
sútari	tanner
svangir	hungry
svara	answer, to-answer
svarað	answered
svaraði	answered
svarar	answered
Svarfaðardal	Svarfadardal (place)
svefni	sleep
sveini	this-lad
sveltir	starving
sverð	sword
sverði	a-sword, sword
sverðið	sword

Word List (Old Icelandic to English)

Old Icelandic	English
svífst	shrinks-from
svíni	swine
svo	so, then
sýlt	sleek
sýna	showed
sýnast	appear
sýndi	showed
sýndist	thought
sýnir	show
sýnist	seems
synjuðu	refused
sýr	sow
sýslu	business, stewardship
systkinum	siblings

T, t

Old Icelandic	English
tæki	take
tak	take
taka	take
taki	takes
takið	take
takist	take
tala	speak, speaking
talað	talking
talaði	talked
talast	speak
tangar	tongs
taum	leash
taumsendanum	the-leash
taumsins	the-leash
tekið	taken
tekist	taken
tíðinda	news
tíðindi	news
tignari	nobler
tigulegur	dignified
til	about, as, for, into, that, to, towards, until, up-to
tíma	time
tíu	ten
tjöru	tar
tók	received, took
tóku	took
tókuð	took
tókum	took
töluðu	spoke
torf	turf
trog	trough
trúa	believe
túngarði	hayfield-wall
Túta	Tuta (name)
Tútu	Tuta (name)
tveföld	two-fold
tveggja	both
tveir	two
tví	tut
tvíræði	ambiguous
tvíræðisorð	ambiguous
tvo	two

Þ, þ

Old Icelandic	English
þá	then
það	it, than, that, the, this
þaðan	from-there
þær	there
þætti	seems
þættist	thought
þagna	silence
þagnaði	silenced
þakkaði	thanked
þangað	from-there
þann	that, then
þar	that, there, they, they
þarmr	intestines
þars	there
þau	that, there
þegar	as-soon-as, early, from-there, straight-away, then
þegnar	men
þeim	for-them, them, they
þeir	the, them, they
þeirra	theirs, them
þeirri	of-them, theirs
þenna	then, this
þér	to-you, you, yours

Word List (Old Icelandic to English)

Old Icelandic	English
þess	this
þessa	this
þessar	this
þessi	these, this
þessu	this
þetta	it, that, these, this
þið	you-two
þig	you
þiggi	receives
þing	assembly
þinga	assemble
þingið	the-assembly
þinginu	the-assembly
þings	the-assembly
þingsins	the-assembly
Þingvallar	Thingvellir (place)
þinn	yours
þíns	yours
þínu	yours
þínum	about
þitt	yours
Þjóðólf	Thjodolf (name)
Þjóðólfs	Thjodolf's (name)
Þjóðólfur	Thjodolf (name)
þjófur	thief
þjón	servant
þjóna	serve
þjónusta	service
þjónustu	service
þjónustumenn	the-servants
Þjóttu	Thjotta (place)
þó	though
þögnuðu	silenced
þökk	thanks
þola	enduring
þoldi	endured
þolir	endures
þöngul	there
Þór	Thor (name)
Þóra	Thora (name)
Þorbergs	Thorberg's (name)
þorði	dared
þörf	of-need
þori	dare
Þorleifi	Thorleif (name)
Þorleifur	Thorleif (name)
Þorljóti	Thorljot (name)
Þorljótur	Thorljot (name)
þorpi	village
Þórr	Thor (name)
Þóru	Thora (name)
þótt	though
þótti	seemed, thought
þóttir	thought
þóttist	seemed, thought
þóttu	thought
þóttust	thought
þræta	argued
þrætu	threatening
Þrándheim	Trondheim (place)
Þrándheims	Trondheim (place)
þrevett	three-winters-old
þriðja	a-third, third
þrjár	three
þrjú	three
þú	you
þulu	thula (poem)
þunga	heavy-cargo
þurfti	needed
þverlega	crossly
því	accordingly, because, before, if, since, then, therefore, why
þyki	seems, think
þykir	consider, considered, seems, think
þykja	seemed

U, u

Old Icelandic	English
um	about, at
undan	out-from, under
undarlegt	scandalous
undir	under
undur	wonder
undurskapaður	wonder-created
unnið	won
uns	until
upp	up, upped, up-to

Word List (Old Icelandic to English)

Old Icelandic	English	Old Icelandic	English
upphaf	beginning	vekja	awaken
utan	out, without	vel	well
utar	out	veltur	hung
		ver	be
		vér	are-we, we

Ú, ú

Old Icelandic	English	Old Icelandic	English
úr	from, out, out-of	vera	be, become, being, to-be, was
úrleysingur	over-praised	verða	be, becomes, have-been, worth
út	about, out, outside	verði	being
úthlaupi	out-running	verðrat	worthy-that
úti	extended-out, out	verður	becomes, worthy
útivist	out-journey	verið	become, been
útróður	out-rowing (fishing)	verk	work
		verkmanns	workman's

V, v

Old Icelandic	English	Old Icelandic	English
vændishöfðingjar	wicked-chieftain	verkum	actions
vænstur	promising	verr	worse
væri	being, was, were, would, would-be	verra	worse, worst
vætti	expected	verri	worse
vakið	awake	vert	worth
vaknaði	awoke	vetri	winter
válegrar	wretched	vetur	winter
vandi	difficult	veturinn	winter
vanr	custom	veturvistar	winter-lodgings, winter-provisions
var	was, were, who	við	about, against, at, from, of, to, we, with
varð	became, came, was, were	víg	slaying
varði	were	vil	will, wish
varðist	guarded	vildi	wanted, willed, wished
varla	hardly	vilja	wished
varlega	warily	viljið	wish
varp	threw	viljum	we-wish, wish
veðja	wager	vill	wishes
veðjanin	the-wager	vilt	will, wish
veðjanina	wager	viltu	will-you
veg	way	vinskapur	friendship
vegar	way	virti	worthied
veginn	killed	vísan	the-verse, verse
veik	turned	vissi	knew
veit	know, known	vissu	knew
veita	grant	vist	provisions
veitt	given	víst	certainly
		vistaðist	found-a-place
		vistar	lodgings

Word List (Old Icelandic to English)

Old Icelandic	English
vistin	the-supply
vistina	the-provisions
vísu	a-verse
vit	know, wit
vita	knew, know, to-know
vitið	know
vitrastur	the-wisest
vitsmuna	intellect
von	expected
vopnast	armed
vor	our
vorið	spring
vorkunn	understandable
voru	our, was, were, where
voruð	were
vorum	were

Y, y

yðrum	yours
yður	you
yðvar	of-you, you
yðvart	your, yours
yfir	over, sitting
ykkur	you
ynni	won
yrði	became
yrk	compose, write
yrkisefnin	the-themes
yrkja	compose, to-compose

Ý, ý

ýmsu	about
ýttum	pushed

Word List (English to Old Icelandic)

Word List *(English to Old Icelandic)*

English	*Old Icelandic*	*English*	*Old Icelandic*

A, a

English	Old Icelandic
a	á, á
about	á, á, á, á, á, á, á
an	á
at	á, á, á, á, á
and	að, að, að, að, að
as	að, að, að, að, að
another	aðra, áður, áður, áður, æpir, æptu, ær
after	áður, áður, áður
awed	ær
again	aftur
Agdanes (place)	Agðanes, Agðaness
Agdi (name)	Agði, Agði
age	aldri
all	allir, allir, allra, allreiður, allt, allur, allvel
all-angry	allreiður
all-well	allvel
all-year	ári
ate	át, át
always	ávallt, bað
asked	bað, bað, bað, báðir, bæði
a-child	barn
a-better	betri
ask	biðja
at-table	borðum
away	brott, brott, brottu, brynju, brynju
a-plate	diskur
a-drapa (poem)	drápu
a-dream	draumur
alone	einn
am	er, er
am-I	er
are	er, er, er, er
are-you	ertu
are-we	erum, eta
accomplished	fær
a-few	fám
ahead	fram
agreeable	gæfur
a-delight	gaman
amusement	gamans
a-gold-ring	gullhring
autumn	haustið, haustum
avenge	hefna
avenged	hefnt
a-horse	hest
a-lot-of	hlaut
a-hearing	hljóð
a-thing	hluti
a-threat	hótun
afraid	hræddir
awhile	hríð, hringum, hroðið, hróður
a-house	hús
an-Icelander	íslenskur
an-earl	jarl
accuse	kæra
a-calf	kálf
a-man	karlmanni, kastað
a-bell	klukku
a-choice	kostur
assigned	lagin
allow	láta, láta
answered	leyst, líf, lífi, lífinu
a-little	litlu
appetite	lysti
as-might	mátti
as-long-as	meðan
a-mark	mörk
against	móti, móti
any	nokkra
anything	nokkuð
also	og
ashes	ösku
an-axe	öxi
axe	öxi
advice	ráð
advisable	ráð
advised	ráði
appointed	ráðinn, ráðleitinn

Word List (English to Old Icelandic)

English	Old Icelandic
agreement	ráðs
a-search	rannsóknar
anger	reiði
actually	reyndar
afterwards	síðan, síðar
a-custom	siður
a-poet	skáld, skáldskapar
announced	sögðuð
a-spoon	spón
asking	spurði
a-stone	steinn
ascending	stígandi
answer	svara
a-sword	sverði
appear	sýnast
as-soon-as	þegar
assembly	þing
assemble	þinga
argued	þræta
a-third	þriðja
accordingly	því
ambiguous	tvíræði, tvíræðisorð
awake	vakið
awoke	vaknaði
awaken	vekja
actions	verkum
a-verse	vísu
armed	vopnast

B, b

English	Old Icelandic
be	á, á, á, á, á
by	á, á, á
before	áðr, aðra, áður, áður, áður, æpir, æptu, ær
back	áður, áður, æpir, æptu
bid	bað
both	báðir, bæði, bændur, bæta
bears	bar
bore	bar
Bard (name)	Bárð, Bárður
belt	belti
best	best
better	betr, betra
bites	bita
bite	bitar
biting	bitið
bigger-men	bokkar
Bolli (name)	Bolla
boards	borð
brought	borin, borinn, bótunum, brá, brákar, brauði, brenndan
breaker	brákar
bread	brauði
burnt	brenndan
brother	bróðir, bróður
boys	drengi
but	eða, ef, eftir, eftir
back-from	eftir
brow	enni
beam	erðr
bring	færa
because-of	fyrir
became	gerðist, gerðu, gerðu, geri
beguile	gilja, giljum
beside	hjá
be-heard	hljóðs
boldly	hraustlega
bad	illa
badly	illa
be-called	kallaðir
blame	kennt
bought	keyptuð
bowed	laut
Byzantium (place)	miklagarði
between	milli
below	neðan
benefit	njótum
become	orðið, ort, ösku
barter	selja
bench-companion	sessunaut, sessunautur
boil	sjóða
bag	skreppa
bag-tackle	skreppuskrúði
buttered	smjörvan
burst	sprengja, sprungið, spryngi

149

Word List (English to Old Icelandic)

English	Old Icelandic	English	Old Icelandic
big-man-like	stórmannlega	cheerful	kátur
battles	stríði	come	kem, kemur, kemur, kemur, kenn
business	sýslu		
because	því	came	kemur, kemur, kemur, kenn, kenna, kenndi, kennt
believe	trúa		
beginning	upphaf		
being	væri, vætti, vakið		
becomes	verða, verða	comes	kemur
been	verið	cow-verses	kolluvísur
		come-forward	koma

C, c

English	Old Icelandic	English	Old Icelandic
		coming	komið, kominn, komnir
cried-out	æpir	could	kunnu, kurfaldi, kvaddi
called-out	æptu	composed	kvæði, kveða, kveðinn
completely	alla, allir	compose	kveða, kveðinn, kveðju
compensation	bæta, bæti, bætti	cows	kýr
compensate	bæti	cow-buying	kýrkaupi
compensated	bætti	coloured	lít
carried	bar, Bárð, Bárður	concluded	lokið
child	barn	could-be	mundi
children	barna	close-to	nærri
cunning	brögðóttan, brosti	cause	olli
chain-mail	brynju	common	samir
coat-of-mail	brynju, brynjuna	chatter	sennur
command	býð	cuts	skerði
can	fæ, fær	crawled	skreið
carry-out	færð	crossly	þverlega
companion	félagi	consider	þykir
caught	fengu	considered	þykir
commotion	háreysti	custom	vanr
call	heita, heitir	certainly	víst
court	hirðarinnar		
care	hirði	## D, d	
courtiers	hirðin		
court-man	hirðmaður	descent	ætt
court-men	hirðmanna	descended	ættaður
calm	hljóða	disrespected	afvirti
chieftains	höfðingja	dead	andaður, andróða, annað
chief-poet	höfuðskáld		
circles	hringum	difficulty	andróða
cleared	hroðið, hróður	death-sentence	banasök
called	kallaði, kallaðir, kallaður, kann	death	bani, bar
		drew	brá, brákar, brauði
can-it	kann	day	dag, dagana
cast	kastað, kastaði	Denmark (place)	Danmerkur
		daring	djarfan
		daughter	dóttur

150

Word List (English to Old Icelandic)

English	Old Icelandic
drapa (poem)	drápa
drapa	drápu
dream	draum, draumur
draws	dregr
draw	dregst
dragon	dreki
drinking	drekka
dreamed	dreymt
drink	drykk, drykkjar
denied	duldu
dwarf	dvergur
delivered	flutt
delight	gaman, gaman
do	ger, ger, gera, gera
does	ger, gera
doing	gera
done	gera, gera, gera
did	gerði, gerði, gerðir
deception	ginning
dug	grafið
deep-red	gruntrauðustum
danger	hættu
disappeared	hverft
dear-friendship	kærleikum
down	niður
decide	ráða
decided	ráða, ráði
delivery	sendingum
disgrace	skömm
debt	skuld
dined	snætt
dared	þorði
dare	þori
dignified	tigulegur
difficult	vandi

E, e

English	Old Icelandic
excellent	ágætur
estate	búi
examples	dæmi
Einar (name)	Einar, Einari, Einars
Einar's (name)	Einars
elderly	eldilegt
Emma (name)	Emmu
ended	enda, enda
England (place)	Englandi, Englands
errand	erindi
eat	eta, eta
eating	eta
extremely	furðulega
enjoyment	gaman
entertaining	gaman
equipped	gyrti
Earl-of-Lade (name)	Hlaðajarli
each	hverjum, hvern, hvers, hversu, hvert
encouraged-lightning	hvofteldingum
each-way	hvorttveggja
evil	illa, illan
evil-ways	ilvegs
equally	jafnan
equally-badly	jafngreypilega
equal	jafnir, jafnsleppt
equally-slip	jafnsleppt
earl	jarl
even	jöfnum
evening	kveldið
easily-satisfied	lítilþægir
end	lýk
educated	menntur
except	nema
enjoy	njót
enough	nóg
eachother	öðrum
Elegant (name)	Prúða
extended	rétti
entertainment	skemmt
entertain	skemmta
exchange	skipt
early	þegar
enduring	þola
endured	þoldi
endures	þolir
extended-out	úti
expected	vætti, vakið

F, f

English	Old Icelandic
for	á, á, á, á, að

Word List (English to Old Icelandic)

English	Old Icelandic	English	Old Icelandic
from	á, á, á, að, að, að, að, að	force	hér
family-small	ættsmár	fallen	hnigið
farmers	bændur, bæta	fame	hróður
farmer	bóndi	friendship	kærleikum, kálf
fair-wind	byr	felt	kenndi
fine	dýran	flesh	kjöts
fire-house (kitchen)	eldahús	folded	kurfaldi
fire	eldi, eldilegt	finished	lokið
forehead	enni	food	mat, matar, matr, mátti
few	fá	for-me	mér
father	faðir, fæ	finished-eating	mettir, mettur
Fafnir (name)	Fáfni	finery	prýði
found	fann, far, fara	filthy	saurugt
fare	fara	for-him	sér
fee-taken	fátækur	food-trough-verses	soðtrogsvísur
fee-servant	féhirði, féhirðinn	for-them	þeim
fell	féll, felldan, fellt	found-a-place	vistaðist
five	fimm		
find	finna, finna, finnferð		
Finland-voyages (place)	finnferð		

G, g

English	Old Icelandic
fishermen	fiskimenn
fee	fjár
followers	fjölmennt, fjör
four	fjóra, fjórar
fourth	fjórðung
fourteen	fjórtán
fleeing	flærat
Fljot (place)	Fljótum
Fly (name)	Fluga, Flugu
flew	flugust
father's-killer	föðurbana
fore-knowing	forvitnar
feet	fótum
forwards	fram
from-saying	frásagnar
Frisian (name)	frísa
Frisian	frískur
full	fullt, fullur
follow	fylgja
first	fyrst, fyrstu
fun	gaman
famine	hallæri
from-there	héðan, hefði, hefðir, hefðu

English	Old Icelandic
greatly	ærið
grinned	brosti
get	fá, fá, faðir
give	fá, faðir, fæ, fær
go	far, fara, fara, fara, fara, farist
goes	fara, fara
going	fara, farist, fátækur, fáum, fé
gone	farist
got	fékk, fékk
gave	gæfi, gæfur
guarded	gætti, gaf
gaping	gap
garden	garðinn
Gasir (place)	Gásum
granted	gefa
given	gefið, gefin, Geirröð
Geirrod (name)	Geirröð, Geirröðr
guest	gista
gladly	gjarna
glad	glaðr, glaður
gnawing	gnadda

Word List (English to Old Icelandic)

English	Old Icelandic
good	góð, góða, góðan, góðum, góður, göngum
grasped	greppr
Godwinson (name)	Guðinason
good-rightly	guðréttilegast
Gula-assembly (name)	gulaþing, gulaþings
gold-band	gullhlað
gold-ring	gullhring
gold-inlaid	gullrekin
goat	hafra
giant	jötni
greeted	kvaddi
greeting	kveðju
games	leika
great	mikið, mikið, mikill, mikill, mikinn
greatest	mikla
gluttony	offylli
genitals	reðri
greater	stærri
grant	veita

H, h

English	Old Icelandic
had	ætti, ættsmár, af, af, af, af, aftur, aftur, afvirti, ágætur, Agðanes, Agðaness, Agði, Agði, aldri, alla, allir, allir
hat	átti
higher	hærra, hærri
high	hæst, hættu
have	haf, hafa, hafa, hafa, hafa, hafði, hafðir, hafðir, hafðist
has	hafa, hafa, hafa
having	hafa
Hakon (name)	Hákon, Hákoni
hold	halda
held	haldið, hálfa, Halla
half	hálfa
Halli (name)	Halla, Halla
Halli's (name)	Halla
Halogaland (place)	Hálogaland, Hálogalandi
her	hana
hand-washing	handlaugar
he	hann, hann, hans
him	hann, hans, hans, hans, hár
his	hans, hár, Haraldi, Haraldi, haraldr, Haraldr, Haralds, Haralds, Haraldur, Háreks, háreysti, hásætið, haustið
Harald (name)	Haraldi, Haraldi, haraldr, Haraldr
Harald's (name)	Haraldi, haraldr, Haraldr
Harek's (name)	Háreks
high-seat	hásætið
has-been	hefir
health	heill
home	heim
hone	hein
honing-grease	heinasmjör
hung	hékk, hélt
hand	hendi, hendi, hendur, hér
hands	hendi
here	hér
hostel	herbergi
horse	hestr, hesturinn
hear	heyra
heard	heyra, heyrði, heyrðu, heyrt, hilmis
helmsman's	hilmis
Hitra (place)	Hítrar
helmet	hjálm
head	höfuð, höfuðið
horn-spoon	hornspónu
hide	húðar
hungry	hungrar, hús
how	hve
how-so	hvers, hversu
hammering	klappar
his-life	lífinu
harm	mein, meir

Word List (English to Old Icelandic)

English	Old Icelandic
himself	sér, sér, sessunaut, sessunautur, séuð
hit	skall
heading	stillir
heavy-cargo	þunga
hayfield-wall	túngarði
hardly	varla
have-been	verða

I, i

English	Old Icelandic
in	á, á, að, að, að, að, að, að
it	á, að, að, að, að
intended	ætlað, ætluðu
invited	bað, báðir
if	ef, eftir
I	eg, eg, Einar
in-the-end	enda
is	er
islands	eyjar
intestines	fyrir, fyrr
is-named	heitir
into	í, illa
ill	illt
inside	innan
Iceland (place)	Ísland, Íslandi, Íslands
Iceland-voyage	íslandsfari
Icelanders	íslendinga, íslendingar
Icelander	íslenska, íslenskan, íslenskur
iron-weapon	járn
ironsmith	járnsmiður
intellect	vitsmuna

J, j

English	Old Icelandic
journey	förum
jumped	hljóp
Jutland (place)	Jótlands

K, k

English	Old Icelandic
killed	drap, drápa, drápu, drápu, draum
kill	drepa, drepið
kinsman	frændi, frændunum
kinsmen	frændunum
knife	hníf, hnífi, hnífinum
knife-handle	hnífskafti
knocked-down	hnúskum
knows	kann
know-you	kanntu
Kapuang (place)	Kaupangs
Kaupang (place)	Kaupangur
know	kenn, kenna, kenndi, kennt, keyptuð, kjöts, klappar
knee	kné
knorrs	knörru
kings	konunga
king	konungr
king's	konungr
kin	kyns
known	veit
knew	vissi, vissu, víst

L, l

English	Old Icelandic
lived	bjó
laughed	brosti
lodgings	búð, búfinna
loved	elskaði
lost	firrst, fiskimenn, fjár
life	fjör, fjóra, fjórar
leg	fót
last	fyrra
look-to	gervan
long-neck	hálslangur
long-armed	handsíður
lord	herra
ladened	hlaðna
listen	hlýði
lobsters	humrum
lay	lá, læt, læt, lagði, lagði

Word List (English to Old Icelandic)

English	Old Icelandic
let	læt, lagði
laid	lagði, lagðist, lagin, lágu, láguð
land	land, landi, langa
long	langa, langskip, lát
longships	langskip
leave	látir
lead	leiða
look-for	leita
lands	lendi
leaned	lér
let-up	létti, léttum
lie	liggja, líkaði
liked	líkaði, líkar
like	líkar, líkar
likely	líklegur
looked	lítast, lítið, lítil
little	lítið, lítil, lítilla, lítils, lítilþægir, lítilþægur
little-behaving	lítilþægur
light	ljóst
legal-settlement	lögskilum
lifting	lyftingunni
lies	lýgur
lying	lýgur
less	minna
lesser	minna
lose	missa
long-nosed	neflangr
look	séuð
later	síðar
least	síst
learned	spurði
large-repaying (generous)	stórlyndur
leash	taum

M, m

English	Old Icelandic
man	af, aftur, aftur, afvirti, ágætur
married	átti
master	bóndi
mockery	dáruskapur, dauðan
master-wounder	drottinserðr
me	eg, Einar, Einari
message	erindi
money	fé, fébætur, féhirði
money-bribe	fémúta
many	fjölda, fjöldi, fjölmennt, fjör, fjóra, fjórar
more	fleira, fleiri, flesta, Fljótum, Fluga, Flugu
most	flesta, Fljótum, Fluga, Flugu
mistakes	föll
met	fundumst, furðulega
magic	galdra
made	gera, gera, gerast, gerði
make	gera
moustache	grön
mocking	háðyrðum
most-hardy	herðimestur
mind	hug, hugar
minds	hugar
molars	jaxlar
merchant-men	kaupmennirnir
merchant-ship	kaupskipinu
may	má, maður, maður
matter	mæla, mæla, mættum, Magnús
matters	mæla, mættum, Magnús
Magnus (name)	Magnús
more-suitable	maklegri
men	mann, manna, manna, manni
man's-son	mannsbarn
many-things	margs
mine	mér, mér, merkur, mest, mesta, mestum, mettir, mettur
my	mér, merkur
marks	merkur
much	mikið, mikill, mikill, mikinn, mikla, mikla
mis-liked	mislíkaði
miss	missa
meal	mjöl
morning	morguninn
meet	móti

Word List (English to Old Icelandic)

English	Old Icelandic
mouth	munni
must	munt
most-angry	reiðasti
mood-dragon	skapdreki
mood	skapi

N, n

English	Old Icelandic
never	aldrei, aldrei
not	ei, eiga, eiga, eigi, eigu, eina, einhugi
nothing	einkis, einmælt
nonsense	endilausu
no	engan, engi, engi, enginn, engu, engum, enn
none	engi, enginn, engu, engum, enn
neck	háls, hárinu
named	heita, heitan, heitir, held, heldr, hella
narrow-shouldered	herðilítill
nearby	hjá
nowhere	hvergi
neither	hvorigum
noose	lykkja
neared	næði
near	nær, nærri, næst
next	næsta
necessary	nauðsyn
needs	nauðsynja
necessarily	nauðulega
Njord (name)	Njörðr
north	norður
northern-lands	norðurlönd
Norway (place)	Noreg, Noregi, Noregs
night	nótt
nights	nóttum
now	nú
needed	þurfti
news	tíðinda, tíðindi
nobler	tignari

O, o

English	Old Icelandic
of	á, á, á, á, á, á, ábyrgst, að
on	á, á
other	aðra, aðra, aðrir, ætla, ætla, ætla
others	aðra, aðrir
off	af
of-all	allra, allra
one	annan, annan, annar, annarra, annars, Árnasonar, átti
otherwise	annar
ordered	bað
order	bið, biðja
offered	býður
or	eða
own	eiga
ownership	eigu
one-minded	einhugi
one-meal	einmælt
one-decision	einráðir
once	eitt
or-else	ella
over	fyrir, fyrri, gamall
old	gamall
of-the-floor	gólfið
of-porridge	grautar
obeying	hlýða
of-him	honum
obscenities	hrópyrði
onboard	innanborðs
obscene	klámyrði
obscene-words	klámyrðum
on-way	leiðar
of-footwear	leista
of-your-hair	loðir
one-mark	mörk
obtain	ná
ox-skin	nautaleðrs
one-of	nokkru
other-knowing	öðruvís
open	opið
of-words	orðinn

Word List (English to Old Icelandic)

English	Old Icelandic
of-silver	silfurs
occasion	sinn
on-his-side	sínumegin
of-skins	skinna
of-the-smith	smiðju
one-summer-old	sumargamlan
of-them	þeirri
of-need	þörf
out-from	undan
out	úr, úr, úrleysingur, út, út
out-of	úr
over-praised	úrleysingur
outside	út
out-running	úthlaupi
out-journey	útivist
out-rowing (fishing)	útróður
our	vor, vorið
of-you	yðvar

P, p

English	Old Icelandic
power	afli
pale	blakir, bleikr
prepared	búinn, búinn
plate	disk
provoke	etja
performed	færði
passage	far
poor	fátæka
payment	fé, féð
pierced	festi
people	fólk, föng, fór, fór
procession	för
pay	gjalda
porridge	graut, grautar, grauti, grautinn
peace	grið, griðníðingur
possessions	gripi
possession	gripur
pig	grís
pour	hella
poured	hella
part	hlotist, hlut, hlut
polite	kurteis
poem	kvæði, kvæði
poems	kvæði, kvæði
poem-reward	kvæðislaun
poem-image	kvæðismynd
peaceful	kyrrt
passed	leið
play	leika
permission	lof
praise	lof
promise	lofa
praised	loft, lofuðu
prove	prófa
plan	ráð
proved	reyndust
persistent	seinþreyttur
purse	sjóði
poet	skáld
poets	skáld, skáld
poetry	skáldskap
place	staðar, standa
piece	stykki
promising	vænstur
provisions	vist
pushed	ýttum

Q, q

English	Old Icelandic
queen	drottning
quickly	flýta, fólk
quickly-cleared	rymskyndir
questions	spurt

R, r

English	Old Icelandic
responsible	ábyrgst
returning	aftur
related-to	átti
ring-land	bauglands
ready	búnir
room	deild
received	fékkst, fer
rhymes	föng
ready-made	gjör
revenge	hefnt

Word List (English to Old Icelandic)

English	Old Icelandic
rather	heldr, hella, hella
running	hlaupi, hleyp
ran	hleypur, hljóð
reasonable	hófi
roaring	hröng
rapped	klappaði
recited	kvað, kvað, kvað, kváðu, kvæði, kvæði
recite	kveð, kveð
reciting	kveðið
reward	launa
rewarded	launaði
repay	launin, leðr
rented	leigðu
remembered	munað, munaður, mundi
reversed	öfugt
robbery	rán
Ran (name)	Ránar
round	randa
Raud (name)	Rauð, rauðan
red	rauðar, rauðum
ruled	réð
Reine (place)	Rein
rowing	reru
richer	ríkari
rye-loaf	rúghleifa
rooms	rúms
row	runa
rattled	skall
rapidly	skjótt
rushed	snaraði
return	snúa
roasted	steiktur
refused	synjuðu
receives	þiggi

S, s

English	Old Icelandic
suppose	ætla, ætla
supposed	ætla
Son-of-Arni (name)	Árnasonar
settled	bjó, blakir, bleikr, boði, borði, borði
soon	brátt
smiled	brosti
shop-keeping	búðarvörð
spears	dörrum
spent	eyddust
Slayer-of-Fafnir (name)	Fáfnisbana
sent-for	fara
stout	feitur
Sami-goods	finnskrepp
stories	frásagnir
stopped	hætti
sound-advice	heilræði
sleeping-quarters	herbergjum
silence	hljóð, hljóðgreipum, hljóðið
sound-grippers (ears)	hljóðgreipum
share	hlut
suits	hlýða
shaken	hrökkviskafls
spine	hryggurinn
she	hún
sole-bucket	ilfat
struck	klappaði
said	kvað, kvað, kváðu, kvæði, kvæði, kvæði, kvæðið, kvæðið, kvæðin, kvæðinu, kvæðisins
spoke	kvað, kváðu, kvæði
say	kveð, kveða, kveðið, kveðið
spoken	kveðið
short-poem	kviðlingur
skin	leðr
seek	leita, leita
seeking	leita
sought	leitaði, leitaðir
speak	mæl, mæla, mæla, mælti, mæltist
satisfied	mettir, mettur
shall	mun, mun, mun, mun, mun, mun, munað, munaður
should	mun, mun, mun, mun, mun, munað, munaður, mundi, mundi, mundi

Word List (English to Old Icelandic)

English	Old Icelandic	English	Old Icelandic
should-be	mun, mun, mun	sick	sjúkur
shall-you	muntu, muntu	scarlet	skarlatsklæðum
serpent	naðri	ship	skip, skip
slander	níð	ship-smiths	skipsmiðir
some	nokkru, nokkru, nokkru, nokkrum, nokkuð	ships	skipuðu
		shield	skjöld
		shoes	skó
somehow	nokkru	scandal	skömm
somewhat	nokkru, nokkrum	sheathed	slíðrar
something	nokkuð, nokkuð	such	slík, slíka, slíkir, slíkt
shouting	óp	smith-bellows	smiðbelgja
sharp-tongued	orðhvass	snake	snák
saw	sá, sá, sæhafa	Sarcastic-Halli (name)	Sneglu-Halla, Sneglu-Halli
so	sá, sæhafa, sækir, sæsjúkur		
		sleep	sofa, sögðu
sea-scattered	sæhafa	son	son
seasick	sæsjúkur	sickness	sótt
sit	sæti, sætis, sættir	Stad (place)	Stað
seat	sætis	standing	standa, standið, steiktur
settlements	sættir		
sake	sakir	stone-kettle	steinkatli
sake-less	saklausa	stands	stendur
same	sama, saman	stood	stóð
sat	sátu, sátu, sáu, sé, sé	steersman	stýrimaður
see	sé, sé	steers	stýrir
seen	séð	strong	styrk
sold	seldag	south	suður
same-as	sem	southern-men	suðurmenn
send	send	summer	sumar
sent	sendi	Svarfadardal (place)	Svarfaðardal
sees	sér	starving	sveltir
set	setja, settist	sword	sverð, sverði, sverðið
sedately	settlega	shrinks-from	svífst
since	síð, síðan, síðan, síðast	swine	svíni
		sleek	sýlt
side	síðu	showed	sýna, sýndi
sailed	sigldi, sigldu	show	sýnir
Sigurd (name)	Sigurð, Sigurðarson, Sigurði, Sigurðr	seems	sýnist, synjuðu, sýr, sýslu
Sigurdson (name)	Sigurðarson	sow	sýr
silver	silfri, silfrinu	stewardship	sýslu
silver-band	silfurhólkur	siblings	systkinum
silver-wound	silfurvafið	speaking	tala
settle	sitja	silenced	þagnaði, þakkaði
sift	síu	straight-away	þegar
seldom	sjaldan	servant	þjón

Word List (English to Old Icelandic)

English	Old Icelandic	English	Old Icelandic
serve	þjóna	the-dwarf	dverg, dverginn
service	þjónusta, þjónustu	the-fire	eld
seemed	þótti, þótti, þóttir	then	en, enda, endilausu, enga, engan, engi, engi, enginn, engu, engum, enn, enn, enn
scandalous	undarlegt		
slaying	víg		
spring	vorið		
sitting	yfir	the-end	enda
		they-are	eruð
		to-eat	etið

T, t

English	Old Icelandic	English	Old Icelandic
		the-legs	fæturnir
that	á, á, á, á, ábyrgst, að, að, að, að, að, að, að	travel	far, fara, fara, fara
		travelled	farið, fars
to	á, á, á, ábyrgst, að, að, að	the-poor	fátækra
		the-money	féð
than	að, að, að, að	the-Sami (name)	finna
the	að, að, að, að, aðra, aðra, aðrir, ætla, ætla, ætla, af	the-fjord	firðinum
		to-extend	flenna
		the-most	flest
this	að, að, að, aðra, aðra, aðrir, ætla, ætla, ætla, af	to-meet	fund
		to-delight	gaman
		the-house	garðinn
taxes	akta	the-wall	garðinn, garðinum, garðsins, garðurinn
the-next	annan		
the-town	bæjar	to-give	gefa
town	bænum	told	getið, gjalda, gjör, gólf, gólfið
the-boat	báti, báti		
the-ship's-boat	báti	the-floor	gólf, gólfið
the-bench	bekkinn	the-porridge	grautinn
the-best	best, bið	the-poor-thing	greyið
to-ask	biðja	truce-breaker	griðníðingur
table	borði, borði	the-trinkets	gripanna, gripi, gripi
the-table	borði, borðið	treasure	gripi
tables	borðin	the-handle	haddan
the-city	börg	the-lid	haddan
the-children	börnin	to-have	hafa
transformed	brást	the harbour	hafnan
the-day	daginn	to-hold	halda
thick-set	digrastur	the-hairs	hárinu
the-plate	diskinum	the-heath	heiði
the-Danes (name)	dönum	threat	heitan
the-killing	drápi	think	held, heldr, hella, hella
the-drapa (poem)	drápuna	to-hand	hendi
this-dream	draum	the-horse	hestinn
the-dragon-ship	drekanum	to-hear	heyra
the-boy	drengurinn	the-court	hirð, hirðinni
the-queen	drottning, drottningu	the-court-men	hirðinni

Word List (English to Old Icelandic)

English	*Old Icelandic*	*English*	*Old Icelandic*
the-helmet	hjálmfaldinn	*the-border*	mörkina
things	hluti	*take*	ná, naðri, næði, nær, nærri, næst
to-strike	höggva		
the-hall	höllina, höllunni	*took*	nam, námu, nauðsyn, nauðsynja, nauðulega, nautaleðrs, nefndur
to-him	honum		
turn	horfa		
the-ring	hring, hringinn, hringinum	*the-slander*	níðið
		the-night	nótt
the-spine	hrygg	*the-other*	öðru
thought	hugði, hugðu, hún, hvað, hvað, hvar, hver, hver, hverfur	*too-much*	ofraun
		terrible	ógurlegur
		the-serpent	ormr
turned	hverfur, hvergi, hvergi, hverju	*the-whole*	óskert
		to-us	oss
trade	iðnar	*the-axe*	öxarinnar, öxina
the-giant	jötun	*trickery*	prettum
the-calf	kálfinn, kálfurinn	*trick*	prettur
to-call	kalla	*the-ruler*	ræsi
the-kettle	katlinum	*the-trunk*	rana
traded	kaup	*the-red*	rauðan
trading-voyage	kaupferð	*tested*	reynt
the-trading-men	kaupmönnum	*told-of*	sagði
trading-men	kaupmönnum	*told-to*	sagt
trading-ship	kaupskipinu	*together*	saman
teach	kenna	*true-words*	sannmæli
the-binding	kilju	*true*	
the-king	konung, konungi, konungi, konunginn, konunginum, konungr, konungs, konungs, konungsgarð, konungsins	*truth*	satt
		tell	seg, seggr, segi
		to-tell	segja
		to-sell	selja
		themselves	sér, sér
the-king's	konungi, konunginn, konunginum	*to-get-hurt*	serðast
		the-last	síðast
the-poem	kvæðið, kvæðin, kvæðinu	*the-custom*	siður
		the-silver	silfrinu
the-poetry	kvæðunum	*tendon*	sinina
the-evening	kveld	*theirs*	sinn, sinn, sinnar, sinni
the-land	landi, landinu	*their*	sinnar, sinni
the-noose	lykkjan	*these*	sinni, sínum, sínumegin
the-whitings	lýsu		
the-man	maður, maðurinn	*the-purse*	sjóðnum
talked	mæltur, maklegra	*the-shaft*	skaftið
the-matter	málið	*the-poet*	skáld, skálda
to-me	mér	*the-ship*	skip, skipið, skipið
the-middle	mitt	*the-ships*	skipin
the-people	mönnum	*the-hammer*	sleggju

Word List (English to Old Icelandic)

English	Old Icelandic	English	Old Icelandic
the-story	sögu	*tar*	tjöru
the-place	stað	*turf*	torf
the-street	stræti	*trough*	trog
the-shore	ströndu	*Tuta (name)*	Túta, Tútu
the-southerners	suðurmenn	*two-fold*	tveföld
tanner	sútari	*two*	tveir, tví
to-answer	svara	*tut*	tví
this-lad	sveini	*threw*	varp
takes	taki	*the-wager*	veðjanin
talking	talað	*to-be*	vera
tongs	tangar	*the-verse*	vísan
the-leash	taumsendanum, taumsins	*the-supply*	vistin
		the-provisions	vistina
taken	tekið, tekist	*to-know*	vita
there	þær, þætti, þættist, þagna, þagnaði	*the-wisest*	vitrastur
		the-themes	yrkisefnin
thanked	þakkaði	*to-compose*	yrkja
they	þar, þar, þars, þau		
them	þeim, þeim, þeir		
to-you	þér		
the-assembly	þingið, þinginu, þings, þingsins		

U, u

English	Old Icelandic
Thingvellir (place)	Þingvallar
Thjodolf (name)	Þjóðólf, Þjóðólfs
Thjodolf's (name)	Þjóðólfs
thief	þjófur
the-servants	þjónustumenn
Thjotta (place)	Þjóttu
though	þó, þögnuðu
thanks	þökk
Thor (name)	Þór, Þóra
Thora (name)	Þóra, Þorbergs
Thorberg's (name)	Þorbergs
Thorleif (name)	Þorleifi, Þorleifur
Thorljot (name)	Þorljóti, Þorljótur
threatening	þrætu
Trondheim (place)	Þrándheim, Þrándheims
three-winters-old	þrevett
third	þriðja
three	þrjár, þrjú
thula (poem)	þulu
therefore	því
towards	til
time	tíma
ten	tíu

English	Old Icelandic
use	brúki
urged	eggjaði
undertaking	færð
upper-shaft	forskeftinu
usually	jafnan
ugly-limbed	ljótlimaður
unreliable	óeinarðarmaður
un-infatuated	öfundsjúkur
upside-down	öndvert
un-custom-mixing	ósiðblandnir
us	oss
unsettled	ótæpt
un-thanks	óþökk
un-ranking	ótiginna
un-truthful	ótrúlegir
unworthy	óvirðulegt
upright	réttur
until	til, til
up-to	til, tíma
under	undan, undarlegt
up	upp
upped	upp
understandable	vorkunn

Word List (English to Old Icelandic)

English	Old Icelandic

V, v

English	Old Icelandic
very-short	allskammur
vacation	orlofs
village	þorpi
verse	vísan

W, w

English	Old Icelandic
was	á, á, ábyrgst, að, að, að, að
with	á, ábyrgst, að, að, að
waited	beið
what	er, er, er, er, er, eru
when	er
where	er, er, er, eru, eruð
which	er, er, eru
who	er, eru, eruð
we-are	eru
went	færu, fæturnir, Fáfnisbana, fagnar, far, far, fara
welcomed	fagnar
went-you	fórstu
willing	fús
went-before	fyrri
walking	gengju
we-are-going	göngum
was-named	hét
whom	hvern
why	hví, hvorigum
whether	hvort
worded	kveðið, kveðin, kveðin, kveðst, kveður
words	kveður, kveld, kvenna, kviðlingur
women	kvenna
with-footwear	leist
well-deserved	maklegra
while	meðan
will	mun, mun, mun
would	mun, mun, munað, munaður, mundi, mundi, mundi, mundir
would-be	mun, munað
would-you	muntu
word	orð
words-separated	orðaskil
word-fallen	orðfall
word-bold	orðgreppur
word-tall	orðhákur
we	oss, ótæpt, óþökk
well-advising	ráðugastur
wrong	rangt
written	ritað
wounded	sarð
were	sátu, sáu, sé, sé, séð, seen, seg, seggr
withhold	spara
with-bread	sufli
wonder	undur
wonder-created	undurskapaður
won	unnið, uns
without	utan
wicked-chieftain	vændishöfðingjar
wretched	válegrar
warily	varlega
wager	veðja, veðjanin
way	veg, vegar
well	vel
worth	verða, verðrat
worthy-that	verðrat
worthy	verður
work	verk
workman's	verkmanns
worse	verr, verra, verra
worst	verra
winter	vetri, vetur, veturinn
winter-lodgings	veturvistar
winter-provisions	veturvistar
wish	vil, vildi, vildi, vildi
wanted	vildi
willed	vildi
wished	vildi, vilja
we-wish	viljum
wishes	vill
will-you	viltu
worthied	virti
wit	vit
write	yrk

Word List (English to Old Icelandic)

English					Old Icelandic

Y, y

yet					enna
Yule-day				jóladag
Yule					jólin, jólunum
your-life				lífinu
yourself				sjálfur
yours					sú, suður, suðurmenn,
					suðurmenn, sufli,
					sumar, sumargamlan,
					sumir
you					þér, þér, þess, þessa,
					þessar, þessi
you-two					þið
your					yðvart

A Word Comparison of Old Norse and Old Icelandic Words

Old Norse	Old Icelandic	English
áðr	áður	after
áðr	áður	back
áðr	áður	before
ætlat	ætlað	intended
ættaðr	ættaður	descended
aftr	aftur	back
aftr	aftur	returning
ágætr	ágætur	excellent
aldrigi	aldrei	never
allr	allur	all
allreiðr	allreiður	all-angry
allskammr	allskammur	very-short
andaðr	andaður	dead
annarr	annar	another
annarr	annar	otherwise
annat	annað	another
annat	annað	other
at	að	a
at	að	and
at	að	as
at	að	at
at	að	by
at	að	for
at	að	in
at	að	it
at	að	of
at	að	than
at	að	that
at	að	the
at	að	this
at	að	to
at	að	with
átta	átti	related-to
bana-sök	banasök	death-sentence
Bárðr	Bárður	Bard (name)
bátnum	bátinum	the-boat
beidda	beiddi	asked
bezt	best	best
bezt	best	the-best
bitit	bitið	biting
blakkir	blakir	pale
bœjar	bæjar	the-town
bœndr	bændur	farmers
bœnum	bænum	town
bœta	bæta	compensation
bœti	bæti	compensate
bœtti	bætti	compensated
borðit	borðið	table
borðit	borðið	the-table
bú-Finna	búfinna	farmers
burt	brott	away
burt	brott	brought
burtu	brottu	away
býðr	býður	offered
Danmerkr	Danmerkur	Denmark (place)
dáruskapr	dáruskapur	mockery
dauðr	dauður	dead
digrastr	digrastur	thick-set
diskr	diskur	a-plate
dœmi	dæmi	examples
drápu	drápa	drapa (poem)
draumr	draumur	a-dream
draumr	draumur	dream
dregr	dregur	drew
drengrinn	drengurinn	the-boy
drepit	drepið	kill
drepit	drepið	killed
drepr	drepur	killed
dvergr	dvergur	dwarf
eðr	eða	and
eðr	eða	but
eðr	eða	or
eigi	ei	not
eigi	ekki	not
eign	eigu	ownership
Einari	Einar	Einar (name)

A Word Comparison of Old Norse and Old Icelandic

Old Norse	Old Icelandic	English	Old Norse	Old Icelandic	English
Einarr	Einar	Einar (name)	fœra	færa	bring
ek	eg	I	fœra	færa	brought
ek	eg	me	fœra	fara	sent-for
eldr	eldur	fire	fœrði	færði	performed
elliligt	eldilegt	elderly	fœrðr	færðr	brought
endileysu	endilausu	nonsense	fœri	færu	went
engan	öngvan	none	fœrr	fær	accomplished
engi	enginn	none	fœtrnir	fæturnir	the-legs
engum	öngum	no	fór	för	before
enn	en	and	forskeftinn	forskeftinu	upper-shaft
enn	en	but	fórtu	fórstu	went-you
enn	en	than	frískr	frískur	Frisian
enn	en	that	fullr	fullur	full
enn	en	then	fundu	fundum	found
ertú	ertu	are-you	furðanliga	furðulega	extremely
eru	er	is	fúss	fús	willing
eru	eruð	they-are	fyr	fyrir	before
eru	erum	are-we	fyrr	fyrri	went-before
etit	etið	to-eat	gæfr	gæfur	agreeable
eyja	eyjar	islands	ganga	gangi	go
fær	færð	carry-out	gangu	göngum	going
fær	færð	undertaking	garðrinn	garðurinn	the-wall
Fáfnis-bana	Fáfnisbana	Slayer-of-Fafnir (name)	gefi	gæfi	gave
fáim	fáum	get	gefit	gefið	given
farit	farið	travelled	Geirrauð	Geirröð	Geirrod (name)
farit	farist	gone	Geirrauðr	Geirröðr	Geirrod (name)
fátœka	fátæka	poor	gengi	gengju	walking
fátœkr	fátækur	fee-taken	gera	gervan	look-to
fátœkra	fátækra	the-poor	gerir	gerðir	done
fébœtr	fébætur	compensation	gerit	gerið	do
féit	féð	the-money	gerla	gjörla	completely
feitr	feitur	stout	getit	getið	told
fekk	fékk	give	glaðr	glaður	glad
fekk	fékk	got	gnauða	gnadda	gnawing
fekk	fékk	had	góðr	góður	good
fekkst	fékkst	received	gólfit	gólfið	the-floor
feldan	felldan	killed	görr	gjör	ready-made
fell	féll	fell	grafit	grafið	dug
ferr	fer	go	grautr	grautur	porridge
ferr	fer	goes	greyit	greyið	the-poor-thing
ferr	fer	went	griðníðingr	griðníðingur	truce-breaker
flœr-at	flærat	fleeing			

A Word Comparison of Old Norse and Old Icelandic

Old Norse	Old Icelandic	English
gripina	gripuna	the-trinkets
gripr	gripur	possession
gríss	grís	pig
guðréttligast	guðréttilegast	good-rightly
gyrði	gyrti	equipped
hafða	hafði	had
haldit	haldið	held
hálslangr	hálslangur	long-neck
handsiðr	handsíður	long-armed
hanh	hann	he
hann	honum	he
hanu	hann	he
Haraldr	Haraldur	Harald (name)
hásætit	hásætið	high-seat
haustit	haustið	autumn
hávan	hafnan	the harbour
hefði	hafði	had
hefði	hefðu	had
hefðim	hefðum	have
hefr	hefur	had
heilt	hellt	rather
hekk	hékk	hung
helt	hélt	held
helzt	helst	rather
hendr	hendur	hand
herðalítill	herðilítill	narrow-shouldered
herðamestr	herðimestur	most-hardy
hestrinn	hesturinn	horse
heyrða	heyrði	heard
hirðmaðr	hirðmaður	court-man
hit	hið	the
hleypr	hleypur	ran
hljóðit	hljóðið	silence
hlotizt	hlotist	part
hlutr	hlutur	part
hnífskefti	hnífskafti	knife-handle
hnigit	hnigið	fallen
hnígr	hnígur	fell
höfuðit	höfuðið	head
höldnum	höldnu	held
höllinni	höllunni	the-hall
hon	hún	it
hon	hún	she
hornspánu	hornspónu	horn-spoon
hraustliga	hraustlega	boldly
hringnum	hringinum	the-ring
hroðit	hroðið	cleared
hróðr	hróður	fame
hrökkvi-skafls	hrökkviskafls	shaken
hryggrinn	hryggurinn	spine
hugða	hugði	thought
hvárigum	hvorigum	neither
hvárn	hvern	each
hvárr	hvor	each
hvárt	hvort	each
hvárt	hvort	whether
hvárttveggja	hvorttveggja	each-way
hvat	hvað	that
hvat	hvað	what
hvé	hve	how
hverfr	hverfur	turned
hverjar	hvað	that
hverju	hvoru	which
hverr	hver	what
hverr	hver	who
hveru	hvern	each
hveru	hvern	what
hveru	hvern	whom
hví	því	if
hví	því	why
Íslands-fari	íslandsfari	Iceland-voyage
íslenzka	íslenska	Icelander
íslenzkan	íslenskan	Icelander
íslenzkr	íslenskur	an-Icelander
íslenzkr	íslenskur	Icelander
jafngreypiliga	jafngreypilega	equally-badly
járnsmiðr	járnsmiður	ironsmith
jólum	jólunum	Yule
kagtat	kastað	cast
kálfrinn	kálfurinn	the-calf
kallaði	konungur	the-king
kallaðr	kallaður	called
kanntú	kanntu	know-you

A Word Comparison of Old Norse and Old Icelandic

Old Norse	Old Icelandic	English	Old Norse	Old Icelandic	English
kátr	kátur	cheerful	líkr	líkur	like
Kaupang	Kaupangur	Kaupang (place)	lítilþægr	lítilþægur	little-behaving
			lítit	lítið	little
kemr	kemur	came	ljótlimaðr	ljótlimaður	ugly-limbed
kemr	kemur	come	lögðu	lögðum	laid
kemr	kemur	comes	lokit	lokið	concluded
kendi	hendi	hands	lokit	lokið	ended
keyptut	keyptuð	bought	lokit	lokið	finished
kníf	hníf	knife	lönd	lendi	lands
knífi	hnífi	knife	lýgr	lýgur	lies
knífinum	hnífinum	knife	lýgr	lýgur	lying
knúskim	hnúskum	knocked-down	maðr	maður	a-man
köllu	köllum	call	maðr	maður	man
Kollu-vísur	kolluvísur	cow-verses	maðr	maður	the-man
kom	kemur	came	maðrinn	maðurinn	the-man
komit	komið	came	makligra	maklegra	well-deserved
komit	komið	come	makligri	maklegri	more-suitable
komit	komið	coming	makligust	maklegust	the-best
konungr	konungur	the-king	málit	málið	the-matter
konungr	konungur	the-king's	málsþörf	máls	matter
konungr	konungurinn	the-king	matr	matur	food
konungrinn	konungur	the-king	megu	megum	may
konungrinn	konungurinn	the-king	menn	mönnum	people
kostr	kostur	a-choice	menntr	menntur	educated
kurteiss	kurteis	polite	merkr	merkur	marks
kúrvaldi	kurfaldi	folded	mestu	mestum	most
kvæðis-launin	kvæðislaun	poem-reward	mettr	mettur	finished-eating
kvæðis-mynd	kvæðismynd	poem-image	mettr	mettur	satisfied
kvæðit	kvæðið	poem	mik	mér	me
kvæðit	kvæðið	the-poem	mik	mig	me
kveðit	kveðið	spoken	mikit	mikið	great
kveðit	kveðið	worded	mikit	mikið	much
kveðr	kveður	recited	mjök	mjög	much
kveðr	kveður	words	mjöli	mjöl	meal
kveldit	kveldið	evening	mœttum	mættum	met
kviðlingr	kviðlingur	short-poem	morgininn	morguninn	morning
lágu	láguð	laid	mun'k	mun	will
látit	látið	had	muna	mun	would
látit	látið	let	munat	munað	remembered
leggr	leggur	laid	munda	mundi	remembered
lendr	lendur	land	mundu	mundi	could-be
líklegr	líklegur	likely	muntú	muntu	shall-you

A Word Comparison of Old Norse and Old Icelandic

Old Norse	Old Icelandic	English
muntú	muntu	should
muntú	muntu	would-you
munu	munuð	shall
næða	næði	neared
nauðliga	nauðulega	necessarily
nefndr	nefndur	named
níðit	níðið	the-slander
niðr	niður	down
nökkur	nokkur	some
nökkur	nokkur	something
nökkura	nokkra	any
nökkurr	nokkur	something
nökkuru	nokkru	one-of
nökkuru	nokkru	some
nökkuru	nokkru	somehow
nökkuru	nokkru	somewhat
nökkurum	nokkrum	some
nökkut	nokkuð	anything
nökkut	nokkuð	something
nökkut	nokkuð	somewhat
norðr	norður	north
norðrlönd	norðurlönd	northern-lands
öðruvísi	öðruvís	other-knowing
œpir	æpir	cried-out
œptu	æptu	called-out
œrit	ærið	greatly
œrr	ær	awed
óeyrðarmaðr	óeinarðarmaður	unreliable
of	af	off
öfigt	öfugt	reversed
oftar	aftur	again
öfundsjúkr	öfundsjúkur	un-infatuated
ógrligr	ógurlegur	terrible
ok	og	also
ok	og	and
öngan	öngvan	no
opit	opið	open
orðfátt	orðfall	word-fallen
orðgreppr	orðgreppur	word-bold
orðhákr	orðhákur	word-tall
orðit	orðið	become
orðit	orðið	worded
órleysingr	úrleysingur	over-praised
órlofs	orlofs	vacation
orm	ormr	the-serpent
orta	orti	worded
ósiðblendnir	ósiðblandnir	un-custom-mixing
óskerðan	óskert	the-whole
ótíginna	ótiginna	un-ranking
ótrúligir	ótrúlegir	un-truthful
óvirðuligt	óvirðulegt	unworthy
penningar	peningar	money
penningum	peningum	payment
prettr	prettur	trick
ráðar	ráða	decide
ráðigastr	ráðugastur	well-advising
ræð'k	ræð	speak
Rauðr	Rauður	Raud (name)
reðra	reðri	genitals
réttr	réttur	upright
ritat	ritað	written
röru	reru	rowing
sá	sáu	saw
sá	seen	so
sá's	sá	so
sæsjúkr	sæsjúkur	seasick
sagða	sagði	said
sagði	segir	said
sagði	segir	told
sagðir	segir	said
satt?	satt	true
saurigt	saurugt	filthy
sé'k	sé	see
segir	sagði	said
segit	segið	tell
seinþreyttr	seinþreyttur	persistent
séit	séuð	look
sessunautr	sessunautur	bench-companion
sét	séð	seen
setit	setið	sat
settliga	settlega	sedately
sezt	sest	sat

A Word Comparison of Old Norse and Old Icelandic

Old Norse	Old Icelandic	English
siðr	siður	a-custom
siðr	siður	the-custom
síður	síðr	since
Sigurðr	Sigurður	Sigurd (name)
sik	sig	him
sik	sig	himself
silfr	silfur	silver
silfrhólkr	silfurhólkur	silver-band
silfrs	silfurs	of-silver
silfrvafit	silfurvafið	silver-wound
sit'k	sit	sit
sit'k	sitk	one
sitr	situr	sat
sízt	síst	least
sjálfr	sjálfur	yourself
sjúkr	sjúkur	sick
skaftit	skaftið	the-shaft
skaltú	skaltu	shall-you
skemt	skemmt	entertainment
skemta	skemmta	entertain
skift	skipt	exchange
skilat	skilað	settled
skipit	skipið	ship
skipit	skipið	the-ship
skreppu-skrúði	skreppuskrúði	bag-tackle
skulu	skuluð	should
skulut	skuluð	should
skylda	skyldi	would
skyldi	skyldu	should
slíkir	slíkt	such
snöri	sneri	turned
snúit	snúið	turned
sœkir	sækir	sought
sögðu	sögðuð	announced
sögðuzt	sögðust	said
sómir	samir	common
Sorptrogs-vísur	soðtrogsvísur	food-trough-verses
spán	spón	a-spoon
sprungit	sprungið	burst
spyrr	spyr	asked
standit	standið	standing
steiktr	steiktur	roasted
stendr	stendur	stands
stœrri	stærri	greater
stórlyndr	stórlyndur	large-repaying (generous)
stórmannliga	stórmannlega	big-man-like
stórum	steinkatli	stone-kettle
stund	stund	awhile
stýrimaðr	stýrimaður	steersman
suðr	suður	south
suðrmenn	suðurmenn	southern-men
suðrmenn	suðurmenn	the-southerners
svá	svo	so
svá	svo	then
svarat	svarað	answered
sverðit	sverðið	sword
sýndisk	sýnist	seems
sýnna	sýnast	appear
takit	takið	take
talat	talað	talking
taumi	taum	leash
taums-endanum	taumsendanum	the-leash
tekit	tekið	taken
tekizt	tekist	taken
þá	þó	though
það	þau	that
þangat	þangað	from-there
þar's	þars	there
þari	þarmr	intestines
þat	það	it
þat	það	than
þat	það	that
þat	það	the
þat	það	this
þat	þó	though
þeira	þeirra	theirs
þeira	þeirra	them
þeiri	þeirri	of-them
þeiri	þeirri	theirs
þessarrar	þessar	this
þetta	það	that

A Word Comparison of Old Norse and Old Icelandic

Old Norse	Old Icelandic	English	Old Norse	Old Icelandic	English
þik	þig	you	undrskapaðr	undurskapaður	wonder-created
þinginn	þinginu	the-assembly	unnit	unnið	won
þingit	þingið	the-assembly	unz	uns	until
Þingvalla	Þingvallar	Thingvellir (place)	ut	út	out
þit	þið	you-two	útan	utan	out
Þjóðólfr	Þjóðólfur	Thjodolf (name)	útan	utan	without
þjófr	þjófur	thief	útar	utar	out
þó	þá	then	úti	út	out
þœtti	þætti	seems	útróðr	útróður	out-rowing (fishing)
þœttist	þættist	thought	vænstr	vænstur	promising
Þórbergs	Þorbergs	Thorberg's (name)	vænti	vætti	expected
Þórleifi	Þorleifi	Thorleif (name)	vakit	vakið	awake
Þórleifr	Þorleifur	Thorleif (name)	vaknaða	vaknaði	awoke
Þórljóti	Þorljóti	Thorljot (name)	váligrar	válegrar	wretched
Þórljótr	Þorljótur	Thorljot (name)	ván	von	expected
þóttumst	þóttist	seemed	vánligt	von	expected
þóttumst	þóttist	thought	vápnast	vopnast	armed
þula	þulu	thula (poem)	várit	vorið	spring
þverliga	þverlega	crossly	várkunn	vorkunn	understandable
þykki	þyki	seems	varliga	varlega	warily
þykki	þyki	think	várr	vor	our
þykki	þykir	seems	váru	voru	our
þykkir	þykir	consider	váru	voru	was
þykkir	þykir	considered	váru	voru	were
þykkir	þykir	seems	váru	voru	where
þykkir	þykir	think	váru	voruð	were
þykkja	þykja	seemed	várum	vorum	were
þyrði	þorði	dared	veginn	var	was
tiguligr	tigulegur	dignified	veltr	veltur	hung
tœki	tæki	take	vér	við	we
tóku	tókuð	took	vera	vilja	wished
tvá	tvo	two	verða	verði	being
tvíræð	tvíræði	ambiguous	verðr	verður	worthy
tvíræðis-orð	tvíræðisorð	ambiguous	verit	verið	become
tvöföld	tveföld	two-fold	verit	verið	been
undarligt	undarlegt	scandalous	verra	vera	was
undr	undur	wonder	vetr	vetur	winter
			vetrinn	veturinn	winter
			vetrvistar	veturvistar	winter-lodgings

171

A Word Comparison of Old Norse and Old Icelandic

Old Norse	Old Icelandic	English
vetrvistar	veturvistar	winter-provisions
vilda	vildi	wished
vilit	viljið	wish
vilja	vera	to-be
vilju	viljum	wish
vill	vilt	will
vill	vilt	wish
viltú	viltu	will-you
vinskapr	vinskapur	friendship
virði	virti	worthied
vit	við	we
vit	við	with
vitit	vitið	know
vitrastr	vitrastur	the-wisest
yðar	yðvar	you
yðarr	yðvar	of-you
yðart	yðvart	your
yðart	yðvart	yours
yðr	yður	you
ykkr	ykkur	you